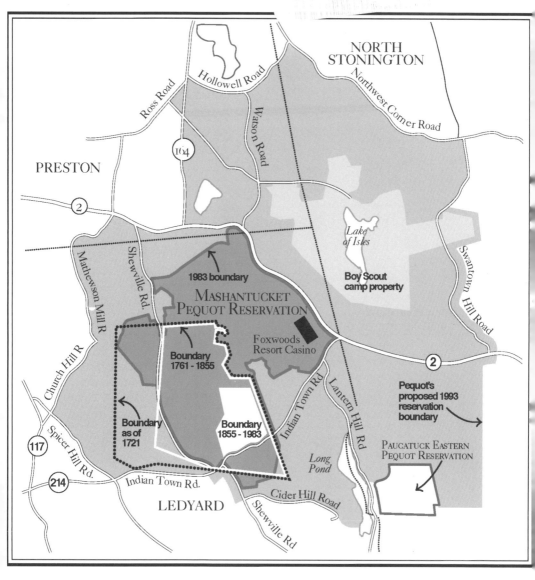

NORTH STONINGTON

Ross Road

Hollowell Road

Watson Road

Northwest Corner Road

PRESTON

104

2

Mathewson Mill R

Shewville Rd.

Lake of Isles

Boy Scout camp property

Swantown Hill Road

1983 boundary

MASHANTUCKET PEQUOT RESERVATION

Foxwoods Resort Casino

2

Church Hill R

Boundary 1761 - 1855

Boundary as of 1721

Boundary 1855 - 1983

Indian Town Rd

Lantern Hill Rd

Pequot's proposed 1993 reservation boundary

PAUCATUCK EASTERN PEQUOT RESERVATION

117

Spicer Hill Rd.

214

Indian Town Rd.

Long Pond

LEDYARD

Shewville Rd

Cider Hill Road

Hitting

the

Jackpot

Hitting
the
Jackpot

The Inside Story of the Richest
Indian Tribe in History

BRETT DUVAL FROMSON

Atlantic Monthly Press
New York

Printed in the United States of America

FIRST EDITION

Library of Congress Cataloging-in-Publication Data

Fromson, Brett Duval, 1955–
Hitting the jackpot : the inside story of the richest Indian tribe in history / by Brett
Fromson.
p. cm.
Includes index.
ISBN 0-87113-904-9
1. Pequot Indians—Gambling. 2. Pequot Indians—History. 3. Pequot
Indians—Social conditions. 4. Gambling on Indian reservations—Connecticut—
Ledyard. 5. Casinos—Government policy—Connecticut—Ledyard. 6. Ledyard
(Conn.)—Economic conditions. I. Title.
E99.P53F76 2003
974.6004'973—dc21   2003052105

Endpaper maps by Milt Moore

Atlantic Monthly Press
841 Broadway
New York, NY 10003
03 04 05 06 07 10 9 8 7 6 5 4 3 2 1

For Carmel and Jamie

CONTENTS

1

DEFEAT AND DECAY

The first Puritans migrated from Massachusetts Bay Colony to Connecticut Colony in 1635 and within two years were at war with the Pequot Indians, the dominant tribe in the region. The Pequots waged a guerrilla war against the Puritan settlements, and the English retaliated with punitive strikes on Pequot villages. The main casualties were civilians—elderly men, women, and children. In the spring of 1637, the Pequots raided Wethersfield, one of the three English settlements along the Connecticut River. Three women and six men were killed, and two young girls were kidnapped.

The colony's leaders met in Hartford and decided to launch a counteroffensive, having already lost more than thirty dead out of a total population of 250. Faced with a superior Pequot population—about three thousand, according to modern estimates—and surrounded by other Indian tribes of uncertain loyalties, the English chose as their military commander a professional soldier named Captain John Mason. Though not a Puritan, Mason was a veteran of the religious wars of the early seventeenth century between Catholic Spain and the Protestants of northern Europe. Tall, powerfully built, and a proven leader in the field, Mason was given a hastily cobbled militia of ninety men. They were joined by seventy Indian warriors under the command of Uncas, chief of the nearby Mohegan tribe, which was already at war with the Pequots.

Mason's motley expeditionary force boarded three small ships on Wednesday, May 20, 1637, for a trip down the Connecticut River to the military garrison at Saybrook, where the river met Long Island Sound. On the way, the Mohegans disembarked, preferring to walk rather than travel in ships that constantly ran aground in the river's low water. The Mohegans skirmished along the way with Pequot war parties but arrived intact as a fighting force at Saybrook. Mason was impressed with the Mohegans' fighting spirit. However, other members of the English expedition doubted their mettle. To test the Mohegans' loyalty, Mason ordered them to track and capture, dead or alive, a small war party of Pequots seen nearby. The Mohegans killed four Pequots and brought a fifth warrior back alive. They lashed the captured warrior—who dared them to do their worst—to a post, tied a rope to one of his legs, and pulled him apart. An Englishman finally put a bullet through the Pequot's head to end the torture.

Mason was under orders to strike the main Pequot fortified village, but en route he decided against a frontal assault, noting that the Pequot fort was likely to be on alert and well defended. Instead, he chose to withdraw from the area, sail east to what is today Rhode Island, and then march back west, surprising the Pequots from the rear. Mason was initially opposed by those soldiers in his force who felt a direct attack on the main Pequot fort was the quickest way to achieve victory. It was only after a minister accompanying the expedition announced that he had received word from God endorsing Mason's proposal that the captain was able to proceed with his plan. Mason sent home those who still doubted his leadership and replaced them with professional soldiers from the garrison at Saybrook.

On Friday, May 29, his small force sailed east toward Rhode Island, which, as planned, led the Pequots to assume that Mason was giving up. Instead, Mason's ships landed in Narragansett territory, recruited several hundred of that tribe's warriors, and quick-marched back into Pequot territory. The weather was exceptionally warm that May, and the English soldiers with their heavy metal armor, leather boots, and matchlock guns labored in the extreme heat. From his Mohegan and Narragansett scouts, Mason learned that the two largest Pequot camps were too far apart for him to attack simultaneously with his small force. He decided to concentrate the attack on the nearer of the two, a hilltop fort overlooking the Mystic River.

The English and their Indian allies pitched camp two miles northeast of the Pequot fort. "The Rocks were our Pillows; yet Rest was pleasant," Mason recorded later. "The Night proved comfortable being clear and Moon Light: We appointed our Guards and placed our Sentinels at some distance; who heard the Enemy Singing at the Fort, who continued that Strain until Midnight, with great Insulting and Rejoicing, as we were afterwards informed: they seeing our Pinnaces sail by them some Days before, concluded we were afraid of them and durst not come near them; the Burthen of their Song tending to that purpose."

The English rose before daybreak on Friday, June 5, praying together to God for victory. They climbed quietly up the hill to the fort, where Mason divided them into two forces, sending one to the south entrance of the fort, while he led a second force to the north entrance. Mason and his soldiers advanced to within twenty feet of the Pequots' wooden palisade before an Indian dog caught their scent and barked. A Pequot warrior cried out, "*Owanux! Owanux!* [Englishmen! Englishmen!]"

Mason and his soldiers rushed into the fort, pushing through a thorny brush pile intended to block the entrance. Once inside the oval-shaped fortification, they formed ranks and let go a volley of musket fire down the main lane. Frightened Pequots remained in their homes. Mason forced his way into one of the dwellings and killed several Pequot warriors with his sword. A fierce battle ensued. Many Pequots were killed, but Mason's force was outmanned. Fearful of losing a protracted fight, Mason shouted to his men, "We must burn them." He seized a firebrand, entered a house constructed of tree bark draped over wooden saplings, and set the dwelling afire. Within minutes, the entire fort was engulfed in a hellish inferno.

The screams of Pequot women and children mingled with the roar of English muskets and the triumphant shouts of the Mohegans and Narragansetts. Some Pequots perished in the flames without attempting to escape; others rushed directly into the flames, either deliberately or in panic. Many warriors fought amid the conflagration until their bowstrings cracked and were rendered useless. Still other Pequot fighters gathered outside the fort and shot their arrows until cut down by musket volleys. About forty of the boldest rushed out and attempted to force their way through the English lines. Only a few escaped. Most were struck down by English swords or Mohegan and Narragansett arrows, tomahawks, and war clubs. In little more than an hour, close to four hundred Pequot men, women, and children were killed. Seven were taken prisoner, and seven escaped. Only two Englishmen died, and twenty were wounded.

To Mason's way of thinking, the hand of God had been at work: "Thus were they now at their Wit's End, who not many Hours before exalted themselves in their great Pride," he wrote. "Threatening and resolving the utter Ruin and Destruction of all the English, Exulting and Rejoycing with Songs and Dances; But God was above them, who laughed at his Enemies and the Enemies of his People to Scorn, making them as a fiery Oven: Thus were the Stout Hearted spoiled, having slept their last Sleep, and none of their Men could find their Hands: Thus did the Lord judge among the Heathens, filling the Place with dead Bodies!"

Following the victory at Mystic, the English hunted down the remnants of the tribe and handed over any survivors to the Mohegans and Narragansetts as spoils of war. A small number of Pequots were also sold into slavery in the Caribbean or indentured as servants to English families in Connecticut. In 1666, the Pequots under the control of the Mohegan tribe were given a two-thousand-acre reservation in what is today Ledyard, Connecticut. Those overseen by the Narragansett were given a reservation in nearby North Stonington. The days of the Pequots as a major force in southern New England appeared to have ended forever.

As a child growing up in the 1890s on the reservation in Ledyard— whittled down over the centuries by land sales and transfers to about two hundred acres—Eliza George heard a somewhat different version of the events of 1637. As one of her half sisters recalled,

> My mother and grandmother told me how the Indians made a blockade to protect the women and children when they were fighting against the settlers. They said that John Mason came with a regiment of soldiers. First, they didn't know what to do, whether to burn them out with their torches. ... They went to the Baptist Church there in Old Mystic and talked. There were four or more ministers that were Protestant ministers to ask them if it would be all right to do that. And so my grandmother and mother told me that they said after talking about a half hour together with the other ministers, they said, "Yes. Go ahead and do it. Get rid of them." I think they called them the Canaanites. "Get rid of the Canaanites, wicked people," which was the Pequot Indians. So they did. They threw torches and put it all aflame.

Eliza George's understanding of the Pequots as victims of history would turn out to be crucial. In her narrative of the Pequots' demise were the seeds of the twentieth-century reinvention of the tribe.

In 1898 in Connecticut, a man clubbed to death was unusual, even in as remote and notorious a place as the Western Pequot Indian reservation in Ledyard. The reservation was essentially a dense patch of dark forest and rock ledge inhabited by a dozen or so impoverished people who claimed descent from the original tribe. By the late nineteenth century, the reservation had become a refuge for a few closely related families of Pequot descent as well as various squatters and tramps. Poor whites, blacks, and others at the bottom of the New England social ladder gravitated to the reservation, often intermarrying with the Pequot descendants. The prevailing attitude of town authorities and state government was that there was by this time no Pequot tribe to speak of, only a sordid assortment of Pequot half-breeds, and reprobates of uncertain lineage and history. When townspeople in Ledyard discussed the reservation, if at all, it was with the smug sympathy of small-town New Englanders. It was the bad part of town.

Cyrus George, Eliya's father, was an impoverished half-Narragansett with uncertain amounts of Pequot, black, and white ancestry. Cy was well known to the barkeeps of the nearby provincial cities of Norwich and New London. Never boisterous or aggressive, he and his half-Pequot, half-Narragansett wife, Martha Hoxie George, and their seven children lived in a tumbledown cottage on the Ledyard reservation. His best friend was a worn-out nag who pulled his battered wagon along the dirt roads of the county.

Cy worked as a common laborer for Everett Whitford, a Yankee who ran a sawmill three miles away. Sawmills were a growth industry in Connecticut in the late 1890s. Marginal pastures were reverting to forestland as farmers abandoned them in the face of competition from the more productive farms of the Midwest. More forests meant more trees for sawmills, which produced lumber for the construction trades in burgeoning New York City and elsewhere along the Eastern Seaboard. Cy was happy to work at Whitford's sawmill cutting and stacking lumber, even if it did keep him away from home for weeks at a time.

One Saturday in October 1898, Cy received his wages from Whitford, but instead of going straight back to the reservation he stopped in at the Red Wing Tavern, a local bar. After treating friends and acquaintances to drinks, Cy left the Red Wing at nine o'clock, carrying half a pint of whiskey for the road. On his way home, he passed a neighbor near the reservation who later recalled that Cy was "under the influence of liquor," but seemed "sober enough to talk rationally and handle his team without any trouble."

About a mile from home, Cy was hit on the head with a club or another blunt instrument, crushing his skull. In the struggle with his attacker, Cy broke his whip trying to save himself. Bleeding profusely from the head, however, Cy fell backward into his wagon. He came to rest on the floor of the wagon, drawn up in a fetal position in a pool of blood.

The horse pulled the wagon, with Cy inside, beyond the usual stopping place outside his family's cottage. That was where his children found their father's body. His wife Martha sent for a nearby farmer, who helped carry Cy's corpse into the house. Upon examining the body, the neighbor concluded that Cy had been struck with a club.

The State of Connecticut's overseer for the reservation, former Judge George Fanning of Ledyard, came the next day. "I cannot give any opinion on the man's method of death until after the inquest," he said. "The mark of the blow on the forehead can be plainly seen and looks as though he was struck with a club. The horse is gentle and does not kick, and I don't see how a man, even if he was drunk, could slip off the seat and cause death." The headline in the *New London Day* newspaper read, "PEQUOT INDIAN MURDERED. Brought Home Dead in Wagon by His Faithful Horse." A proper inquiry into the murder was never conducted. Confidential state records, however, said, "It is reported that Martha (Hoxie) George and Napoleon Langevin made way with Cyrus George while he was drunk. . . . The official report was that he died of heart disease and that the marks on his head and face were cause[d] by a fall."

Cyrus's widow was left with seven young children and the house on the reservation. Luckily, she paid neither rent nor property taxes because the state maintained the house and held the land in trust for the descendants of the Pequots. Martha George also received four dollars a month in public assistance.

Martha supplemented this assistance by renting out rooms to itinerant woodcutters working the forestland surrounding the reservation. She put her children up in the attic to make available four small bedrooms to let. Before Cy's death, Martha had struck up a close friendship with one of her boarders, a skilled lumberjack (he could cut four cords a day) named Napoleon Langevin, the man mentioned in the confidential state records. French-Canadian and a baker by training, he arrived at the reservation after his bakery in Rhode Island went bankrupt. Tall, white, and slim with a full mustache, Napoleon towered over small, dark-skinned Martha.

Within two months of Cyrus's death, Martha was pregnant with Napoleon's child. This caused whispers among her children, one of whom, eleven-year-old Amos, accused Napoleon of having committed the murder. Nothing came of the boy's allegations, and he soon left the reservation, never to return.

Napoleon proved a more reliable provider than had Cy. Napoleon and Martha went on to have four children. It was a happier marriage for her. Napoleon worked hard and abstained from liquor. He and Martha even developed a snake act and entertained people in the area with it. He would dance with live snakes he had trapped on the reservation, while Martha sold ice cream and hot dogs.

Before her marriage to Napoleon, Martha had doted on her daughter Eliza, the baby of the family. Born three years before Cyrus's murder, Eliza was raised practically as an only child because her closest sister was nine years older. Eliza was beloved and a bit spoiled, but her mother's marriage to Napoleon changed all that. The arrival of little half sisters and brothers meant less room in the small house, and as the eldest child at home, Eliza was first to be pushed from the nest. By age sixteen, Eliza was hired out as a maid and cook for families in Norwich. In the summers, she found work with rich families from New York City who vacationed on exclusive Fisher's Island, located in nearby Long Island Sound just off New London.

By the time Eliza turned twenty, she had blossomed into a handsome young woman. Slim with a long, graceful neck, Eliza wore modern, stylish suits and jaunty straw hats with upswept brims. Her pale skin and piercing, wide-set eyes gave little sign of the difficulties of her life. In addition to working, she had already given birth to a boy by a man named Charles Clady, a gambler of African-American descent, with whom she would have two more children before he abandoned her. After Clady, Eliza bore two more children by two different men whose families she worked for as a domestic. She gave both children the surname Clady but their middle names were those of their true fathers.

Now supporting five small children, Eliza moved back to the reservation to live with her mother, Martha. Her half sisters and half brother were by the mid-1920s grown and old enough to leave the reservation. Eliza offered to help Martha, by then in her sixties, take care of Jane Wheeler, Martha's eighty-year-old mother, who was notoriously disagreeable. When Martha died in 1927, Eliza moved back into her childhood house and promptly packed her cranky grandmother off to a neighboring farmer where she lived out the rest of her life.

Eliza finally had her childhood home all to herself. The roof and walls were a patchwork of wood and tarpaper, so it was cold in the winter and hot in the summer. Yet with two floors and five small bedrooms, a kitchen, and a sitting room with a long wooden table that sat eight, the house was also a potential source of income. Like her mother Martha, Eliza took in paying boarders. And like Martha, Eliza had a relationship with one of her boarders, another young French-Canadian woodsman named Arthur Plouffe. Their first child died soon after birth in 1927 and was buried under a tree not far from the house, but she soon gave birth to two more children, giving her a total of at least seven children—by some accounts she had nine—by 1930.

As an unmarried woman with many children, Eliza attracted the attention of state and local authorities, especially since Plouffe had moved back to Canada. Fearful of having to support her and her children, the state arrested Eliza on a charge of "lascivious carriage," a criminal count used to prosecute prostitutes. Having named Plouffe as the father of her children, Eliza asked to have the charges dismissed if Plouffe returned from Canada and married her. The authorities agreed but warned that if Plouffe failed to appear, they would incarcerate her at the state prison for women in nearby Niantic.

Eliza pleaded with Plouffe to return from Canada and marry her. He did, but with one caveat: Eliza agreed to give away her children fathered by Clady and the other men. Her dark-skinned children were shipped off to Ohio, while her light-skinned children were sent to live with families in the area. A few years later, Eliza recovered the light-skinned children. She made no such attempt to retrieve her dark-skinned children and in later years never spoke of them.

Eliza wanted little to do with her dark-skinned relations. Annie George, Eliza's elder sister by nine years, became pregnant in 1929 by a young man named Jesse Sebastian, part black and part American Indian from the Eastern Pequot reservation in nearby North Stonington. Eliza objected violently to her sister's involvement with Sebastian. According to a confidential report written in 1937 by the overseer of the two reservations, the Sebastians descended from an African named Manuel Sebastian, who married an Indian woman named Tamer Brussels in Stonington in 1849. Within a few generations, there were, according to the overseer's report, "more than 150 descendants of different shades of color from blackest black to what appears to be pure white, most of them living in Southeastern Connecticut and Southwestern Rhode Island. They are very prolific, many of them having ten children or more." Eliza had been taught by her mother that Tamer Brussels had not been a Pequot, but rather a squatter incorrectly counted by the overseer. Eliza didn't acknowledge any of the Sebastians as Pequot descendants. She resented the state's unwillingness to intercede in the dispute over "the Sebastian strain," as the overseer's report called it, noting, "as members of this family have been entered on the records of both tribes for over forty years, I have never taken steps to have those names removed. Eighty-eight years have passed since that marriage and it is rather late in the day to find out very much about it."

Late in Annie George's pregnancy by Sebastian, she returned to the reservation to give birth. Eliza played a key role in the family refusal to allow Annie to give birth at the house. Eliza referred to Sebastian as a "nigger Indian" and wanted nothing to do with black half-breeds who might call into question her own identity as a Pequot. Eliza was at most a quarter Pequot by blood and had never participated in any tribal rituals. She knew that the state bureaucracy already harbored severe doubts about the authenticity of the Pequots. As the overseer wrote in the 1937 report, "Of the living members of these Tribes, many have scarcely any Indian blood, for in the past they have not been particular as to the races with which they have intermarried. It would appear that basketmaking, which was formerly an occupation and source of revenue, has been forgotten."

Eliza feared that if blacks like Sebastian and his offspring were allowed on the reservation, the state might throw them all off.

Eliza would not risk losing her house, even for a sister. At Eliza's urging, Annie was ejected from the reservation by the family— stoned off, according to Annie's descendants. Annie moved eventually to New York City with Sebastian, naming her newborn child Clifford Cyrus Sebastian in honor of her murdered father, Cy.

Decades later, two of Annie's grown children, a son and a daughter, drove back to see the reservation. The son was dying of congestive heart failure and had had both legs amputated. They pulled to a stop in front of Eliza's house. Several members of Eliza's family came out, looked the two black visitors over, and called for Eliza. Annie's ailing son said, "Hello, Liza." She looked at him blankly. "Don't you know who I am?" he asked.

"No," she said.

"I'm Cliff, Annie's son Cliff."

Eliza said that she didn't know who he was and that he ought to leave. He and his sister drove away. Before Cliff died, he told his children, "Don't go around those people. Don't ever go around those people."

By 1928, anthropologist Frank G. Speck, the most dedicated student in the early twentieth century of the New England tribes, observed, "The remaining Pequot in Connecticut have become hopelessly deculturated." One of Speck's research assistants, Gladys Tantaquidgeon, a college-educated Mohegan from nearby Montville, Connecticut, wrote a paper on New England Indians for the U.S. Interior Department's Bureau of Indian Affairs (BIA), and concurred with Speck's assessment.

> With the exception of the tribes in Maine, the remaining Indian population in New England is made up of deculturated remnant groups. In southern New England, our Indian communities have been, and still are, melting pots. Beginning with the early French and English contacts, and

continuing through the later period of intensive whaling industries along the coast during which time the men from
many lands married and settled in the Indian communities,
the march had gone on and the Indian blood continues to
become diluted. The infusion of Negro blood was strong in
this portion of the area in certain tribes and scientists are of
the opinion that many of the smaller tribes along the coast
became completely absorbed. Here there are but few who
are of ½ Indian blood and a mere handful who can claim ¾
Indian blood. The majority [has] ¼ Indian blood or less.

By 1941 the state Welfare Department, responsible for the Ledyard
reservation, had set strict rules for who was allowed to live on the
reservation. Eliza supported the department's regulations, which
included securing written permission from the state to reside permanently. The new requirements also included at least two months
of full-time residency per year, keeping a clean house, and not com-
mitting any illegal acts—all under threat of eviction if the regulations were not followed. All buildings erected on the reservation
were considered part of the reservation, not private property. Additionally, if you died or abandoned your house, it became property
of the state. Intentional or not, these rules made it practically im-
possible for anyone but Eliza to live on the reservation, which was
fine with her.

    Not that anyone had much of a desire to live in a remote area
without decent paying jobs, electricity, or indoor plumbing. Even
Eliza appreciated that. As her children reached adulthood, she
encouraged them to head out into the world. She was especially
pleased when her eldest daughter by Plouffe, Theresa Victoria,
married a young navy medical corpsman, Richard Hayward, who
traced his ancestry back to the *Mayflower*.

* * *

By the 1950s, Eliza's two daughters by Plouffe—Theresa and
Loretta—had grown up and moved away, returning only in the
summers with their children. Those visits were a source of tremendous joy to Eliza. She especially enjoyed seeing her Hayward
grandchildren—Theresa and Richard Hayward's children—who
were navy brats and lived primarily on military bases far from
Ledyard. The grandchildren's visits offered Eliza a welcome break
from the isolation of the reservation. In summertime, the population on the reservation frequently comprised just Eliza, her half
sister Martha Langevin, and ten Haywards.

Eliza liked to tell her grandchildren her version of the
bloody defeat of the Pequots at Mystic, only ten miles from the
reservation. In the middle of the night when the sky was ablaze
with lightning, Eliza, who was deathly afraid of lightning, would
rise from her bed, light the kerosene lamps, fire up the stove,
and put on the kettle to make tea for herself and hot chocolate
for the grandchildren. She knew her banging around the kitchen
would wake them up. Trooping into the kitchen a few minutes
later, the grandchildren would complain about being woken up.
But they were not overly cranky because they knew Eliza would
have hot chocolate and tales of the distant past when, as she said,
"Our lands went to the ocean, before the white man pushed us
back." Eliza's telling of the Pequot War made it a relevant topic,
not an historical footnote from more than three hundred years
ago. "Whenever she talked about the incident at Mystic, she
would get extremely upset, very angry," recalled her eldest
grandson, Richard A. (Skip) Hayward. "Those are things you
don't forget."

Visiting Eliza, who was known to her Hayward grandchildren
as "Nanny," was for Skip Hayward like stepping into another
world. Skip's visits to the reservation were filled with the kind of
outdoor adventure missing from his suburban life on or near various navy bases. Nanny's wooden floors creaked, and the ceilings
were low. Skip played cowboys and Indians in the woods and took

walks with his grandmother on the land surrounding the reservation. She told him that all the land had once been the Pequots'. Whenever they came upon a surveying stake in the ground representing possible development by neighboring landowners, she would send Skip or another of her grandchildren to rip it out . She would periodically berate landowners if she found them building a house near the reservation. "You're on my land," she would yell. "Get off my land." When her neighbors reminded her that they owned the land they were building on, Eliza would shout back, "You couldn't have bought it. That's our land."

Meanwhile, the Connecticut Welfare Department had less time and money for the state's depopulated reservations. In 1962 there were only thirty-nine residents on the state's four reservations, and by 1967 the number had dropped to eighteen. The man responsible for overseeing Eliza and the Ledyard reservation was Edward A. Danielczuk, an ex–small businessman who had joined the Welfare Department as an investigator in 1962, a second career to help pay for his retirement. It had seemed, on paper, a mutually beneficial arrangement. Ed wanted a quiet job, and the department wanted an employee who would willingly follow its policy of neglect toward the reservations. Ed oversaw the Ledyard reservation in a part-time fashion. He liked Eliza, but he did not consider her "a real Indian. As far as I was concerned, she was just an old lady. I didn't really distinguish her as an Indian." Ed's primary task was to make sure that welfare recipients like Eliza did not cheat the state. Eliza and the reservation were perhaps "one-twentieth" of Ed's responsibility. They really weren't that important. As far as his department was concerned, it was just a necessary evil, something they had to take care of.

Ed understood that Eliza disdained him for his department's indifference. He got used to Eliza ignoring him when he drove down from Hartford for the annual inspection of the reservation.

Eliza would lock herself inside her house and have another family member deal with him. Ed managed as best he could with the state's minuscule $5,000 annual budget for all four reservations. In 1968 he secured money for a bathroom addition so that for the first time Eliza could have indoor plumbing. Eliza, by then seventy-three, was still tromping out to a two-hole outhouse fifty feet off the back door. She had long wanted an indoor toilet. In 1956, one of her sons-in-law had written a letter on her behalf to the Welfare Department requesting one. "It is approximately 70 feet to the outhouse," he wrote. "And it would be an insult to you to go into explanations why a woman of [Eliza's] age should require what is today mandatory in every home." Fourteen years later, Ed installed her bathroom at a cost of $2,400. "That was a lot of money in those days," Ed recalled. "That was practically half the entire annual budget for all the reservations."

By the late 1960s, Eliza's family had shown little interest in returning to live on the reservation. She expected to die alone and that afterward the reservation would be turned into a state park. Eliza was terribly disappointed in her family, especially in her grandchildren who were coming of age.

Eliza was determined to establish in her grandchildren some kind of interest in their Indian ancestry. In 1971, when one of her granddaughters, Theresa Darnice Hayward, decided to get married, Eliza argued that the young woman should have "an Indian wedding. There has not been one here in three hundred years." The ceremony was held on the reservation atop a flat rock outcropping where the original Pequots were said by local historians to have held their tribal councils. Theresa, wearing a miniskirt with leather fringes, was given away by her big brother Skip, who wore a store-bought, Western-style feather headdress. Afterward, they served succotash and turkey, and the children played cowboys and

Indians because they were already dressed for the parts. Robert Hayward, Skip's younger brother, later recalled, "So it was authentic Pequot, even though, you know, it was done in the fashion of guesswork. There were probably a lot of different cultures like Middle or Western Native American because a lot of the heritage and culture was wiped out through the history. Even my grandmother didn't practice it."

Despite such efforts to foster a sense of Indian identity, Eliza's grandchildren remained uninterested. Skip Hayward, a broad-shouldered, six-foot, two-inch tall young man, particularly disappointed Eliza. Of all her grandchildren, she felt that he had the greatest potential to organize the family and hold on to the reservation after she died.

It was not clear to anyone else that Skip was a natural-born leader. Armed only with a high school degree, Skip was just one of thousands of unskilled New England kids scraping by in a slow-growth economy. His father wanted him to go into the navy as he had, but instead Skip—or "Skipper," as he was known within the family—never got around to it. He floated from job to unskilled job until he made a deal to take over a clam shack near the Mystic Seaport. The Sea Mist Haven served fried seafood and hamburgers to locals and tourists. Skip took out a small loan from a local credit union, flipped burgers and clam fritters seven days a week, and worked nights as a pipe fitter at nearby defense contractor Electric Boat, where they built nuclear-powered submarines for the U.S. Navy. Skip hoped to show his father that he could make something of himself. Hayward Sr. was a taskmaster who had used corporal punishment liberally on Skip and his siblings when they were younger. As a teenager, Skip appeared one day at a cousin's house. He looked terrible. His feet were horribly blistered. It turned out that Skip had walked more than twenty miles to his cousin's house after having been beaten by his father.

The last thing Hayward Sr. wanted, however, was for Skip to get involved with old Eliza and her derelict reservation. So in early 1973 when Eliza visited Skip at his clam shack to ask him to take more of an interest in the reservation, he declined. She told him that the state was forming some kind of Indian Council in Hartford, and she wanted Skip to represent the family. He told her, "Between this restaurant and everything else I'm doing, Nanny, there's just no way I can do it. I'm just too busy." After she left, Skip didn't think much more about it.

In the spring of 1973, Eliza had a formal photographic portrait taken of herself. She had been feeling weaker and weaker and wanted a photo before she died as a visual legacy for her children and grand-children to remind them of their Pequot ancestry. She called a local photographer whose motto was "A Touch of Elegance." Like most Americans, he had a stereotypical image of American Indians—red skin, high cheekbones, thick straight hair. The Indians in Connecticut had always disappointed him, looking either too white or too black. In Eliza, he saw potential. He gave her a false hairpiece—two long, thick braids—and a plaid workman's jacket akin to the Pendleton blanket jackets worn by Western Indian tribes. He posed Eliza on the banks of a local pond in front of a tree-covered hill and an arching sky. Eliza never looked more Indian.

On June 8, 1973, a fine late spring day, Eliza died alone, as she had anticipated, in her old house. The peach, cherry, apple, and pear trees were in blossom. Her vegetable garden was beginning to fill up with green beans and peas and summer squash. In the rhubarb patch, a small forest of reddish stalks poked above the ground. Out front, hollyhocks, roses, daffodils, and lilies were in various stages of bloom. Inside, Eliza's body rested in her old rocker. Her heart had simply given out.

2

REINVENTION

Whereas public policy in the immediate post–World War II period had emphasized the assimilation of Indians, the late 1960s marked a commitment to increased political autonomy for tribes. At the federal level, Indian lobbyists on Capitol Hill made sure that the eligibility sections of new anti-poverty legislation included tribes as governmental organizations through which federal money could be funneled. In 1970, members of the American Indian Movement seized the headquarters of the Bureau of Indian Affairs in Washington, D.C. In February 1973, armed members of AIM took over the entire town of Wounded Knee, South Dakota, in order to focus public attention on their demand for monetary compensation for lands taken from the Oglala Sioux, and for greater self-determination on the Pine Ridge reservation. Largely in response to these acts, Congress passed that year the Indian Self-Determination and Education Act, which encouraged tribal development through a variety of federal aid programs.

The political tailwind for Indian tribes reached even Connecticut. Federal money became available to provide jobs and services to Indians, mainly those from other states who had moved to Connecticut for work. While no members of Skip Hayward's family were involved in the new movement for Indian rights, the political shift was noted by another Indian band in the northwest corner of Connecticut—the tiny Schaghticoke tribe of Litchfield

County. The state administered a small, nearly empty reservation in the town of Kent that the Schaghticokes wanted Hartford to transfer to them. Their leader was Irving Harris, and Harris had friends in the United Auto Workers union, a power within the state Democratic party. He asked the UAW for advice in how to mount a lobbying campaign to have the reservation turned over, and was advised to include other Indian bands in the state in his petition if he wanted broader political support. Harris wrote to the Welfare Department, asking for names and addresses of other Indian groups in Connecticut.

"Would it be possible for you," he wrote, "to send me the names and addresses of either the Chiefs or main representatives from the Reservations in Stonington and Ledyard? I understand that there is only one Indian on the Golden Hill Reservation in Trumbull, also."

Ed Danielczuk, the welfare inspector whom Eliza had so disliked, responded by letter, explaining that "people residing in the Indian reservations of Connecticut are classified as private citizens, therefore, their names and addresses are not available to the public through this department. We do not know of any existing list designating which people are Chiefs or representatives of specific tribes."

Ed's reply articulated the Welfare Department's policy regarding people living on the reservations. They deemed the inhabitants as remnant populations of uncertain ancestry who through historical accident happened to have access to state land. Underlying his reply was a fear of granting any political legitimacy to populations not considered tribal. Ed warned his boss at Welfare that if the state gave the reservations any autonomy, "Indians would come out of the woodwork."

Backed by the UAW union and the Democratic party in Connecticut, the state legislature in 1973 passed legislation transferring responsibility for the reservations from the Welfare Department to the newly created Connecticut Indian Affairs Council. CIAC, which operated under the aegis of the Department of Environmental Protection (DEP), was explicitly intended to empower Indians. For the first time in over three hundred years, the residents of the state reservations had a sympathetic governmental forum.

The Ledyard reservation was no longer Ed Danielczuk's headache. It was now Brendan Keleher's, who was a twenty-five-year-old dropout from the master's degree program in anthropology at the University of Connecticut when he was named "Indian Affairs Coordinator" for CIAC. A charming kid from Boston, Brendan had been hired as a temporary worker by DEP to help out on a summer project mapping Connecticut's underground aquifers. One day, DEP's commissioner was complaining to Brendan's summer boss about the creation of the CIAC and how no one on the DEP staff knew anything about Indians. DEP was good on fields and streams, not Indians. Brendan's supervisor said, "I've got a young anthropologist who needs work." Brendan was promptly hired to staff CIAC for $12,000 a year, despite knowing next to nothing about Indians or Indian tribes. Like most people in New England, he didn't even know that Connecticut had reservations.

Brendan spent his first few months as head of CIAC trying to acquaint himself with the reservations. He was welcomed on the Schaghticoke reservation because they had been involved in the lobbying campaign to establish the CIAC and knew they stood to benefit. This was not the case at Ledyard. About three months after Eliza's death, her daughter Theresa Hayward—Skip Hayward's mother—and children moved to Connecticut from Maryland, where they had been living, and staked their claim to the family house and surrounding acreage. They were not interested in CIAC telling them what to do, and did not even bother to send a representative to the CIAC meetings in Hartford.

Brendan's first contact with the Hayward family was "quite negative." He received a phone call at his desk in Hartford from Skip's sister Theresa (Terry) Darnice Bell, who announced that she was moving a mobile home onto the reservation, with or without state approval. "I'm bringing my trailer on," Bell said. "I cleared this lot with my grandmother, and this is where she wanted me, and I'm coming. She might not be here, but I'm coming." Brendan was nonplussed. He had no intention of evicting anyone but, at the same time, he could not simply allow state land to be claimed by individuals on a first-come, first-served basis. There needed to be some kind of collective—i.e., tribal—decision-making process before anyone moved onto the land.

Not sure how to handle the situation, Brendan drove down to Ledyard to talk to Bell. Before he had a chance to explain why he was there, she loudly informed him that she was not moving, that it was her land, and that he ought to get the hell off. She then slammed the door in his face.

Brendan telephoned Skip, whose number he had from Welfare Department records. Brendan arranged to meet Skip at a greasy spoon one morning after Skip got off work at Electric Boat in nearby Groton. Over eggs and toast, Skip explained that his sister and the rest of the Hayward family were frustrated that they could not just move trailers onto land they considered theirs. "I want to get access to the land and do something on it. I want to get access to the money that the state is holding," Skip said, referring to a small state-controlled trust fund. He told Brendan that the reservation rightly belonged to his family because of Eliza's residency and that he saw the reservation as a place where they could make homes for themselves.

Brendan Keleher was touched by Skip's sincerity, but he realized that Skip did not speak about his relationship to the reservation in tribal terms; to him, the reservation was a family affair, not a tribal matter. This lack of tribal consciousness posed a problem for Brendan. His mandate as head of CIAC was to help

Indians and Indian tribes, not just a single family. He explained to Skip that his family needed to form itself into a tribe. He advised, "You need to have meetings, and you need to call these meetings something other than family meetings. You need some tribal structure. You should start thinking about treating yourselves as an organization and start acting like an organization rather than just a family if you want to be taken seriously."

Pine Tree Legal Assistance was a federally funded, nonprofit legal services organization intended to provide legal aid to poor people, which included Indian tribes. A legacy of President Lyndon Johnson's war on poverty, Pine Tree had established itself as a leading advocate for Indian tribes seeking to reinvigorate themselves economically via bold legal strategies. Pine Tree's lawyer in Connecticut was a recent law school graduate named David Crosby.

When Crosby arrived in Connecticut, Pine Tree was years into a path-breaking lawsuit against the State of Maine on behalf of two poverty-stricken Maine tribes, the Passamaquoddy and the Penobscot. Pine Tree's lawsuit alleged that millions of acres of land had been illegally transferred from the two tribes' reservations in the eighteenth and nineteenth centuries. The land sales had been illegal, Pine Tree argued in federal court, because both Maine and Massachusetts, which administered the territory before Maine became a state, had allowed the land sales without first notifying the federal government. Congress had in 1790 passed, and President George Washington had signed, the Non-Intercourse Act, which stated that no Indian lands could be transferred without federal approval.

The act further stated:

> That no sale of lands made by any Indians, or any nation or tribe of Indians within the United States, shall be valid to any person or persons, or to any state, whether having the

right of preemption to such lands or not, unless the same
shall be made and duly executed at some public treaty, held
under the authority of the United States.

Crosby had come to Connecticut to determine whether the
state's Indian bands might also be eligible to sue for land, monetary damages, and federal services. As the most junior member of
the Pine Tree legal staff, Crosby was given Connecticut on the
assumption that any potential land claims there would be small
because the Indian bands were tiny and unorganized.

Through Brendan Keleher at CIAC, Crosby made contact
with Skip Hayward. Crosby drove down to Ledyard and met with
about eight members of Skip's family at a local church. Crosby
told them that any sales or transfers of Pequot land after 1790
were potentially in violation of federal law, and that no statute
of limitations prevented Pine Tree from bringing suit to recover
the lands. Crosby explained that a claim would be relatively easy
to put together because they had a long-standing reservation,
which should have been held in trust for them by the state. To
the extent that the reservation had been whittled down through
the years by land sales, the land was subject to a claim. He offered them a deal. Crosby would, he said, research the land and
court records to see whether they had a land-claim case. If so,
Pine Tree would represent them in federal court. It would not
cost them a penny.

At the church meeting, Skip's family was already putting him
forward as their representative. To Crosby, Skip seemed an ear-
nest young man who felt the responsibility being thrust on him
to be a burden, a cup that he preferred to pass. Skip said little at
the meeting, but unlike many Indians Crosby had met in California and Maine, he was not an angry young man. Crosby felt he
could work with him. At the end of the meeting, Skip's family
enthusiastically agreed to authorize Crosby to begin the legal research for a land-claim case.

While Crosby was pleased to have their confidence, he wondered also whether Skip's family constituted a tribe. The Ledyard Pequots could be considered one extended family. Unlike the tribes in Maine, the Pequots, as far as he could tell, had no tribal council or tribal leader. To legally assert tribal rights required leaping specific legal hurdles that would not exist if, say, they merely sought acknowledgment of Indian ancestry. The reason was that Indian tribes had special rights that did not pertain to individuals of Indian heritage. Crosby feared a legal defense by the surrounding land owners or the state that argued the Pequots had long ago ceased to exist as a unique cultural and political entity—i.e., a tribe—an argument Crosby hoped to deflect by asserting that the Pequots had been recognized by the State of Connecticut for hundreds of years. Crosby did not know if they were a legitimate tribe, but he was there to put together a land-claim suit, not to pass judgment on their tribal authenticity.

August 18, 1974, was an historic day for Skip's family and Eliza's other descendants. At Brendan Keleher's urging, seventeen family members gathered for the first official meeting in memory of the Pequot tribe of Ledyard, Connecticut. They met at Eliza's old house on the reservation, which was too cramped to fit everyone, so they congregated outside in lawn chairs.

The first order of business was to establish themselves as a corporation—The Western Pequot Indians of Connecticut, Inc.—then elect a board of directors. Modeling themselves after a company and not a government, there was neither tribal council nor chief. It was no coincidence that the initial legal structure of the Pequot tribe was corporate. The primary objective of the group was practical—to obtain plots of land on the reservation for family members.

At this first meeting, they chose one of Skip's uncles, Amos George, to be "president of the board of directors" and representative to CIAC. Amos was an elderly, mild-mannered, retired caretaker of an estate in Simsbury. Amos was not the Hayward family's first choice. His flaw was that his father had been Cyrus George's son, who left the reservation in anger after Cy's murder. Because Eliza had stayed, the Haywards, her descendants, felt a greater sense of entitlement, a conviction that they were the land's rightful heirs. Amos was simply a temporary fix until Skip was ready to take over. Even at this embryonic stage, the Pequots were already divided into two groups: the descendants of Elizabeth George Plouffe and everybody else.

In 1974, Skip discovered that running a greasy spoon was not as glamorous or as profitable as he had imagined. Inexperienced and undercapitalized, he went bust after OPEC tripled the price of oil and precipitated a recession in the United States. He was unemployed, twenty-seven years old, and married to Aline Champoux, a twenty-three-year old he had married when she was still in high school. Skip moved to Maryland, his father's home state, to become a preacher in the Church of God, a fundamentalist Christian sect. It did not work out. By 1975 he was once again unemployed and living in rural Missouri. When his family urged him to return to Connecticut and get involved in their effort to establish themselves on the reservation, the offer looked much more attractive than when Eliza had approached him in 1973. He once again got a job at the Electric Boat shipyard in Groton, Connecticut and moved into cheap rental housing.

Now, Skip leapt with enthusiasm into his new role as tribal leader. He began to lobby CIAC to give the Pequots the funds in the state-controlled trust to buy a pickup truck to use around the reservation. Skip wrote to Brendan Keleher, "This truck will be for tribal use only. We would use it for hauling and selling cordwood. Also for general labor around Mushintuxit. The truck is a necessity at the present time. We ask that there be no delays

if possible. . . . We raised $62.80 at our last meeting for this pur-
pose and the ladies are having a bake sale this Saturday in Mystic. We have put $25.00 on deposit on the truck." He signed the
letter, "Richard A. Hayward, President, Western Pequots, Inc.,
Acting Council Chairman." According to confidential tribal minutes, Skip was neither "president" nor "acting council chairman"
at the time. Skip was not then, nor would he be in the future, especially concerned about the legal formalities of governance. This
was his family's tribe, and he was going to run things.

3

TNT

On January 20, 1975, federal Judge Edward Ginoux ruled in a case brought by Pine Tree Legal on behalf of the Passamaquoddy of Maine that the Non-Intercourse Act of 1790 applied to the tribe even though the federal government did not recognize the Passamaquoddy as a tribe. Before Ginoux's decision, only federally recognized tribes were thought to have their land safeguarded by the Non-Intercourse Act. Ginoux agreed with Pine Tree's argument that the original intent of the Non-Intercourse Act had been to protect the land of all tribes in existence at the time of its signing. The federal government, Ginoux ruled, could not now pick and choose which tribes to protect. The Pequot's lead attorney, Thomas N. Tureen of Pine Tree, referred to this logic as the "Indians-always-win" rule. "Because the federal government took control of the Indians," Tureen said, "it has always had a trust relationship with those tribes. Therefore, we argued that the courts must interpret laws like the Non-Intercourse Act as the Indians would have understood them—favorably. You must, in essence, give the Indians the benefit of the doubt. The Non-Intercourse Act says nothing about a tribe having to be formally recognized by the federal government for the statute to apply."

Judge Ginoux's decision had enormous ramifications for the Ledyard Pequots. It cleared the way for any existing tribe that had sold land after 1790 without congressional approval to sue in court to recover it.

Pine Tree possessed the only list in existence that showed every group of Indians along the Eastern Seaboard that might now be able to bring a land-claim suit in federal court. Seventeen pages long with more than two hundred Indian groups named, the document was a virtual client list for a pro bono firm like Pine Tree. No one was more excited by the Ginoux decision than Tureen, the senior attorney and driving force behind Pine Tree.

Thomas Norton Tureen had always tried to live up to the initials—TNT—his father had given him at birth. (Years later, Tureen took to wearing a gold belt buckle emblazoned with his initials in capital letters.) His father had great expectations for young Tom. He hoped his son would achieve what he himself had not. The father had pursued a legal career but the Great Depression forced him to withdraw from law school. He instead became a serial entrepreneur, running first a regional chain of drugstores that ended in collapse, then venturing into the aspirin manufacturing business until World War II, when the ensuing shortage of raw materials netted him the same result. It was only after the war that he found success as a hotel proprietor in St. Louis, affording his son Tom a private day school and, later, a Princeton education.

Tom's father was also inadvertently responsible for his son's interest in Indians. In an effort to break up Tom's romantic entanglement with a girl whose father's failing business represented a financially "drowning man," threatening to pull the Tureens under, he asked a friend at the Bureau of Indian Affairs to find Tom a summer job far away from St. Louis. His friend at the BIA obliged, and Tom soon found himself working at a BIA-administered Indian boarding school outside Pierre, South Dakota. A far cry from Tom's own St. Louis Country Day School, the BIA school was an ugly set of barracks that housed several hundred Indian children, mainly Sioux, between six and fourteen years of age. Run in a military fashion, the school was essentially a re-education camp for Indian children. They were not allowed to see their families—even on holidays—without school permission. If a child rebelled against the strict disciplinary rules, he could be punished physically with a leather strap or a wooden paddle. The school was typical of educational facilities found within the BIA system. The intent was to remove children as much as possible from their respective reservations and tribal cultures in order to speed their assimilation into American society. "This was one of the things that led into what I later did in life," Tureen recalled. "There was something obviously wrong here. It didn't take much to see this was a pretty dismal situation."

After his summer in South Dakota, Tom considered becoming a teacher or a social worker on a reservation. "But the problem was intrinsically legal and political, the result of the inequitable relationship between the U.S. government and the tribes," he said. Instead, he went to law school at George Washington University in Washington, D.C. Tom became bored, and was about to drop out in the second semester when he heard a speech given by left-wing legal advocate Edgar Cahn. Cahn introduced Tom to the idea that a lawyer could be a "change agent," one who utilized the legal and political process to advance the interests of the poor. "Congress might make the laws," Cahn said. "But the courts adjudicate and interpret the laws." After the speech, Tom volunteered to help Cahn on his latest project—an exposé of the BIA and its treatment of Indians. Their research was published as a book titled *Our Brother's Keeper: The Indian in White America.* The book prompted U.S. Senate hearings on federal Indian policy and helped push public opinion and federal policy in the direction of granting tribes additional powers of self-determination.

Tom had tasted the excitement of pushing the political agenda, which led him after law school to join Pine Tree Legal in

Maine. Tom loved working with the Passamaquoddy tribe. "They were a real community," he recalled. "They were a population of two thousand on seventeen thousand acres of land. They spoke their own language. They had lived in the same place for many centuries. They had a unique cultural tradition. But they were downtrodden and they could use my help." In 1969, Tom returned full-time to work for the tribe. He believed he could win the Passamaquoddy federal services and maybe even get them some of the land they said had been stolen from them over the centuries. Such confidence was typical of Tom.

While studying the issue of federal recognition on behalf of the Passamaquoddy who, like the Pequots, were not recognized as a tribe by the federal government, Tom researched the Non-Intercourse Act of 1790. He immediately saw the act as a way for the Passamaquoddy to recover lost land. They had sold millions of acres after the Revolutionary War to Massachusetts, which then included the territory of Maine. Massachusetts had never sought the blessing of the new Congress, and as a result, Tom's first application of the Non-Intercourse Act led to Ginoux's favorable decision in January 1975. An exuberant Tureen sent scouts up and down the Eastern Seaboard looking for similar suits to file. He was in particular looking for groups with reservations. A land base implied tribal existence, which was, according to the Ginoux decision, a prerequisite for bringing a suit in court. By spring 1975, Tureen had compiled a list of potential Indian groups for Pine Tree to represent, which included the Ledyard Pequots.

Tom knew almost nothing about the Pequots because David Crosby had done Pine Tree's work in Connecticut. Crosby had already laid the groundwork for a lawsuit by determining what land could be subject to a Pequot claim. The harder part was establishing the Pequots' authenticity as an Indian tribe. "The Pequots were essentially invisible to the point of being nonexistent," Tureen recalled. "I knew very early on that what was left in southern New England was dramatically less than what was left in northern New

England. This was a huge challenge. The Non-Intercourse Act applied to any nation or tribe of Indians, but you have to be a nation or tribe of Indians. Not an Indian, but a tribe. Not a collection of Indians, but a tribe. Not a remnant of a tribe, but a tribe." The State of Maine had never contested the tribal authenticity of the Passamoquoddy or the Penobscot. Tureen worried that Connecticut might question the Pequots'.

"They had this reservation, but as a practical matter, if we had ever had to prove tribal existence for the Pequot, it would have been extremely difficult," Tureen explained. "There were so few people. The hook we had with them was that the state had not terminated them and still held a reservation in trust for them. It was therefore our view that Connecticut would be stopped from denying their existence. They were such a small group that they were not worth terminating. They were so small as to be invisible. Would we have won on that if we had gone to court? I sure never wanted the question of Pequot tribal existence to go to court. A court could have simply looked at the Pequots and said, 'They stopped being a tribe a long time ago. The reservation may have been held in trust for them, but that was a mistake.'"

Tom met Skip Hayward for the first time in Boston, Massachusetts, at a meeting in 1975 organized by a former BIA administrator eager to help unrecognized tribes in New England attain access to federal aid programs. Tom spoke to the group in his capacity as the head of the Coalition of Eastern Native Americans (CENA), a nonprofit organization he had put together with a few hundred dollars of grant money from foundations beginning to take an interest in American Indian issues. "Once we understood the legal theory of the Non-Intercourse Act," Tom recalled, "the question was, 'How can we use this to bring about change for other tribes who have been forgotten?' And one of the major organizing vehicles was the land claim because that was the news, that was the hope. The idea of the land claim had the power to make these people believe that change was possible. I held out the dream that they could get back together, that they could actually get on top, that they could begin to take charge of their lives. I was telling them that we would bring a legal action on their behalf that could have huge positive consequences for them. We could get them federal services, and money, and land. That was incredibly empowering for them. It was electric."

After Tom's talk, Skip began to see the reservation as much more than simply a place for him and his immediate family to get plots of land to live on. He began to envision bringing more people to the Ledyard reservation. He wanted to obtain federal services and development aid to attract them. Skip had a reservation but he needed Indians. Tom appreciated Skip's streak of self-invention. "Skip was imagining a tribe before it actually existed, but he did not have any choice. If you don't have it, you have to make it," he recalled. "Skip had a sense from his grandmother Eliza never to let go of the land. Remember, this is the moment of the back-to-the-earth movement of the 1970s. Skip went back to the reservation imbued with this notion from his grandmother: Don't give up what we got here. If you had two hundred acres of beautiful land in Connecticut with this history of being a Pequot Indian, would you let it go? You have to understand Skip and his family had nothing to lose. It was all gain for them. In theory, Connecticut could've gotten pissed off and terminated them, arguing that they were not really a tribe. But it was never like that in Connecticut. No one was even thinking about these issues."

Skip became head of the Pequots officially at the second annual meeting on August 10, 1975. One of his aunts nominated him, and his family promptly elected him chairman to replace old Amos George. His mother Theresa was voted vice chairman. Once again it was held at Eliza's old house, and once again it was a muggy Sunday afternoon. At the meeting, they established membership criteria for the group, as Brendan Keleher had asked they do in June when he visited the reservation. Unlike most Indian tribes, Skip and his family decided that no minimum amount of Pequot blood would be required. Instead, "an authentic descendant of the Western Pequot Tribe of Indians" was anyone who could prove through birth certificate or other legal record that he or she was related to an Indian who was recorded by the state as a Pequot. The rejection of a "blood quantum" was in line with a CIAC-inspired piece of legislation that had passed the state legislature earlier in the year eliminating the one-eighth blood requirement for residency on a reservation. CIAC convinced the legislature that the one-eighth requirement constituted a de facto death sentence for Connecticut's tribes. If they maintained a blood quantum, eventually none of the Indians could qualify because of continued intermarriage with non-Indians. Since there were already so few people, Skip's family was not looking for reasons to reject fellow family members. A spouse of a Pequot descendant could become "an honorary member," as long as he or she paid a five-dollar-a-year membership fee.

Suffering from terminal lung cancer, Amos George was relieved to pass his duties on to Skip. With cigarettes in hand and a tank of oxygen to help him breathe, Amos wrote to a friend, "[Skip] was elected president of the Tribal Council and he is doing very well. . . . [The reservation] has been surveyed out into 2-acre lots. . . . It is, shall I say, a load off my back." Amos died a year later. He did not live long enough to witness Skip's reinvention of the Pequots.

4

LAND CLAIM

In April 1975, David Crosby, his legal research complete, presented the case to Skip and his family on the first Sunday of the month. Crosby explained that in 1666, twenty-nine years after the Pequot War, the Connecticut Colony allowed the Pequots the right to live separately on a two-thousand-acre reservation in Ledyard. By 1790, when the Non-Intercourse Act was signed into law, the Ledyard reservation had already been whittled down by about a thousand acres. None of that land was subject to a claim. However, a subsequent land transfer took place in 1855, when the State of Connecticut sold about eight hundred acres of Pequot land to raise funds for the remaining, impoverished reservation population. Judge Ginoux's January 1975 ruling in the Passamaquoddy case implied that those eight hundred acres had been transferred illegally and could therefore be reclaimed in court. Skip was delighted and urged his family to authorize Pine Tree to bring a land-claim suit.

Dave Holdridge's family had lived in Ledyard just about as long as there had been an Indian reservation. The first Holdridge arrived to farm the land in 1670, and three hundred years later the family still ran a plant nursery in town. As a child, Holdridge had been acquainted with Eliza Plouffe, as he knew her. His father had been first selectman of Ledyard in the 1950s and used to bring his young son to the reservation when he had business with Eliza. (She'd let her dogs run wild in violation of local ordinances.) These visits were tricky for Dave's father since Eliza made it clear she did not think a town official had any business on the reservation. When Dave came along, Eliza would sometimes offer him milk and cookies.

In the 1950s, Dave's father bought about eighty acres of raw land near the reservation. It was rugged woodlot with frontage on Indiantown Road. He bought the land for about $15,000, a good deal because the seller was leaving town, and nobody else wanted it. The property originally had been part of the reservation but was sold off by the state in the 1855 land sale. For estate planning purposes, Dave's father put this and some other land into a family corporation called Holdridge Enterprises. He named Dave, by then a teacher at the local community college, president of the company.

On the morning of May 10, 1976, the tall, skinny, thirty-four-year-old teacher was home grading papers during finals week for his introductory course on U.S. government. He heard a rap on the front door of his ranch house. A black man in a suit and tie flashed a metal badge and photo identification card that read U.S. MARSHAL.

"Are you David Holdridge? I have a legal summons and papers to serve on you. Will you sign for them?"

"What is this all about," Dave asked.

"It's an Indian land claim. Some of your land is being claimed," the marshal replied. "You probably want to get a lawyer."

Dave read the complaint. It had been filed with the United States District Court in Hartford. The plaintiffs were "Richard Hayward and the Western Pequot Tribe." The list of defendants was headed by "Holdridge Enterprises, President David Holdridge." The complaint alleged, "This is a civil action to restore the Western Pequot Tribe of Indians to possession of certain aboriginal and reservation lands in the town of Ledyard." The marshal was right. Dave had to get a lawyer.

* * *

Lawyer Jackson King first learned of the Pequot land-claim suit through a telephone call from another of the defendants, Lois Tefft, a woman in her late forties who served with him on the local land conservation commission. Thirty-something with a boyish mop of light brown hair, Jackson had graduated first in his class at the University of Connecticut Law School. He later joined Brown, Jacobson, Jewett & Laudone, one of eastern Connecticut's most respected and politically connected firms, and by 1971 was made a partner. Intelligent, polite, and fair minded, Jackson King had what it took to be a successful lawyer.

Lois Tefft and her husband, a technical draftsman at Electric Boat, owned a 150-acre farm next to the reservation and, like Dave Holdridge, had received a visit from the U.S. marshal. Tefft was even more outraged than Holdridge. She feared losing her home if the Pequot land claim succeeded. This was the house where she and her husband had raised their children. The farm was their only major financial asset.

"How can they claim our land?" Tefft asked King. "How could it be that our land is not ours?"

"Obviously, you own your house and property," King replied. "They cannot just take your property away. It's part of our legal system that you own it. It's yours." King had been in grade school when the Teffts had bought their farm, but he presumed the transaction had been legal and felt sure enough of that to reassure her.

Promptly at six, the Teffts made the short drive to Jackson King's house. Over the kitchen table, the three went through the legal papers.

King was confident that there couldn't be a successful claim based on what was presented in the documents. "We have legal doctrines to protect people like you, like the 'statute of limitations,'" he assured the Teffts. "It limits the length of time people have to sue. State law sets a twenty-year time limit on bringing trespassing suits. And we have things like 'adverse possession,' which says that you have the right to this land simply because you have been living on it for so long and no one ever complained before. There is no possible claim here. Nobody can take your land from you."

While King asserted the case was groundless, a legal defense still needed to be mounted, and it wouldn't be cheap. The Teffts didn't want to exhaust their savings defending themselves in federal court. King reminded them that all the other defendants were presumably going through similar conversations that evening. They ought to pool their resources to pay for as much legal research as possible. Tefft agreed to call the other defendants and organize a common defense.

As Jackson King began his legal research, he learned that the Pequot claim was not as frivolous as he had initially thought. He and one of the most senior partners at Brown, Jacobson—Wayne Tillinghast—dug into the history of the Non-Intercourse Act and were concerned by their findings. In Judge Ginoux's decision in *Passamaquoddy v. Morgan*, both of the legal defenses King had discussed with Lois Tefft—statute of limitations and adverse possession—had been rejected. Ginoux's rulings in Maine did not necessarily mean that a federal judge in Connecticut would rule similarly, but it signaled that this was a credible case waged by successful attorneys. Of particular note to Jackson was George Washington's role in this obscure piece of American history. Soon after passage of the Non-Intercourse Act in 1790, Washington told the Seneca tribe of Indians in New York, "When you find it in your interest to sell any part of your lands, the United States must be present, by their agent, and will be your security that you shall not be defrauded in the bargain you make." That America's first president had explicitly stated the primacy of the federal government in land transactions involving an Indian tribe gave King pause.

He and Tillinghast called a meeting of the defendants at Brown, Jacobson's offices in the old Hartford National Bank building, a three-story neoclassical pile in downtown Norwich. About a dozen worried and angry people trudged up the stairs to the firm's library to hear what many had already suspected: the case was more serious than the lawyers had thought. "They should have sued the State of Connecticut," Dave Holdridge said. "It was the state that sold the land. The landowners are really innocent bystanders."

King expected that the defense would be costly, perhaps in the tens of thousands of dollars. The lawyers would have to do extensive legal research because they were unfamiliar with Indian law. In addition, historical research needed to be done on the land transactions and on the tribe. This could drag on for years. Holdridge and others raised the issue of cost. Who was going to pay for the legal defense and possible litigation? No one had title insurance on their land, which meant that there was no insurance company with deep enough pockets to finance a fight. The burden of defending the case would fall directly to the landowners, many of whom felt the land was not worth a protracted legal fight. Some of the land had been picked up for as little as five to ten dollars an acre. Also, few of the defendants actually lived on the land at issue and therefore lacked deep attachments to it.

Why not just give up now and spare everyone the cost? Holdridge and his family weren't about to cut and run, at least not without some kind of a fight. King and Tillinghast agreed. If the landowners didn't defend themselves, not only could they lose the land but the tribe also might be able to sue for monetary damages—lost rents, for example—for the years the defendants had owned the land. King said the best resolution might be a negotiated settlement whereby the tribe paid them for the land through federal government grants. If the Pequots, or anyone else for that matter, wanted to buy them out at a good price, that would be fine too.

King and Tillinghast said they would pursue the legal research necessary to mount a preliminary response to the court.
They also suggested that to keep costs down, the landowners
themselves do some of the historical research. Dave Holdridge
volunteered to lead the research effort at the state archive and
the state library in Hartford.

King and Tillinghast filed for a three-month extension from
the court to give them time to get up to speed. Meanwhile, they
called on their local political representatives for help. King contacted the Connecticut attorney general's office to see whether
the state might join the defense effort as it was the state that had
allegedly botched the reservation land sale back in 1855. The
attorney general's office responded that the state did not litigate
private civil actions. Pine Tree Legal had intentionally refrained
from suing the State of Connecticut in order to avoid giving it a
reason to intervene.

5

HOUSES

While King and his clients searched the state archives, Skip Hayward was pushing ahead on other fronts. His family, especially his sisters, wanted Skip to petition the state to deed the reservation to the remaining members of the tribe, primarily the Hayward family. Their plan was to divide the land into two-acre and four-acre plots that would be individually owned. Skip didn't like the idea of dividing the land. He was one of the few members who favored treating the land as common, or tribal, property. Yet he didn't have an attractive housing alternative to offer to his siblings, who wanted houses most of all. He needed to find out if the federal government would subsidize new housing.

Skip drove up to Hartford to introduce himself to the local office of the U.S. Department of Housing and Urban Development. HUD's local community planning development representative was Alan Hayes. Previously a planner for the city of Springfield, Massachusetts, the thirty-seven-year-old Hayes arrived at HUD already jaded about the federal housing bureaucracy, questioning its commitment to its housing mandate. He was intent on helping poor people. Skip arrived at Hayes's office wearing his usual outfit of blue jeans and a T-shirt with a pack of Marlboro cigarettes rolled up in one sleeve. He sat down on Hayes's desk and said, "I'm the chairman of the Western Pequots down in Ledyard."

Skip explained that he had learned from the Passamaquoddy that the tribes in Maine had qualified for subsidized housing, and Skip felt the Pequots should be next in line. He said that HUD housing also had a second objective: to bolster the tribe's case for federal recognition. If HUD recognized the Pequots, then that would get the ball rolling toward full-fledged federal recognition from the BIA.

Hayes promised to look into how the Maine tribes had received HUD assistance, then get back to Skip. As soon as Skip left, Hayes raced into his boss's office. "You'll never believe the conversation I just had," he said. "I just met an Indian chief from Connecticut."

Hayes discovered that under the HUD Indian housing assistance program, the Pequots must first be deemed "an autonomous unit of government" by the state. In essence, Connecticut needed to certify that the tribal government functioned akin to a town or city government. Hayes needed to plot a strategy to overcome this potential bureaucratic obstacle, so he contacted CIAC, which suggested that the Schaghticoke and Golden Hill Paugussett be included in any HUD-inspired designation of Connecticut tribes as "autonomous units of government" by the state. The broader the coalition, according to CIAC, the more effective the political lobbying effort.

As it turned out, granting these minuscule Indian groups the same legal status as Ledyard, Norwich, New London, or, for that matter, Hartford was remarkably easy because of the fact that HUD—not Connecticut—would pay for any future subsidized housing. HUD had enormous bureaucratic clout in Connecticut at the time by virtue of its community development block grant program, which had just been funded by Congress. Over the next several years, HUD handed out more than $1 billion throughout the state.

"I asked the state what criteria were required for a municipality to qualify for revenue sharing," Hayes recalled. "The State of Connecticut gave me a set of parameters. I then took this box of parameters and made the Pequots fit into the box. I went to my lawyers at HUD and I asked, 'Is this legal?' They said it was. We were dealing pretty much with the lawyers at the state attorney general's office. We are not dealing with political people. This is taking place at the staff level. We got it done very quietly. After about nine months, the lawyers for Connecticut said, 'Okay. The Western Pequots are now recognized for revenue sharing.' Once I had them recognized for revenue sharing, they were a legitimate Connecticut governmental entity. Once they were a legitimate Connecticut entity, I could then accept Skip's application for grants from the federal government and HUD."

In March 1976, Governor Ella Grasso, a liberal Democrat and the first female governor of Connecticut, notified the federal government that the Pequots should "be included as [a unit] of Connecticut local government for revenue sharing purposes." Grasso determined that the Pequots and the two other tribes "have recognized tribal governing bodies, which exercise substantial governmental functions." The total Pequot population, according to information Skip Hayward had provided to the state, was thirty-two men, women, and children, most his close relations.

Hayes visited the reservation several times in 1976 and was impressed. Skip took him up to Council Rocks, where his sister Terry Bell had been married. High atop the rocky bluff, the two men could smell the salt air blowing in from Long Island Sound. Skip walked Alan around the reservation and showed him where he planned to build houses. Later, Hayes came to the reservation on his own time, on weekends with family and friends, to help cut wood and bearing gifts of government-issue pens and paper and notepads from the HUD supply closet.

In 1978, Skip formed a Pequot housing authority with the permission of the state and was ready to apply for HUD loans and grants. HUD grants were fiercely competitive, so Hayes was enlisted to rewrite the Pequot grant applications himself. "My fingerprints were on the applications," Hayes recalled. "Skip was not a writer. No one in his family was. I knew the rules and the regulations. I knew the right words, the right language to meet HUD's requirements. I would not literally sit down at the type-writer, but I would review the applications before they were submitted and recommend changes."

Hayes drafted such a compelling narrative of the Pequots' history that in 1979 they won a $12,000 grant to pay for the writing of an economic development plan for the reservation, a prerequisite for subsequent housing grants. With Skip's input, Hayes sketched out a vision of a repopulated reservation with federal housing, a community center, a public health facility, roads, even a wind-driven energy generating plant to be set on a high bluff. Hayes portrayed the reservation as a center of agricultural entrepreneurial activity that simply needed more capital to grow. He wrote, for example, of the Pequots' maple sugar operation, making it sound like a profitable venture. It was, in truth, a money loser. (Years later, Skip shut down the ill-fated operation.)

Skip received the planning grant, which financed the writing of the application that convinced HUD to loan the Pequots $1.2 million for the construction of fifteen houses on extremely favorable terms. Skip and his family members were not obliged to make down payments on the houses. They simply had to promise to landscape the property around their houses. HUD further agreed to subsidize their mortgage payments to ensure that no one paid more than 25 percent of household income. Most important, the houses were to be single-family dwellings with basements and garages, not semidetached row houses or apartments. This raised the cost of the project considerably, to 85 percent above HUD's construction guidelines. Hayes made a special trip to Washington, D.C., at Skip's request and convinced HUD that the "unique geology" of the Ledyard reservation required major blasting, which was needed to excavate the land for the basements and garages. In contrast, the typical HUD house on an Indian reservation at the time was built on nothing more than a poured concrete slab.

The housing plan was to build fifteen houses, each on two-acre lots, at a cost of about $125,000 apiece. John Holder, a cousin of Skip's, oversaw the project. (Holder's maternal grandfather had been a brother of Eliza's.) When Skip asked Holder to take the job, John was initially reluctant. He already made a good living as a draftsman at Electric Boat in Groton, and he wasn't sure he wanted to become executive director of the tribe's new housing authority.

"What the hell is a housing authority?" he asked.

"I don't really know," Skip said. "But if you come work, we'll have a lot of fun."

John's hesitation also stemmed from his already being a member of the Eastern Pequots, who had their own reservation next door in North Stonington. John had been a member of the Eastern Pequot tribal council, but he stepped down during a power struggle between lighter-skinned members like himself and darker-skinned members. Skip wooed John to switch to the Ledyard Pequots, which was almost exclusively light-skinned. Skip said he was offering John an opportunity to get in on the ground floor of something big, a new tribe that was going to construct new housing and start new businesses. It was a crazy but seductive dream. After six months of courtship, John switched tribes and became a Western Pequot.

The job of housing director turned out to be more difficult than Skip had led John to believe. The problem wasn't the construction process but dealing with Skip's immediate family. John may have had the title of housing director, and HUD may have been financing the construction, but the Haywards set the rules. John rehung Sheetrock, repapered walls, and ordered better bathroom fixtures for the Haywards. Despite this attention to detail,

Skip's family suspected John of building himself a better house than they were getting. Their discovery of his slightly nicer basement confirmed their suspicions, resulting in their complaining to HUD that John had misappropriated federal funds. John countered that he had paid personally for the improvements and that Skip's family was free to do so as well.

"I got your mother and sisters all over my ass," John complained to Skip. "They're accusing me of doing extra things to my house and not paying for them. Skip, I don't know what to do here."

"Well, John, you better be careful," Skip replied. "Those people can put you in jail."

John was cleared of all charges and in fact was complimented by the HUD inspector, who said the housing was the best-constructed HUD project he had ever seen. At the ribbon-cutting ceremony, Connecticut Governor William O'Neill and other local dignitaries lavishly praised the quality of the construction. It was an enormous political and personal coup for Skip, who saw the housing project as only the beginning.

One winter afternoon after the houses were finished, some of the Pequots and hired laborers were felling trees in the woods. The temperature was a frigid ten degrees below zero. The sun was setting, and it was getting colder. They were cutting by the light from the headlamps of an old pickup. Skip showed up with a case of beer. They stopped work and sat down on tree stumps. As they were drinking, Skip spoke about his vision for the Pequots. "One day, we're going to be rich," he told them. One of Skip's cousins looked at the beer bottle in Skip's hand and said, "This beer is not doing to me what it's doing to you." But when he looked into Skip's eyes, he could see that Skip was deadly serious. Moved, he said to Skip, "Look, things can't get any worse. I'm unemployed. My wife has thrown me out of the house. And I'm living with my mother. I'm just about as down to the bottom of the barrel as you can get. I'll take my chances with you."

6

NEGOTIATIONS

O
n January 15, 1979, the Pequots filed an informal, preliminary tribal recognition petition with the BIA. Historian Jack Campisi, who had previously worked for Tom
Tureen on other Indian land-claim suits, wrote the petition. A
tenacious, prickly defender of Indian rights, Campisi's greatest
challenge was to explain Pequot tribal life, or the lack thereof, in
the twentieth century. He solved this problem by asserting that,
since the mid-1930s, the tribal organization centered on Eliza "but
that other members of her family as well as those from other families were consulted on a regular basis. As might be expected, no
formal records were kept of these meetings." An expanded tribal
roll of fifty-five, still almost exclusively the descendants of Eliza
and her siblings, was sent with the preliminary petition. The roll
was padded with the names of Skip's cousins who, in truth, had
little or no involvement with him or his Pequots. In the case of
his cousin Bill Guevremont, for example, Guevremont did not discover his name had been used on the early tribal roll until he actually got involved with the tribe in 1994.

Campisi told the BIA that the Pequots would submit a formal petition later in the year, but in fact, whether Campisi knew
it or not, his work was a diversion. Tom Tureen had no intention of submitting a completed recognition petition with the
requisite genealogical, anthropological, and historical support.
The BIA already had dozens of petitions from unrecognized

groups like the Pequots to consider, and the Pequots might have to wait years for a complete review, which could easily end in rejection. If the BIA experts were given a chance to scrutinize in detail the authenticity and continuity of the Pequots, Tureen feared the investigation might conclude that the Pequot tribe had died out before Skip and his family had reinvented it. The strongest evidence of continuous Pequot existence was Connecticut's 213-year maintenance of the reservation, which Tureen argued was prima facie evidence of tribal continuity, but the fact could just as easily be interpreted as a sign of Connecticut's political indifference and bureaucratic inertia.

As much as Tureen feared putting the Pequots through the BIA vetting process, he was even more concerned about a court ruling on Pequot tribal existence. In 1978 Pine Tree had lost a land-claim case in Massachusetts on behalf of the Mashpee Indians, who lived on Cape Cod. The town and local landowners had challenged the Mashpee's legitimacy to bring suit, arguing that the Mashpee had ceased to be a tribe before launching the lawsuit. The judge ordered a trial to determine whether the Mashpee were a legitimate tribe. After several weeks of testimony from expert witnesses for both sides, including Campisi for the Mashpee, the case went to the jury. The jurors decided the Mashpee were not a tribe and therefore had no legal standing to recover lost tribal land. The verdict was upheld by the U.S. Court of Appeals, which explicitly outlined its definition of a tribe: "Plaintiff must prove that it meets the definition of 'tribe of Indians' as that phrase is used in the Non-Intercourse Act. By a 'tribe' we understand a body of Indians (1) of the same or similar race, (2) united in a community, (3) under one leadership or government, and (4) inhabiting a particular though sometimes ill-defined territory."

Applying this set of criteria to the Pequots was Tureen's greatest concern. "Why wouldn't a court have simply looked at the Pequots and said, 'This is not a tribe anymore. They stopped being a tribe a long time ago. The fact that the land was held in trust by the state may have been mistaken. It does not have legal significance,'" Tureen recalled. "We did not know what the test would have been to prove the existence of the Pequots as a tribe. Everything we were doing was right on the cutting edge of the law. We had other cases pending for other tribes. We did not want to endanger those cases by a reversal in the Pequot case. There was an enormous question as to whether or not they legally constituted a tribe. . . . If they had had to go through the BIA recognition process, they very well might not have made it."

By mid-1979, Tureen decided to seek an out-of-court settlement. He needed a settlement whereby all the parties in the suit—the Pequots, the landholders, and the State of Connecticut—could agree on a deal. They would then make common cause and petition the federal government to finance the settlement. His logic was that the federal government had helped create this mess by failing to enforce the Non-Intercourse Act and should therefore bear the cost of resolving the dispute that resulted from its inaction. Tureen had already used this strategy in Maine to settle the land-claim cases of the Passamaquoddy and Penobscot tribes. In October 1980, Congress passed a bill that gave the Passamaquoddy and Penobscot $80.6 million to buy disputed land, and also handed them federal recognition and access to federal aid programs for Indians. Maine was Tureen's model for Connecticut.

By this time, Jackson King's legal defenses were variations on a theme; that is, too much time had passed since the land transfer. "I had filed this wonderful defense I thought was going to devastate Tureen," King recalled. "And he just sends me back copies of other decisions in other federal courts that have rolled over similar time defenses. So all the time defenses go right out the window. Also, we had argued that the Non-Intercourse Act was never intended to apply to those tribes vanquished before the Revolutionary War. But again, it was very clear that argument was not prevailing in other federal courts in New England and that it was unlikely to fly in Connecticut either. And I am seeing that all the rulings are rulings on cases involving Tureen. Tureen had been able to establish that the Non-Intercourse Act did apply to eastern tribes who were conquered well before the Revolution."

The federal judge in Connecticut, Joseph Blumenfeld, had upheld Tureen on every major legal issue King raised. King felt his only avenue of attack was to call into question the tribal legitimacy of the Pequots, an argument that would be extremely expensive to make. "The only issue left in the case was the historical issue of whether this was truly a tribe during the entire period of time since 1855," King recalled. "There was our potential point of attack. We were going to have to undermine the idea that they have been a tribe throughout that period of time. Now, we are looking at having to provide some expert testimony about this tribe. We are now talking about hiring expert witnesses—historians and anthropologists and genealogists—to testify."

King called Tureen on the telephone. "We seriously question the authenticity of the tribe," he said. "We are going to go after it."

Tureen bluffed, "We have all the evidence. We have our historians." He then told King that if he wanted a fight over tribal legitimacy, he would get one, and that would mean King's clients spending years and perhaps hundreds of thousands of dollars in the effort. (The defendants in the Mashpee land-claim case paid $350,000 in legal and related bills.) In the Pequot case, there were far fewer landowners to share the cost of the defense—roughly a dozen versus seventeen thousand at Mashpee. The Pequot case had already dragged on for several years, and King had yet to bill his clients for the time he and his firm had spent. Arguing over land that was worth less than $200,000, King concluded, was unwise. "If we try the case and we lose it, then the clients are out the money and their land," he recalled. "If we try the case and win, then the clients are out the money spent, which was probably as much or more than their land was worth."

In October 1981, Tureen contacted King and offered to visit him in Connecticut to discuss resolving the dispute. Accompanied by Skip Hayward, Tureen explained to King that they were going to submit a bill in Congress that would clear all the land titles and provide the tribe with money to buy the land from those property holders who wanted to sell. The legislation would be modeled on the Maine settlement.

"How are you going to get a bill passed?" King asked.

"We're going to go down to Washington, and I need you to come. There's going to be a hearing on this legislation. You and Skip are going to be witnesses. And you are going to testify in favor of legislation. And if you are in favor of this bill, it will be passed."

"Will all my clients have to sell?"

"No, but it won't work unless we get the bulk of them to sell," Tureen said. "If you have certain clients who really don't want to sell, we can work that out. But give me a feeling for who wants to sell and who does not want to sell. They will get market value."

"Okay. Let me talk to my clients. But what about their legal fees? They ought to be reimbursed for their legal expenses."

"You're not going to get that," Tureen said. "The federal government will not pay your legal bills."

"Well, I want you to try," King insisted. "We have spent hundreds of hours on this case."

Tureen offered to see what he could do, and King tentatively agreed to an out-of-court settlement.

Tureen was delighted, having just preempted a messy legal battle. He had just co-opted his primary adversary.

7

DEVELOPMENT

With federal government money courtesy of the grant applications HUD representative Hayes had helped write, Skip managed to sustain and even expand his money-losing attempts at job creation on the Ledyard reservation. Skip's next attempt at economic development on the reservation was to enter the hydroponic lettuce business. In a hydroponic operation, which is invariably expensive and energy-intensive, the plants are grown in trays filled with fertilized water that sit under heat lamps in greenhouses. The plan was to sell lettuce to grocers between Boston and New York City. Using government money, Skip invested in a mammoth greenhouse that could produce ten thousand heads of lettuce a week. Unfortunately, each head of lettuce cost about sixty cents to grow but could be sold for only twenty-three cents. Skip's family members spent days driving trucks to city markets only to return with unsold, rotting lettuce. Skip blamed his troubles on corrupt distributors opposed to Indians trying to make a buck, and the business soon folded.

Skip's "swine project" was next. His idea was to buy piglets and raise them until they were big enough to sell. Skip and his family initially slaughtered a few pigs themselves, but few in the family actually had the stomach for the messy work. So the pigs were shipped off alive and sold for $35 each, which didn't cover the Pequots' production costs, even with government grants. Like lettuce, the swine project was a bust too.

Luckily for Skip there was a small but steady stream of private money willing to keep his small businesses afloat. Two of his staunchest financial backers were Sandy Cadwalader, the young executive secretary of the Indian Rights Association (IRA) based in Philadelphia, and Miss Ruth Thompson, an elderly wealthy lady from Greenwich, Connecticut, both graduates of Smith College.

The IRA was a charity founded in 1882 by Episcopalians to assist impoverished Indian tribes out West. By the 1970s, however, as newer, Indian-led organizations took the lead in lobbying Washington on behalf of western tribes, the IRA turned its attentions east. Cadwalader, a recent law school graduate, had been introduced to Skip by Tom Tureen. She was fascinated by the idea that remnant Indian groups in the East might have claims to lost lands and federal recognition. Cadwalader raised money to finance Pine Tree's efforts, and Miss Thompson was one of Cadwalader's most generous backers. Thompson had inherited her money—some tribal members said it came from real estate while others claimed her family had owned the famous Thompson machine gun company. She had never married and lived alone in a hunting lodge on her family's former estate in Greenwich, Connecticut, giving away tens of thousands of dollars a year to various Indian causes.

Cadwalader's organization agreed to fund the historical research for the preliminary federal recognition petition submitted to the BIA by Skip Hayward, with Cadwalader often acting as the point person between Skip and Miss Thompson, who wrote checks totaling close to $100,000. Thompson loved Skip, but she worried about him and his family. Their simplicity appealed to her, and as long as they remained a small group on a few hundred acres with modest ambitions, they were worth preserving. "I certainly hope they stay small," she said.

Skip managed to obtain an employment grant from the federal government in 1979 via the Comprehensive Employment and

Training Act (CETA) program, a Nixon-era initiative intended to provide jobs and job training for underprivileged Americans. Skip immediately hired himself a receptionist. Her name was Simone Herritt, a young mother of two small children, and she was the first full-time tribal employee other than Skip and his family.

Simone hadn't known there were Indians in the area, let alone a reservation. When she came for her interview, all she found was a small, beat-up, blue-and-white trailer. Inside was a shambles. Field mice periodically scampered up the sides of the walls, and there was no phone. About ten minutes later, Skip's cousin in charge of hiring, Bruce Kirchner, arrived. It was a short interview. He asked Simone if she wanted a job. She said that she did want a job and was willing to do just about anything. She was hired at a salary of $200 a week.

Not long after, Skip bought Simone a telephone. When people called, Simone answered, "Office of the chairman of the Mashantucket Pequot tribe." She spent most of her time writing grants to get money and baby-sitting pigs. There were weeks when she did not receive pay because Skip had not scrounged up enough money to meet payroll. Nonetheless, Simone came to love Skip and her job. Simone's hiring was notable for her being the Pequots' first full-time tribal employee, though she would not be the last.

8

SETTLEMENT

Tom Tureen was familiar with the profit possibilities of bingo because for years the Penobscots had operated a hall on their reservation in Maine. Unfortunately, when Tureen negotiated the Penobscot and Passamaquoddy land-claim settlement in 1980, Maine had insisted on retaining regulatory authority over the reservation. Since Maine regulations prohibited high-stakes gambling, it was also banned on the reservations. Tureen wanted to avoid any such regulatory prohibitions in the Pequot land-claim settlement. He had high hopes for gambling in Connecticut. The Penobscots had been earning several million dollars a year in rural Maine before being forced to close down the operation by the state. The Pequots, whose reservation was located midway between New York City and Boston, had an opportunity to make that amount look like a pittance.

Skip was excited by the prospect of gambling on the Ledyard reservation. His economic development efforts had failed as businesses, and government grants, aid programs, and private charity were not providing the jobs he needed to attract potential new tribal members. Skip agreed with Tureen's suggestion that they design a settlement bill that would leave open the possibility of gambling.

Any settlement deal first required the blessing of the state government. So Tureen asked the State of Connecticut to transfer ownership of the reservation to the federal government, and in exchange the Pequots would drop their claim against the landowners. Washington would then formally recognize the Pequots as a tribe, provide money to buy out the property owners, and permit those acres to be incorporated into an expanded, federally recognized reservation. The state administration in Hartford was eager to sign off on almost any deal. "No one [in state government] really gave a shit," Tureen recalled. "It was such a small matter."

The state's one demand was that it retain legal authority on the reservation for criminal and civil matters. Tureen was happy to agree to that. He knew that criminal and civil jurisdiction would not prevent legalized gambling. Only "regulatory" authority could do that, as Connecticut already prohibited high-stakes gambling. This was a crucial point, as the Supreme Court had ruled that state regulations didn't apply on Indian reservations. If a state permitted bingo, albeit under regulatory restrictions, then similarly a federally recognized Indian tribe could have bingo on its reservation free of state regulations.

In June 1982, the state approved Tureen's proposed settlement. Connecticut did not retain regulatory jurisdiction over the reservation. "The attitude in Hartford was, 'Let's just get this done. It's the right thing for all parties, and the federal government is going to pick up the bill anyway.'" As Tureen recalled, "Never underestimate the ignorance of your opponents. People are real stupid sometimes."

Tureen drafted a settlement bill for Congress, which he planned to have introduced in the ninety-seventh session. He showed the draft to Jackson King, who readily approved it. Based on appraisals of the eight hundred acres at issue, the Pequots were to receive $900,000 from the federal government, money that would be used to buy land from Jackson's clients. As a sweetener for the property owners, Tom included a provision allowing them to sell without incurring capital gains tax, as long as they reinvested the money in real estate.

With the help of Indian lobbyists in Washington, Tureen asked the staff of Connecticut Republican Senator Lowell Weicker if the state's senior senator would introduce the legislation. A proponent of Indian rights, Weicker was ideally positioned to give the bill a strong push in the Senate. Weicker felt deeply that Indians had been "dumped on for far too long." If he could help usher a few toward affluence and economic development, especially if they were constituents from Connecticut, so much the better.

Weicker's staff walked the draft bill over to the Senate Select Committee on Indian Affairs, which had been established in 1977 in response to the "Red Power" protests of the late 1960s and early seventies. The committee staff was well versed in the technical minutiae of Indian legislation, and its general counsel, Peter Taylor, immediately noticed one glaring omission in the draft bill: there was no limit on the location or amount of land in Connecticut that the Pequots would be eligible to buy with the $900,000 settlement.

"We don't want this money just to buy land anywhere—in New Haven or Norwich or wherever. This is only to buy land within a certain defined area. We need a map of precisely what that area is," Taylor told Tureen and King. He knew that property bought by a federally recognized tribe within the settlement area could be taken into trust by the Department of the Interior and added to the reservation. The land within the settlement area would be reclassified as federal "Indian country," which meant the loss of state and local control. The reservation would have a legal status akin to an army base.

Tureen, King, and Skip Hayward found a nearby meeting room in the Senate with a large table and some chairs. They looked at one another. Who was going to draw the map? "I know the land pretty well," said King, who had years of experience handling land transfers in the area. "I can give it a shot, if you guys want." He scrounged around in his briefcase and found an assessor's map of the reservation and the surrounding land. He placed it on a table, sat down, and pulled out a red felt marker.

With Tureen and Skip guiding him, King drew the outlines of the settlement area on the map. He marked out an area intended to include five categories of land. First, the existing reservation. Second, the eight hundred acres of land sold in 1855 at issue in the lawsuit. Third, a twenty-two-acre Pequot cemetery being transferred to the Pequots by the State of Connecticut. Fourth, any land that Tureen and Skip thought might have been part of the original Pequot reservation as of 1666. Finally, he included any land the Pequots might have a shot at acquiring in the relatively near future. The sum total of acreage defined by this hastily drawn settlement map was about two thousand acres, far in excess of the eight hundred acres at issue in the lawsuit. From Skip and Tureen's point of view, the additional acreage meant more reservation land for the gambling establishment they were already discussing in private. King had not been taken into their confidence, but he knew of their desire to buy property along the road for economic development. In October 1981, Skip and Tom had visited King at his law office in Norwich and discussed the Pequots' intention to buy two large parcels of agricultural land along Route 2—a 300-acre piece and another 550-acre site. King had heard Skip say that there were thousands of acres that ultimately should be part of the reservation, and that the Pequots deserved all the land back, meaning far more than the acreage at issue in the lawsuit.

King realized that he, Skip, and Tureen were giving the Pequots the right to dramatically expand the reservation. Why did he do that? He later recalled, "It corresponded roughly with what the reservation was probably two hundred years ago—and I say 'probably' because it's very hard to know. That reservation boundary changed an awful lot from 1666 up until 1855. So, when I say it was about what the reservation was, I can't be absolutely sure of that. . . . That's how the map got drawn, and that thing is written in stone now, and yet that's what went into the process."

As far as King was concerned, giving the Pequots an expanded reservation did not impinge on his clients' interests. They would still get clear title and a ready market for their properties if they wished to sell. He believed it was an amicable arrangement. It did not cross his mind that there was anything odd about the representatives of the two parties to the lawsuit essentially redrawing the map of Ledyard without any input from the town.

On July 14, 1982, the chairman of the Senate Select Committee on Indian Affairs, William S. Cohen (R-Maine), opened congressional hearings on S. 2719: The Mashantucket Pequot Indian Claims Settlement Act. Cohen commended the Pequots, landowners, and the State of Connecticut for having reached a compromise agreement, contrasting the situation with the divisive and lengthy fight in Maine between the state and its tribes. Cohen asked William Coldiron, solicitor general of the Department of the Interior, to speak on behalf of the Reagan administration. Coldiron was a hardnosed Republican lawyer from Montana who had made his career representing the state's energy and power industry. As the Interior Department's top lawyer, Coldiron reviewed legislation involving the federal government's relationship with tribes. He was less impressed than Cohen with the Pequot bill.

"The [Interior] Department recommends against the enactment of S. 2719," Coldiron said, because it allowed the Pequots to circumvent the BIA recognition process established in 1978 to "provide consideration of petitions under a uniform standard based on systematic and detailed examination of historical evidence. Such bypassing would set a precedent which might encourage similar legislative requests from other groups with pending petitions." Coldiron noted that the BIA already had eighty-three pending recognition petitions. In addition, he said, $900,000 might be too much to pay to extinguish the Pequots' land claim, and the Reagan administration wanted Connecticut to pick up more of the cost. Third, and most problematic for Tureen, Coldiron noted, "The Western Pequot group petitioned for federal acknowledgment on January 15, 1979, under the Secretary's regulations, and a final submission of full documentation is apparently imminent. For some reason, there is presently little available information on file to indicate whether the group could meet the requirements for federal acknowledgment under the regulations. Therefore, we do not have sufficient information about the group to support the acknowledgment at this time."

Coldiron argued that the Pequots be subject to the usual BIA vetting: "Even if the Western Pequots' petition were rejected under the regulation, the group would still be able to approach Congress for acknowledgment through legislation. . . . Congress at that time could make a decision based on full and accurate anthropological, historical, and genealogical data collected through extensive research."

Senator Cohen chastised the Interior for not being more familiar with the Pequots and their land claim. Coldiron replied, "With respect to the Western Pequot, they are still knocking at the door, so to speak. They have not filed any materials with us. We do not have it in the files." Cohen complained that a senior official of the Interior Department ought to be better informed before coming to testify on Capitol Hill. Coldiron was ill informed, of course, because at Tureen's suggestion the Pequots had intentionally withheld submission of the formal acknowledgment petition to the BIA. In doing so, they had ensured that the Interior lacked the anthropological, historical, and genealogical proof necessary to testify convincingly one way or the other on tribal authenticity.

Coldiron's questions about tribal credibility had effectively redirected the hearing, and the supporters in Congress of the Pequot claims were forced to respond. No one spoke more passionately in favor of the bill than Representative Sam Gejdenson, the newly elected liberal Democratic representative from southeastern Connecticut. "This bill meets the criterion of a [credible] claim. The Indians have lived on this land. They have a commitment to it. They are certainly a tribe," he said. When Gejdenson finished, Cohen said, "The only question I have is that I was surprised to hear the Solicitor say that they have no real information on which to base a settlement specification and that they have had no real participation in the negotiations, that they have been almost totally removed from the process. That struck me as odd."

Gejdenson replied, "I find it difficult to believe that they have not heard of it at all."

Cohen then asked, "Has there been no participation by the Interior Department? Has the Interior Department worked with you at all?"

Gejdenson bucked Cohen's question on to Skip, who replied, "Almost all of the federal agencies were involved." Gejdenson jumped in to explain that the tribe had worked closely with HUD and other federal agencies, but not with the Interior. "That may be partially our fault," Gejdenson admitted.

Cohen said, "It seems to me that we ought to have the Interior Department involved in this settlement before we go ahead."

Gejdenson replied, "We will certainly do some more homework immediately."

Skip spoke next. He gave a moving rendition of the Pequot narrative—the unjust treatment by the Puritans, the Pequots' stubborn survival, and their miraculous rebirth under his leadership.

The Mashantucket Pequot Tribe and the Mashantucket Pequot Reservation was once part of the powerful Pequot Nation, which inhabited the area centered in southeastern Connecticut prior to the Pequot massacre in the year 1637. . . . It was the desire of our predecessors that we hold and maintain the land. It is the desire of the Mashantucket people to continue to exist on its land as a tribe and to be self governing, maintain a good standard of living for its people, and become self determining and self sufficient through its economic development projects. . . .

In closing, I would like to read the last paragraph of a letter sent by Robin Cassacinamon, Sachem of the Pequot Tribe at Mashantucket to the Governor at Hartford on May 11, 1721: "I in behalf of myself & people do humbly Pray this Honorable Assembly that your Honors would be pleased to do us Justice by Nulling and making void what Groton Gentlemen have done in letting out and fencing as aforesaid and yet your Honors would be pleased to Confirm and Quiet us in our Ancient possessions at Mashantuxit as aforesaid. All which I in behalf of myself & people do humbly Pray."

Senator Cohen observed, looking at Tureen, "It sounds as though [Skip] has a Harvard Law education."

Tureen jumped in to address the concerns raised by Coldiron. "I am very pleased to see the apparent interest which Interior has in looking into the merits of the claim," he said. "As soon as this hearing is over, I shall contact them, and I will be discussing it with them. I will provide all of the information to them. Certainly, it should not be difficult for them to determine that the claim is . . . on par with the Maine claim. The federal acknowledgment people [from the BIA] have been in Connecticut. They are familiar with both tribes. It is my understanding that they believe that [the Pequots] could easily establish recognition status through that process. I feel that it would be a terrible waste of the federal government's resources and the tribe's very limited resources to have to go through that process. I think it far more efficient all around, inasmuch as we all know that they will be recognized, to simply do it in legislation."

It was a brilliant performance, in particular Tureen's assertion that the Pequots would sail through the BIA recognition process when in private he believed precisely the opposite. As he wrote later in a January 1983 memo to another attorney working for the Pequots, "Insofar as the submission of a recognition petition is concerned, I think that the Tribe should . . . see where its legislation stands before making a decision on submission of the petition. I say this because the pendency of a petition might make Congress less willing to go along with a settlement which grants recognition to the Band simply because it could be argued that the recognition petition had already been submitted and that the issue should be decided administratively [i.e., by the BIA]."

The day after the Senate hearing, the House of Representatives held its own hearing chaired by Representative Gejdenson. The son of Jewish survivors of the Nazi death camps, Gejdenson was born in 1948 in a refugee camp in postwar Germany. He came with his family to southeastern Connecticut where his father and uncle established themselves as dairy farmers. As a child, Gejdenson attended 4-H camp where he was taught outdoor skills and camping by one of the leaders of the nearby Mohegan tribe, Harold Tantaquidgeon. Gejdenson admired Tantaquidgeon, who taught the campers to appreciate and sympathize with Indian history. Gejdenson had cut his political teeth as an anti–Vietnam War protester at the University of Connecticut at Storrs, later becoming a Democratic party operative and establishing himself as a leading member of its liberal wing. He served two terms in the State House before going to work for Governor Ella Grasso. Gejdenson knew Skip from the late 1970s, when he attended the ground breaking for the Pequots' hydroponic lettuce operation, and he was eager to push the legislation through the House as quickly as possible. Coldiron had other ideas. At the house he was even more pointed in his opposition to the Pequot bill than he had been the day before, noting the inequity of the Pequots receiving instant federal recognition when so many other tribes awaited BIA approval.

Gejdenson interrupted, stating, "Even though this tribe has been recognized in state law over the last two hundred years or more, you still think that we should go through the federal recognition process. It seems that if we have a tribe in the State of Connecticut, and they call it a tribe, and they have paid for the tribe's services through the last one hundred years, and that tribe has lived on the land for all that period of time, it is a tribe. Why should we be forced to go through a long regulatory process if we are trying to simplify all that, and if we are given an opportunity to do it, let us do it quickly and cleanly."

Coldiron countered that if the Pequots would submit a completed petition with all the relevant supporting information, then the BIA could quickly make an informed decision.

Gejdenson pressed Coldiron to admit that state recognition of the Pequots and their reservation was tantamount to proof that they were a tribe. "Wouldn't you say that makes them a tribe?" he insisted.

"Not necessarily," replied Coldiron. "We would have to examine the evidence. There is a possibility that they might not be. If it is so simple, why haven't they come in the last three years?"

The deadlock between Coldiron and Gejdenson made things awkward for the other members of the House Interior Committee. "I think we are in a tough spot on this," offered Representative Bruce Vento (D-Minn.).

Gejdenson did his best to conclude the hearing on a conciliatory note. It was obvious to him that his committee colleagues had mixed feelings about rushing to recognize the Pequots, so he asked Tureen to provide the Interior with all the supporting documentation of Pequot tribal existence. Tureen replied, "We have spoken with [Coldiron] today. We have arranged for a process by which we will provide them with the information they want. . . . We should be able to get them up to speed very quickly. We will be doing that next week."

*   *   *

Despite Tureen's promise, the Pequots did not submit a final recognition petition to the BIA. Nonetheless, the House passed H.R.
6612 on October 1, 1982, and the Senate passed its version of the
bill on December 21. Tureen was sufficiently optimistic about the
bill's chances in the ninety-eighth Congress that he recommended
the Pequots continue to hold off on submission of a formal recognition petition. On February 24, 1983, the Senate passed the
Pequot bill by voice vote, and the House did the same on March
22. The legislation was sent to President Reagan for his signature.

To everyone's surprise, Reagan vetoed the bill. He wanted
the federal government to pay less because he feared setting a
precedent for other tribes that could cost the federal government "billions of dollars." Second, he objected to the "unaccept-
ably low level of State contribution to the settlement—only
20 acres of State land with an estimated value of about $50,000
[the adjacent Pequot cemetery]." Third, Reagan expressed
doubts as to Pequot tribal identity. "The Tribe may not meet
the standard requirements for Federal recognition or services
that are required of other tribes," he wrote. "The government-
to-government relationship between the Western Pequot Tribe
and the Federal Government that would be established by this
bill is not warranted at this time, pending further study by Interior. Extending Federal recognition to the Tribe would bypass
the Department of the Interior's administrative procedures that
apply a consistent set of eligibility standards in determining
whether or not Federal recognition should be extended to Indian
groups."

No one was more outraged at Reagan's veto than Senator
Lowell Weicker. A man of towering height with an ego to match,
Weicker took Reagan's veto as a personal insult. He knew next to
nothing about the Pequots but he was "damned if he was going
to let Reagan screw things up," he recalled. Weicker counted
heads in the Senate and figured he had a good chance to override
the president, which at that time had yet to happen on any piece

of his adminstration's legislation. Weicker loved the idea of sock-
ing it to an ideological enemy who was driving political moder-
ates like him to the fringes of the Republican party, and he felt
that with some skillful horse trading he could pull off a major political upset against the president.

Tureen went to work rounding up Skip, King, Sandy Cadwalader of the Indian Rights Association, and a few tribal employees
for two weeks of intensive door-to-door lobbying on the Hill. Indian lobbyist Suzanne Harjo set the schedule, organizing them into
pairs. Using Weicker's office as a base, they met each morning over
coffee. Harjo gave each pair a list of people to visit and a script to
follow. To save time and effort, she told them to focus on swing
votes, those senators who were not already known to be for or against
the legislation. Knowing she was dealing mainly with political rook-
ies, Harjo explained the basics of retail lobbying. "You just knock
on the door," she said. "You identify yourself and you ask to see the
senator and you tell them what you want to talk about."

Two key political assets for the Pequots were the relatively
small size of the actual settlement—$900,000—and having Skip—
"a real live Indian chief," according to Tureen—available to take
to the meetings. Skip was humble, patient, and almost apologetic
for taking up people's time, valuable traits as the conversations
with Senate staffers were typically short and to the point.

A prime example was the conversation between an aide to
Senator Henry (Scoop) Jackson (D-Washington) and Pequot anthropologist James Wherry.

Jackson's aide said, "I'm a busy guy. Tell me one thing. How
much is this legislation going to cost?"

"Nine hundred thousand," said Wherry.

"Do you have local support, state support?"

"Yes."

"Okay. The Senator will vote for it. We're done."

And off they would go, down the great, marble halls to the
next senatorial office.

When they met a senator who was wavering in his support for the bill, they would bring in Weicker. For instance, Senator Cohen of Maine wanted a bill to finance the preservation of lighthouses in Maine before he would vote for the Pequot bill. Weicker complained about trading votes, but in the end he did. "All right," bellowed Weicker. "Get that motherfucking son of a bitch his lighthouse."

By mid-April, the Pequot team of lobbyists counted at least sixty-seven votes in the Senate in favor of the Pequot legislation, enough for an override. Weicker and his staff quietly approached then–Senate Majority Leader Howard Baker of Tennessee to see if he would broker a deal with the White House, sparing Reagan the embarrassment of being defeated on a minor bill. Baker brokered a compromise. The State of Connecticut would agree to chip in another $200,000 in the form of road improvements on the reservation, and the president would sign the bill.

Both sides appeared for one last congressional hearing on the bill in July 1983. The administration was represented by a rather grumpy Interior Department assistant secretary for Indian affairs, John W. Fritz, who said that the president would "not object to enactment of S. 1499" and noted the increase in Connecticut's contribution to the $900,000 trust fund for the Pequots. The Interior official was, however, clearly annoyed about a bill being rammed through giving the Pequots federal recognition without BIA vetting. "As to federal recognition, we received the Mashantucket Pequots' petition only a few weeks ago," he said. "Therefore we have not had sufficient time to thoroughly review it and cannot categorically state that they would meet the criteria of our federal acknowledgment project."

However, the politics of the moment required some sort of endorsement of the legislation the president had agreed to sign. The Interior's Fritz said, "The Mashantucket Pequot tribe has, however, held title to their present state reservation of 220 acres for over 250 years. Thus it would appear that the tribe has a prima

facie case for federal recognition status, and we do not object to
their recognition." On October 18, 1983, President Reagan signed
S. 1499 into law, which officially granted the Pequots recognition
from the U.S. government.

Skip and his family reacted joyously when they heard the news.
It was an unbelievable end to Skip's dream, and he wanted to
celebrate. He invited everyone—with the exception of the landowners—to the reservation for a feast, held on one of those lovely
autumn days in New England, cool and sunny and dotted with
bursts of technicolor foliage. Skip had erected a striped tent in
the clearing alongside Eliza's old house and he filled it with long
tables and folding chairs. They piled on the food—dozens of roast
turkeys, gallons of succotash, corn bread, and pies of all descrip-
tion—and drank beer and wine late into the night.

Tureen basked in the moment. He had gotten Skip more
than even he had ever dreamed possible—land, money, federal
recognition, and, soon, he saw a major gambling enterprise on the
new, expanded reservation. As Skip's future chief business adviser,
Tureen's career would veer away from pure legal representation
and toward the more lucrative world of investment banking for
the new tribe. The Pequots looked like they might become his
biggest client.

Skip spoke to the crowd at a standing microphone. As his
cousin Bruce Kirchner recalled, "There was a sense of unity that
came from federal recognition and the land settlement." Skip
retold Eliza's story. But that was all in the past. "From here
on out," he said, "things will be different for us. Things will be
better."

9

BINGO!

In early November 1983, only weeks after Reagan signed the settlement bill, the Penobscot tribe announced plans to invest $2.5 million in a gambling operation on the Pequot reservation that could accommodate thirty-five hundred players. The Penobscots said negotiations between the two tribes had been going on for months. In response to press reports about the announcement, Connecticut's deputy attorney general said that the state would go to court to stop gambling on the reservation, but that it was not well acquainted with federal laws governing Indian reservations.

Skip denied to the media that the Pequots had any agreement with the Penobscots, adding that bingo was not a "serious consideration." Skip found the public controversy over gambling and land purchases embarrassing. First, gambling was at that time still identified in the public mind with organized crime. Second, Skip had yet to officially propose to his family that they set up a gambling operation. And finally, he had not yet discussed gambling with politicians like Sam Gejdenson who had worked so energetically to get the Pequots' land and federal recognition. Commenting on the ensuing furor, Skip said, "It's enough to drive you nuts." He played down gambling's importance and noted that his people were overlooking the many other business opportunities open to the Pequots, such as hydroponic lettuce.

In truth, Skip was extremely interested in the financial possibilities of gambling. He flew down to the Seminole reservation in Florida to see the biggest high-stakes bingo operation in Indian country. He returned from Florida all excited; he was convinced that bingo was the way to get money, to create jobs. "We're going to build a bingo," he told tribal members. "High-stakes bingo. You wouldn't believe it. We have got to build this bingo. This is what's happening."

Skip's only concern was organized crime. The Seminoles had financed their bingo operation with money from sources alleged to be associated with organized crime. "We're just down the road from Providence," Skip said, referring to the capital of a state notorious for Mafia-related corruption. "If we started a bingo operation here, those guys are going to come down here and say, 'We want in.' And how are we going to stop them? It's not worth having our lives become a nightmare. For money."

Tureen was similarly concerned. "I told [Skip] he was absolutely right to be concerned. It took me a little while to figure out the answer. But then I realized, and I remember telling Skip this, that you would only have a problem if what the tribe is doing is not recognized by the law. I said to him, 'Where does the mob get in? It gets in when you are doing something illegal like dealing heroin. If you are dealing heroin, and the mob wants a piece of the action, you cannot call in the police to stop the mob from trying to extort money from you. The basic business of the mob is protection—extorting money from people who are engaged in illegal activities. So what you should do is not make any major moves until we can get legal clearance for bingo. Second, I will get you money from a clean source; then we won't have to depend on organized crime to finance the project.'"

In early 1984, Skip drove up to Maine to see the Penobscots. Anthropologist James Wherry, working as a socioeconomic development specialist, organized the trip. Wherry supported bringing gambling to the reservation, mainly out of a concern that Skip might otherwise strip-mine the steeply graded reservation for sand and gravel. The two of them rented a big Lincoln Continental and made the drive to Maine in about ten hours. When they arrived at the Penobscot reservation, the tribe's leaders proposed that the Penobscots manage the Pequots' high-stakes bingo parlor. The Penobscot leaders noted that before the State of Maine shuttered their bingo parlor, it had sales of $800,000 a year. They asked Skip to consider how much money he could make if the Pequots had the only high-stakes bingo hall in southern New England. Skip was sold on bingo, and on Lincoln Continentals too. Not long after his return from Maine, he bought himself a new brown Continental with leather seats.

No one taught Skip more about high-stakes bingo than Howard Wilson, a former carnival promoter who had married a Penobscot woman and run that tribe's bingo operation until it was shut down. Wilson was a veteran bingo operator with tattoos up and down his arms. (His father had been an advance man for Buffalo Bill Cody's Wild West show.) The old ladies at the Penobscot bingo hall, the best customers, had loved him, as he would often hand out money—usually $500—to the oldest person in the house.

Wilson participated in negotiations between the leaders of the Penobscots and the Pequots. The goal was to find a way for the Penobscots to combine their bingo expertise with the Pequots' unique market opportunity in southern New England. Wilson discussed with Skip the enormous opportunity of a Penobscot/ Pequot partnership. "The first thing we did was we drew a dot on a map in Ledyard, Connecticut," Wilson recalled, explaining the attractive economics of high-stakes bingo. "And then we drew a one-hundred-twenty-mile radius. I went to the Pequot tribal council with this map when we were negotiating the bingo arrangement. And I said, 'Within this hundred-twenty-mile radius, you have one tenth of the entire population of the United States.

That is a lot of people. You got a gold mine. You are an hour-and-a-half drive from New York City and you are an hour and a half from Boston.' I was trying to explain to them the size of the market they might have for high-stakes bingo and what we could do with that." You could sell people cards for a dollar with an average payoff in prize money of only sixty to seventy cents. The house keeps the difference. Wilson estimated that if the tribe built a twenty-five-hundred-seat hall and ran it just five nights a week, the yearly profits—what the Pequots would actually keep after deducting all costs—could reach $7 million.

Opposition to bingo within the Hayward family was minor. Skip's aunt, Loretta Libby, a stout, stubborn woman with a beehive hairdo, didn't like gambling and didn't care much for anything that would bring outsiders onto the family's land. To placate her, Skip revealed the next phase of his plan. "We're going to buy all this land on Route 2 and that will become part of the reservation," he said. "Only the property that fronts on Route 2 will we allow people on. There will not be a connecting road that goes from the bingo hall to the real reservation, where we live." Libby dropped her objections, and on April 30, 1984, at a tribal meeting, the Pequots held a vote on high-stakes bingo. Tureen flew down from Maine in his Beechcraft airplane to urge them on. In a fifteen-person vote, bingo won twelve to one with two abstentions.

Not long after the vote, Howard Wilson sat down with Skip to give him a sense of what the future might hold for the Pequots when they got into the gambling business. "Skip," he said. "You have to picture this table with money stacked to the roof. I can take five people and put them in a room with a million dollars and I could have them killing each other over that money. I could scoop a hundred thousand dollars of that money out without them knowing it, and they would be killing each other over the missing hundred thousand. Don't let the money get the best of you. It's like space—there is no end."

10

THE LAWYER AND
THE BUILDER

The task of winning Skip a high-stakes bingo hall fell primarily to Tom Tureen's law partner Barry Margolin. Margolin was, if anything, a more brilliant legal strategist than Tureen. A baby boomer, Margolin was raised in Queens, New York, in a politically progressive, middle-class family. By high school, he was already an activist marching for civil rights for black Americans. An excellent student, Margolin entered Harvard College in 1966. Over the next four years, he became a committed leftist and anti–Vietnam War protester, one of the leaders of the Harvard chapter of Students for a Democratic Society (SDS), the foremost radical organization on campus. In 1969, he received a three-month jail sentence for his participation in a sit-in at the Massachusetts State House. Later that year, he helped lead the student occupation of Harvard's administration building and came within a whisker of being thrown out of school. He graduated in 1970 and promptly began work as a welfare rights organizer in Boston. He found, however, that he lacked the outgoing personality necessary for successful organizing. He decided to go to law school, choosing Northeastern University, which billed itself as a center for public interest law and poverty law. Margolin soon gained a reputation as the most brilliant student in the short history of the school.

Margolin signed up to spend the summer after his first year of law school working for Tureen in Maine. Rural Maine was a

shock to the city kid from New York. "It was the middle of no-
where," he recalled. "The nearest movie theater was a hundred
miles away." But Margolin liked Tureen right away. Margolin appreciated Tureen's willingness to challenge the legal establishment on behalf of the underprivileged. Tom put him to work
immediately. With only nine months of law school under his belt,
Margolin was asked to write the first major brief in the Passamaquoddy land-claim case. The former campus radical also bought
his first Brooks Brothers suit. The suit was part of Tureen's be-
lief that they present themselves as sober lawyers, not radicals,
in order to disarm opponents.

Margolin graduated from Northeastern Law ranked first in
his class and had his choice of offers from prestigious firms. He
chose to return to Maine. Tureen was playing an increasingly larger
role as financial adviser to his Indian clients. The task of writing
the briefs and devising the legal strategy for the Pequots fell
mainly to Margolin.

Margolin felt confident he could convince a federal judge that
the Pequots had the right to have bingo. Connecticut had a general criminal statute penalizing any form of gambling, but it also
had a statute exempting licensed bingo games from criminal
prohibition. (Bingo was permissible at church fund-raisers, for
instance.) Margolin argued in his legal brief that since federally
recognized tribes like the Pequots are exempt from state regulation, their bingo games need not comply with Connecticut's criminal statute prohibiting gambling. Such reasoning had already been
upheld in other federal district courts. Federal sanction was crucial, otherwise there was always the threat of the State of Connecticut closing the hall for months or years while the legal issues
were hashed out in court.

Margolin did not expect to face enormous political opposition from the Connecticut state government. "Skip had done the
most critical thing—he had made friends with the politicians,"
Margolin recalled. "So that even if they did not support what the

tribe wanted to do [with bingo], it was not their personal goal to smash the tribe either. They were not committed to winning. They just could not afford to be seen saying 'Yes' to the Indians." Margolin's political analysis was spot on. After being presented with Margolin's extensive legal research, Connecticut's attorney general—and later U.S. senator—Joseph Lieberman concluded that Connecticut could not legally prevent the Pequots from opening a bingo hall as long as it allowed bingo for charitable purposes.

The only challenge Margolin faced was from Connecticut's chief state's attorney Austin J. McGuigan, who enforced criminal statutes for the state. McGuigan refused to accept Margolin's argument that high-stakes bingo was a regulatory issue and not a criminal matter. Margolin thought McGuigan could be beaten in court, and the quickest way to court was for McGuigan to threaten the Pequots with criminal prosecution if they opened a bingo hall. Margolin baited McGuigan in a letter saying that the Pequots would begin high-stakes bingo operations in February 1985. Margolin wrote in the letter,

> We believe that these operations are not subject to the jurisdiction of the State of Connecticut and that your office lacks jurisdiction to prosecute persons participating in these games. You have advised us informally that your office will take a contrary position. We have agreed that it would be best to resolve this controversy through a civil action prior to commencement of bingo operations on the Reservation in order to avoid an unintended criminal violation by our clients should the courts sustain your position. . . . If the Chief State's Attorney intends to prosecute, we plan to seek relief in a civil action in the United States District Court for the District of Connecticut.

McGuigan took the bait, warning in writing that Connecticut would shut the Pequots down if they proceeded as planned. Margolin immediately filed an injunction in federal court against the State of Connecticut to permanently prevent it from closing a high-stakes bingo on the reservation. On January 9, 1986, federal Judge Peter C. Dorsey granted the injunction, writing, "The parties agree that there are no genuine issues of material fact. Thus, the issue framed is whether the tribe's conduct of bingo games remains solely with its sovereignty or is subject to the regulation and control of the State of Connecticut by reason of its bingo laws." Dorsey found that Connecticut's bingo laws were not part of its criminal code. "There is no blanket prohibition of bingo," he wrote. "Nor is it a part of an overall criminalization of gambling." Taking note of Connecticut's lottery, Dorsey added, "Bingo can hardly be deemed to contravene a public policy against gambling in view of the state's daily encouragement and broad enticement of its citizens to participate in the state run which generates substantial revenue for its governmental functions." Accordingly, Dorsey declared Connecticut's bingo laws unenforceable on the reservation and permanently enjoined the state from prosecuting the Pequots, their employees, or their customers. It was a complete victory for Margolin. It would not be the last.

Skip met Charlie Klewin, a tough, young contractor from nearby Norwich, Connecticut, in early 1983. Klewin had just started out and was struggling to find construction jobs to manage. They met through a Narragansett Indian carpenter named Harry Mars, who called Klewin one day to say that he had a contract to build some government-subsidized houses on the Pequot reservation but that he could not get a bond, that is, a guarantee from a third party to insure the project's completion in case the general contractor went bust and could not pay the subcontractors. Mars was considered too high a risk to insure. He asked Klewin if he would provide a bond.

"What's the job?" Klewin asked.

"It's an Indian-only job," said Mars, meaning the contractor had to be majority-owned by someone recognized as American Indian by the government. "It's fifteen houses."

"How did you get the job?" asked Klewin.

"I was the only bidder."

"What did you bid?" asked Klewin.

"Nine hundred thousand dollars."

"How did you come up with that number?" asked Klewin.

"That's their budget."

Klewin did some back-of-the-envelope calculations and figured he could build the houses for about $700,000, leaving $200,000 as profit. Klewin agreed to put up the bond on one condition—he would be the general contractor. The company would be majority-owned by Mars, but Klewin would oversee the actual work.

Klewin did not make as much money as he'd planned on the Pequot housing project because he and Mars did not work well together, but he made a friend in Skip, who would be worth far more in the long run to Klewin. He and Skip were similar in many ways. They were both ambitious, twenty-something working-class guys who loved to drink and carouse. They went out just about every night drinking at the Brookside Tavern, a local dive not far from the reservation. Fights were common occurrences at the Brookside, which was fine with Klewin and Skip. Both loved a good barroom brawl. Klewin was compact but powerfully built and practiced in the martial arts. Skip was built like an ox. He liked to impress people with his physical strength. It was one of the ways he maintained control on the reservation. One night, he and Klewin returned to the reservation after a night of hard drinking. Skip challenged Klewin to a test of strength. They were standing outside the newly built HUD house of Skip's mother and father. Skip said, "Watch this." He hauled off and hit one of the new thirty-foot aluminum street lamps with his bare fist. The light flickered and went out. He punched the metal pole again, and the light went back on. "You try it," he said to Klewin, who did and almost broke his hand.

Skip's plan for the bingo hall called for a 34,000-square-foot steel-framed building with parking for eight hundred cars and twenty buses, all at a cost of about $2 million, excluding the purchase price of the land. The problem was that Tureen had not yet arranged project financing. Nonetheless, by April 1985, Klewin had signed a construction contract with Skip and begun blasting for the foundation. Klewin planned to start building even before the Pequots had money to pay him, in essence, personally financing Skip's bingo hall. This was an unusual arrangement. Typically, a general contractor doesn't begin construction until financing is in place, or he receives an advance of money for some portion of the project. A contractor relies on subcontractors to do much of the actual work and is liable to pay them even if the client fails to pay him. If Skip did not get the money to go ahead with the project, Klewin would be stuck paying the subcontractors.

Risk aside, Klewin desperately needed the business. He was a fledgling builder who could only afford to remain in business because he had an "in" with the local phone company to put up telephone poles. Klewin needed a big project, and if the bingo hall was the business success Skip said it would be—"We will all be millionaires"—Klewin knew there would be a lot more construction jobs for him down the road. By September 1985, Klewin had erected the steel girders and built the frame of the hall. But he was out of money. It was up to Tureen to find him some more.

11

FINANCING

Tureen knew that the Pequots did not have the money to pay Klewin. The $900,000 received in the 1983 settlement would have been an ideal source had it not already been spent; $600,000 was used to buy land to expand the reservation. The remaining $300,000, intended for economic development on the reservation, was allocated largely to the purchase of a pizza restaurant. Skip had decided to buy Mr. Pizza, a popular restaurant near the reservation along Route 2, just outside the settlement boundary. Skip was Mr. Pizza's biggest customer. He hung out there all day long and into the night. He used Mr. Pizza as his office instead of the tribe's ratty office trailers on the reservation. At Mr. Pizza, Skip had a private booth in the back. He would sit there for hours discussing tribal business, talking about how they were all going to be rich some day, downing pitchers of beer and glasses of schnapps and jug wine. Skip reasoned that if the Pequots owned the eatery, instead of all the money they spent there going to Lenny LaCroix, who owned Mr. Pizza, the revenues would remain in the family. Skip approached LaCroix and asked him how much he wanted for the place. He was told $515,000. Without so much as an appraisal, Skip shook hands on the deal.

Several advisers to Skip, including Jim Wherry and Tom Tureen, opposed the purchase of Mr. Pizza, telling him that

$515,000 was too high a price. They noted Skip's prior lack of success at the Sea Mist clam shack in Mystic and argued it was imprudent to invest so much of the economic development funds into one business. But they could argue only so much. As advisers, not tribal members, their objections could be ignored. Skip told them that he had given LaCroix his word and that his word was his bond. On February 13, 1984, Skip and his aunt Loretta Libby went to Jackson King's law office in Norwich for the closing. King was serving as LaCroix's lawyer. Skip handed over the money: $350,000 for the building and land; $11,000 for the pizza ovens and other equipment; $15,000 for supplies and inventory; $4,000 for the furniture and fixtures; $5,000 for the leasehold improvements; and $130,000 for "goodwill," which represented the difference between the purchase price and the appraised value of the restaurant.

To finance Skip's purchase, the Pequots used $207,153.66 of the $300,000 allotted by Congress for economic development. The BIA provided a $128,750 grant. Finally, the seller took back a ten-year, $200,000 fixed-rate mortgage at 12 percent per annum, with monthly payments of $2,869.42. LaCroix happily took the money, moved to New Hampshire, and opened a baseball card store.

Skip put his sister Terry Bell—previously known as Darnice —in charge of Mr. Pizza. Unfortunately, Bell—who was soon identifying herself in the press as "Princess Teresa Bell, the highest-ranking woman in the Mashantucket hierarchy"—was inept. Her prior food-service career consisted of helping Skip at his failed clam shack and working in the employee cafeteria at Electric Boat. Her problem, according to a tribal adviser who studied the Mr. Pizza operation and declined to be identified, "was that to make Mr. Pizza profitable required a small and dedicated staff. This was a restaurant that had been owned and operated by a guy [LaCroix] who routinely worked sixty-five-hour weeks. Terry ran Mr. Pizza as more of a public works project than a profit-making enterprise. There were too many employees, and they certainly did not want to work sixty-five-hour weeks. Terry was an inept manager. Food costs were too high. Labor costs were too high. And she would not listen to suggestions from anyone else about changes she might want to consider making."

Mr. Pizza under Bell's management was a financial sinkhole. Instead of creating a river of revenue for the Pequots to finance their expansion, the restaurant produced an ever-widening stream of losses. Sales peaked in the first year at around $500,000 and declined steadily each year thereafter. The restaurant never made a dime.

Tureen was under enormous pressure to find other sources of income to finance Skip's bingo palace. He especially worried because Skip was considering a financing deal with a bingo-management company that Tureen thought might be associated with the Mafia. The outfit proposed investing $400,000 to $600,000 to build the bingo hall in exchange for 65 percent of the profits. Tureen soon found Skip a better arrangement.

Tureen set up a tax-shelter deal with a computer leasing company that generated income for the Pequots and outsized tax deductions for investors. Tom calculated that the Pequots would receive $117,000 a year in lease payments, plus another $375,000 at the end of the deal. He named the partnership Autochthon, a Greek word meaning, "One supposed to have risen or sprung from the ground or from the soil he inhabits; one of the original inhabitants or aborigines; a native." While the tax shelter brought Skip desperately needed cash, both Skip and Tureen kept the existence of the tax shelter secret. Tureen was uncomfortable using the Pequots' special tax status as an Indian tribe to help wealthy people avoid paying taxes and worried that if the tax-shelter deal became common knowledge, Congress might view it as abusive and propose legislation to plug the loophole.

Autochthon paid off, ultimately netting the Pequots about $1 million. However, Tureen was still about $3 million short. He started looking for a bank loan to finance the bingo project. He visited the banks in Connecticut but to no avail. No bank wanted to lend money to the Pequots. While Barry Margolin had removed most of the legal obstacles, the State of Connecticut had not yet exhausted its possible appeals. The bankers worried that if somehow Connecticut prevailed, the construction loan would not be repaid. What was the value of an empty building on a remote Indian reservation that generated no income? In the event of loan default, the bank could not even seize the building because it was on the reservation. The banks also doubted the ability of Skip and his family to run a bingo hall. The Pequots had no experience. All they had was a business plan written by Tureen and his associates. Tureen offered the banks various repayment schemes in case of default, but these were too complex for bankers used to simpler lending arrangements.

Tureen persisted, and by August 1985 he developed the outlines of a financing deal he thought could get the Pequots the remaining money they needed. He and his associates had just done a deal for the Fond du Lac tribe in Wisconsin. The tribe had bought an electronic test equipment factory located near its reservation, borrowing all the money to make the acquisition in what was essentially a leveraged buyout. (In a leveraged buyout, the buyer finances the purchase by borrowing against the assets of the company being bought.) One of the bankers in the deal was the UBAF Arab American Bank. In the Fond du Lac deal, Tureen had asked UBAF if it would lend $6 million to the tribe if the BIA guaranteed 90 percent of the face value of the loan. The bank would not otherwise have agreed to the deal because there was not sufficient collateral underpinning the loan. The BIA loan guarantee basically shifted the credit risk from the bank to the taxpayers. The BIA agreed, and UBAF made the loan to the Wisconsin tribe. Tureen hoped to structure a similar loan for the Pequots.

He approached UBAF and explained to its loan officers that the Pequots had a reasonable chance of winning their bingo lawsuit with the State of Connecticut. A Pequot high-stakes bingo operation would have no competition in the entire Northeast, and the tribe was willing to devote most of the bingo profits to a sinking fund to repay the loan before using the money for any other purposes. Tureen even offered as security any income from Mr. Pizza or the sand and gravel operation. "The Tribe does not have a great deal of available income that could be pledged as additional security for a loan," he said. "The Tribe presently operates a gravel mining operation on the reservation, and the income from this operation could be pledged to debt repayment. . . . The Tribe owns and operates a restaurant adjacent to the reservation (Mr. Pizza), on which there still exists a first and second mortgage, but after those have been paid off, the income from the restaurant also would be available." Tureen had correctly sized up UBAF. The bank was less strictly regulated than were its U.S. competitors, and it had an appetite for risk. If he could get the BIA to guarantee 90 percent of the bank's exposure, he felt UBAF would make the loan.

Two bankers from UBAF soon came to Ledyard to meet Skip. They walked into his office. Skip was hungover that day. He hadn't shaved, and his long hair was disheveled. Seeing him, the bankers were ready to walk out the door. Luckily, Jim Wherry was there to take the bankers into his own office. He explained to them the enormous potential for high-stakes bingo. Wherry told them the sky was the limit. They asked him who the audience would be. Wherry had a map in his office that showed only three places— New York City, Boston, and the Mashantucket Pequot reservation in Ledyard. With a protractor, he drew an arc one hundred miles in either direction with Mashantucket as the epicenter. Then he said, "There are twenty-eight million people within this circle. That is the audience." UBAF signed on.

Financing in hand, Tureen turned his attention to obtaining the loan guarantee from the BIA. Even with Skip's excellent connections at the bureau, it would not be easy. In early

September, Tureen asked Bill Ott, head of the BIA's Eastern
Area Office, about the possibility of a guarantee. He argued that
the Pequots had shown success in past development projects and
explained that no bank would lend for the bingo project without such a guarantee. He promised the BIA that the Pequots
would wait for legal clearance from the courts before setting up
shop, that they would run a clean game, and that bingo was the
only feasible economic development project for the Pequots.
The BIA said they would look favorably on a loan guarantee if
UBAF asked for one. Later that month, the UBAF bankers did
precisely that. There was only one hitch. The BIA had already
given the Pequots a $300,000 grant for the bingo hall. Federal
regulations prohibited the BIA from giving both a grant and a
loan guarantee to the same project. Tureen resolved that problem easily enough. He gave the BIA its grant money back.

On January 9, 1986, Judge Dorsey ruled that Connecticut's
bingo laws did not apply to the Pequot reservation. The BIA
promptly issued the loan guarantee to UBAF, and the bank agreed
to lend the Pequots $5 million. The final financing package was a
virtual parfait of loans, loan guarantees, grants, and tax gimmicks.
At the top was the BIA-guaranteed loan from UBAF. The next
layer was $752,000 of construction financing to reimburse Charlie
Klewin. (The Penobscots, who received a three-year contract to
manage the bingo hall, had guaranteed the Klewin loan.) Then
came $375,000 from the land-claim settlement fund. The final
piece of financing came from the Autochthon tax shelter. In sum,
the bingo hall was financed almost entirely via debt. This was to
be the pattern under Skip Hayward. He couldn't make every
Pequot a millionaire without taking chances.

Skip's bingo hall opened on July 5, 1986. The parking lot filled
up immediately, so people simply left their cars alongside Route 2,
creating a traffic jam for miles in both directions. The Pequots

charged a $500 entrance fee, and emcee Howard Wilson gave away thirty new cars as door prizes. "I had them lined up in the street and I had to send about three hundred people away," he recalled. "The state police were going crazy because Route 2 was backed up. We were packed. I would say we probably grossed around seventy thousand dollars that night. That was wow." Despite the hall's legal capacity of twelve hundred people, Wilson had crammed closer to fifteen hundred into the hall by putting in smaller tables. Customers came from as far away as New Hampshire and New York and stayed all night.

The bingo business turned out to be more profitable than Skip had anticipated. According to confidential tribal records, during the first month, bingo profits were roughly $275,000. They dropped as the novelty wore off but recovered over the next two years. By mid-1988 profits were running at about $300,000 per month. In the first year, the bingo operation earned $3.7 million for the Pequots. From opening day in July 1986 through October 1988, bingo attracted more than 400,000 customers, generated about $30 million in revenues, and earned the Pequots slightly more than $4.5 million. Frustrated with the management contract that paid their Penobscot partners 20 percent of the profits, the Pequots bought out the Penobscots in 1988 for $500,000, taking over management of bingo themselves. Cutting out the Penobscots gave the Pequots 100 percent of the annual profits, to be shared among the ninety tribal members. Skip was not satisfied, however. He had an infinite wish list to finance. He wanted more land and more tribal members, and he wanted to make them all millionaires. Not even bingo could pay for all that. Yet Skip and his advisers already had a pretty good idea of what might—casino gambling.

12

SECOND-CLASS
PEQUOTS

As word spread of the success of Pequot bingo, more and more people sought membership in the tribe. These next waves of immigrants were often different from Skip's family in one significant respect. They were black, descendants of Eliza's banished sister Annie, who had married Jesse Sebastian. According to the Pequot constitution, the tribe did not discriminate on the basis of race, creed, or color. Yet Skip's family had never been in a hurry to bring their black relations into the tribe, who as second and third cousins were not that distant. It wasn't until August 1978 that the tribal council decided to accept a Sebastian as a Pequot.

One of the first blacks to join was a middle-aged granddaughter of Annie named Phyllis Monroe. Monroe had been born in 1929 in Rhode Island, and raised in New York City. Her only tribal affiliation as a child was Narragansett and she hardly ever visited the reservation in Ledyard. On one occasion, however, not long after World War II, she arrived unannounced while Eliza was entertaining her new, white son-in-law Richard Hayward. Seeing the black-skinned Monroe, Eliza hurried Hayward around to the other side of the house to avoid his seeing her black niece. Monroe stayed away from the reservation after that. She lived on the Lower East Side of Manhattan and, in the 1970s, in Rhode Island, where she was a black community organizer. In 1978, Phyllis heard that the Haywards were organizing the tribe and trying to get federal housing, and she decided she had as much right to Pequot housing as anyone else. She went to a CIAC meeting in Hartford with one of her sisters to stake a claim to tribal membership. She explained to CIAC that they were Annie George Sebastian's granddaughters. Skip, who was representing the Pequots, said, "Well, if they are who they say they are, our grandmothers were sisters." Monroe replied angrily, "Oh, you can believe I am who I say I am."

Skip did not oppose Phyllis joining the tribe. He needed members. However, many of the other Haywards felt threatened. One of the most virulent race baiters was Skip's father, Richard Hayward. When Skip argued for letting blacks in—his point was that the Pequots needed numbers to be taken seriously—his father would complain, "The goddamn niggers are going to take over this place."

The Sebastians had floated for generations between the African-American and Narragansett and Eastern Pequot communities of Rhode Island and Connecticut and elsewhere, with many migrating to urban ghettos and assimilating into African-American and Latino communities. Although the Haywards were by far the largest family within the Pequot tribe, the Sebastians were potentially far more numerous.

They were also angry. Phyllis Monroe, for example, demanded equal pay, housing, and benefits. To the Haywards, she was a Johnny-come-lately with a big mouth. Behind her back, and sometimes to her face, members of the Hayward family would call her "nigger" and say, "Go back where you came from."

Phyllis felt she was treated as a second-class Pequot. For example, she received a HUD house on the reservation, but only because the white Pequot who had been chosen to occupy the house had unexpectedly died. Phyllis asked herself, "Why did I come here? Why am I putting myself through this kind of torture? Why am I doing it? Why don't I just pack up and leave?" But she did not. She would say to members of Skip's family, "Get used to looking at me because I'm not going anywhere."

Skip declined to play the peacemaker between his family and the new black Pequots. He hated confrontations, and those revolving around issues of race and history were particularly unpleasant. Skip absented himself from the reservation, spending more time lobbying in Washington, D.C., or Hartford. Unfortunately, racial tensions within the tribe were growing. The blacks wanted housing and higher-paying tribal jobs like those offered to the whites. The Pequots had a reservation, federal recognition, and self-government. They were about to have the most successful Indian-owned bingo in history. As a group, however, they barely knew one another and had little in common other than the promise of a higher standard of living. There were fistfights, including, for instance, between one of Skip's sisters and one of Phyllis Monroe's nieces, who had to be pulled off each other.

Skip decided to do what leaders often do when faced with a problem they would prefer not to address directly. In 1986 he called in a consultant: James L. West, a Baptist minister and Cheyenne medicine man who specialized in conflict resolution for Indian tribes. Skip chose West because he felt he would be sensitive to the Pequots' cultural insecurity. West was the picture of an American Indian with his long, straight, braided black hair framing a chiseled face with high cheekbones. The meeting room in one of the office trailers on the reservation was packed for his arrival. West opened the meeting with a Cheyenne pipe ceremony. He passed an unlit pipe to the four corners of the room. He spoke in Cheyenne, which impressed the Pequots, as they had no tribal language of their own. For the first time in quite a while, a tribal meeting began without whites and blacks shouting at one another.

Over the next several months, West studied the Pequots. He submitted a confidential report to the tribal council. In his nineteen-page "Report to Mashantucket Pequot in Regards to Analysis of Factors Dividing Reservation Population," West began by noting, "The community being formed by the re-population of the reservation is new. This re-population is the result of the recent reformation of the Western Pequot tribal government with resulting availability of housing and services. The 'new' reservation residents of the Mashantucket Pequots come from varying geographic locations. They bring varying socioeconomic backgrounds, educational backgrounds as well as a variety of life styles." While acknowledging their financial and political success, West described the new Pequots as "people from diverse backgrounds and only a small degree of identification with their Pequot backgrounds."

He also described the Pequots as suffering from "sociological stress." He wrote, "A nation is being created of people who identify with different cultures (or, in this case, sub-cultures of the U.S.). Tribal members bring different values with them . . . different ways of talking; different ways of dressing; different ways of raising their children; different ways of caring for their homes and community; and different social identities."

West described the three subgroups he saw on the reservation. The blacks, he wrote, were mainly poor or working-class people from the inner city with little schooling. They were living in the less attractive HUD apartments on the reservation, as opposed to single-family houses, and were employed in the lower-paying sand and gravel jobs. The whites, West wrote, came from the suburbs or the countryside and they were working or middle class with high school or some college education. They occupied the single-family houses on the reservation and held the higher-paying managerial jobs in the tribe. They were focused on economic success and "have, by [their] own admission and with exceptions, known and identified very little, if at all, with their Pequot heritage before coming to the reservation." He noted that half of the whites "openly state their intent to leave the reservation if their sub-group becomes a minority to the Black sub-group." According to West, there was a subgroup of whites he defined as "Indian." Here, he had the Haywards in mind. They were "rural in social background" with "high school education only" and, like the blacks, were "verbally aggressive." He noted their "attachment and identification with the land of the Pequot people not exemplified by either the White or Black sub-groups." He wrote that they "perceive themselves as having sacrificed socioeconomic gain for their identification as Pequots, as Indians, and for their identification with the land. . . . They perceive the re-population [of the reservation] as invasion by the other sub-groups, White and Black, and will sometimes use their history on the land to try to establish some kind of prior rights."

West described the inequitable manner in which the tribe was governed. There were no blacks on the tribal council because the Pequot constitution, as revised when the tribe was seeking federal recognition, stated that a descendant of a person named on either the 1900 or 1910 reservation was eligible for membership only if he or she was of one-eighth Pequot blood. They computed the "blood quantum" by assuming, without any evidence, that Martha Hoxie, the mother of Eliza and Annie George, was 100 percent Pequot. Any great-grandchild of Martha then automatically met the one-eighth rule, which was how the whites in the tribe could claim to be one-eighth Pequot. Many of the blacks, however, were Martha Hoxie's great-great-grandchildren, one-sixteenth Pequot by this calculation, and therefore ineligible for full membership. They had to be "adopted" into the tribe, and the tribal constitution proscribed adopted Pequots from sitting on council.

Consequently, wrote West, black Pequots resorted to other means of political expression. "The Black sub-group uses the only means of power it perceives it has—the voice. It uses its voice in the same way it has learned to use it as a powerless sub-group in the [inner] city, a fact which the White (& Indian) sub-group perceives as unconstructive and abrasive." West also criticized Skip's near total control. West believed that Skip did not have time to be both political leader and chief operating officer of the fast-growing enterprise. "The development of the bingo operation brings a whole new business and financial chapter to the Tribe," West wrote. "It is apparent that the pace of business development has been far faster than this Tribe or any Indian tribe might be able to grow [with] socially or politically."

West saved the most sensitive issue of them all—enroll-ment—for last. "Why is the issue explosive?" he asked in the re-port. Because the Pequots had a majoritarian form of government. The Haywards and the other whites were the majority, but if they loosened eligibility requirements—i.e., lessened the blood quan-tum for enrollment—Annie George's Sebastian descendants would become the new majority. West wrote, "Within the great, grandchildren of Martha Hoxie, who are the largest sibling group active in the Tribe, the White sub-group holds predominance by number. Because the next generation of the Black sub-group (the great, great grandchildren of Martha Hoxie) are older, full enfran-chisement of this generation would add voting members of this sub-group. The extent of the change in balance is not clearly understood, although both sides *perceive* that the scale of political power would change to predominance by the Black sub-group."

West appealed to the Pequots to put aside their black and white identities and begin to think of themselves as Indians. "The simple truth would seem to be that a tribe with as tenuous a hold on its political existence as the Mashantucket Pequot Tribe needs *all* its members. The question becomes: Who are the rightful mem-bers? Simply put, they are now the descendants of Martha Hoxie until another full-blood Western Pequot shows up in the Tribe's genealogical history. . . . It is very clear that to subject the entire generation identified as great, great grandchildren of Martha Hoxie to the adoption process is to leave the Tribe leaderless at some future time. In another 35 to 40 years, the Mashantucket Pequot Tribe could have no one eligible to lead it." West suggested they get rid of the "one-eighth" rule and embrace a "one-sixteenth rule." To bring the tribe together, he also suggested they hire instructors to teach them "tribal values" and Pequot history, and he advised them to institute "cultural activities which identify and affirm tribal values." Perhaps they should develop a "festival" of some kind.

His bottom line on the Pequots? They were a collection of individuals from various ethnic backgrounds who "have literally been put next door to each other in order to repopulate the reservation. . . . Each person has brought the sum total of his/her life's experience—an identity. The very difficult thing being asked of each person who has voluntarily joined this experiment in tribal reformation is that he or she actually *gives up* some portion of his or her identity. Each person is being asked to subjugate some portion of the social characteristics described in detail by this report and join together with distant relatives who, in come cases, may be total strangers for the purposes of reforming an ancient identity called Mashantucket Pequot." He characterized the attempt as an "incredible sociological transformation."

West ended with a warning aimed directly at Skip's assumption that money would solve all their problems. "The tremendous business development and potential financial prosperity of the Tribe is not, of itself, enough to close the growing gap among the forming political factions. It is crucial that tribal leadership begin to put some time and energy into planning and into social, cultural and financial development of the Tribe at this time."

Skip hated the West report and grew to resent West as well. "I think mainly Skip hates Jim West because 'Jim West took power from me,'" said one longtime tribal aide, who declined to be identified. Tribal member Bruce Kirchner said, "Skip took the attitude that Jim West had no business here, that he was interfering." Skip even prevented West from presenting his report to the tribe, but copies circulated privately and people discussed West's observations and recommendations.

At the annual tribal meeting in early November 1986, the thirty or so tribal members voted to drop the blood quantum from one-eighth to one-sixteenth, a direct result of West's analysis. At that meeting, Phyllis Monroe proposed the direct election of the tribal chairman. The chairman had always been elected by the tribal council, which Skip controlled. Phyllis was preparing the way for a future run for the chairmanship by one of her family members, the Sebastians. One of her nephews, Kenny Reels, a self-confident young black man who had quit the Narragansett tribe for the Pequots in 1984, had already expressed a desire to become Pequot chairman some day. Phyllis's proposal to have the chairman elected by the tribal members, not the council, would make Kenny's dream more likely. Her motion passed, and the tribal constitution was amended to provide for direct election of the chairman. Skip, unsurprisingly, was reelected chairman, and remained in control. But no one could say for how long.

Kenny Reels was emerging as the leader of the black Pequots. A descendant of Annie George Sebastian, Kenny grew up in a rural, black ghetto outside Kingston, Rhode Island. The fourth of fourteen children, he was a large, physically imposing man. Joining the Pequots in December 1984, he announced at his initial membership meeting, to the horror of Skip's family, "Good. Now, I can be chief."

Backed by his own large family and an ever expanding network of relatives he helped recruit to the tribe, Kenny increasingly challenged Skip at tribal meetings. Skip took to chain-smoking Marlboro cigarettes at tribal council meetings when Kenny, who was not even a council member, acted up. At one meeting, Skip complained, "I am tired of our meeting getting out of control. I want to remind people that the tribal council, not the general membership, is responsible for conducting the business of the tribe. I am tired of people who aren't on council raising issues not on the council agenda."

By 1988, Skip, who still controlled the job patronage machine, had named Kenny manager of the tribal Sand & Gravel operation. As "Gravel manager," Kenny ran the crew of workers who mined the reservation's ample supply of surface rock and stone. Under his leadership, in fiscal 1988, for example, Sand & Gravel managed to lose $256,000 on sales of only $538,000 while employing just seven full-time workers and four part-timers. In a report to the tribe on the problems at Sand & Gravel, Kenny explained, "One of our problems at Gravel is some days it seems as if everyone wants to be the boss, but know body [*sic*] wants to work." To Skip, Sand & Gravel was essentially a make-work program for unskilled members of Kenny's extended family. The staff would grow to forty full-time employees, including one of Kenny's relations named Stewart Sebastian, who had served time in prison for armed robbery and often failed to show up for work. The employees were given many expensive pieces of construction equipment—a $152,000 backhoe, a $35,000 rock crusher, and dump trucks galore. But the bigger Sand & Gravel grew, the bigger the losses. By the early 1990s, Kenny's operation would be losing as much as $5 million a year.

Kenny's failure at Sand & Gravel did not, however, imperil his political ascent. He possessed the sole qualification necessary for political success within the majoritarian governance structure of the new Pequots: he came from what was emerging as the biggest family in the tiny tribe. In November 1989, he was elected to the tribal council and set about advancing the interests of the Sebastian family. He took control of the tribe's enrollment committee, which Skip had previously controlled. He further relaxed the entrance requirements. His enrollment committee expanded its reach beyond the direct descendants of people on the 1900 and 1910 census lists to include descendants of brothers and sisters of people on those lists. Kenny achieved a second milestone in 1991 when he convinced membership to pay him a salary. Until then, only Skip had received a salary. Now that Kenny was being paid too, he had the financial freedom to work full-time on wresting control of the tribe away from Skip.

13

THE COMPACT

By 1987, Skip was ready to move from bingo to casino gambling. Other federally recognized tribes, most notably the tiny Cabazon and Morongo of California, had already added high-stakes poker rooms to their bingo halls. The State of California tried to stop them in federal court, claiming that the tribes were required to comply with state laws limiting wagers and cash prizes. The case went to the U.S. Supreme Court, and in 1987 in *California v. Cabazon Band of Mission Indians* the court held that California lacked authority to regulate gambling on a federally recognized Indian reservation. Congress, the court ruled, had not explicitly given states that power.

The implications of the Supreme Court decision meant that states had no control over Indian gambling. The state governments promptly lobbied Congress to give them authority. The result was the Indian Gaming Regulatory Act (IGRA), which Congress passed on October 17, 1988. The law established three classes of Indian gambling. Class I included gambling without cash prizes, say, for a school or church fund-raiser. Class II included bingo of any kind, whether high-stakes or otherwise. Class III gambling was defined as casino games including card games and slot machines. Under IGRA, federally recognized tribes were allowed Class I gambling. Class II gambling was allowed in states where bingo was regulated, not prohibited. However, IGRA set more stringent restrictions on Class III casino gambling. For a tribe to set up a high-stakes casino, the reservation had to be located in a state that allowed gambling. The tribe also had to negotiate an agreement, a "compact," with the state to set the rules and regulations governing the casino. Finally, the secretary of the interior was required to approve any Class III compact between a tribe and a state. Upon passage of IGRA, many state governments were satisfied that Congress had effectively placed a lid on Indian gambling.

Tom Tureen and Barry Margolin thought otherwise. "We took a look at the statute," recalled Tureen. "We said, 'Wait a second. If a state allows "such gaming," then they have to allow the Indians to do it.' And we looked at Connecticut, and we saw that Connecticut had a charitable 'casino night' statute. Once a year, if you were a nonprofit, you could get a license from the State of Connecticut, and you could set up a card table, and you could play blackjack, and you could raise money for your charity. So we said, 'That is casino gaming. That is "such gaming."' Connecticut allows casino gaming." Connecticut allowed charities and nonprofits to hold "Las Vegas nights" once or twice a year to raise money. IGRA asserts that any state that "permits such gaming for any purpose by any person, organization, or entity" must enter into a compact with a tribe seeking to operate a Class III game. Tureen and Margolin reasoned that the State of Connecticut would have to enter into good faith negotiations with the Pequots to allow them to have a full-scale casino akin to those in Las Vegas and Atlantic City. Margolin was the crucial architect behind this legal interpretation. Margolin and his younger associate Rob Gips would handle the legal battle to turn Ledyard into the next Atlantic City.

In March 1989, after a meeting with Connecticut governor William O'Neill's staff in Hartford to discuss the implications of IGRA for the Pequots, Margolin and Gips formally declared the Pequots' intentions in a letter to O'Neill. "On behalf of the

Mashantucket Pequot Tribe," Gips wrote, "[I want to] request that the State of Connecticut enter into negotiations with the Tribe for the purpose of entering into a Tribal-State compact governing the conduct of expanded gaming activities on the Tribe's reservation in Ledyard." Gips explained that the Pequots needed gambling "to raise critically needed revenues to fund tribal government operations and related programs, to fund the development, construction and operation of new facilities, including a tribal museum and community center, to promote tribal economic development, and to provide jobs for tribal members and for people from the surrounding communities. The Tribe also expects that the increased tourist activity likely to result from expanded gaming activities will benefit greatly the southeastern Connecticut economy."

O'Neill's response was noncommittal. He had asked Connecticut's acting attorney general to review IGRA and determine the state's obligations. "If in the final analysis, the State of Connecticut does have an obligation to engage in negotiations," O'Neill concluded, "please be assured we will do so in good faith, working with the Mashantucket Pequot Tribe to reach a result beneficial to both parties."

A month later, Margolin and Gips met again with lawyers from the state attorney general's office and the governor's office. The state's lawyers asked Margolin and Gips to describe in writing the kind of gambling the Pequots wanted and why the state was obliged to negotiate with them. This was a distinctly firmer line than O'Neill had taken in his letter. Margolin decided to put his cards on the table. In a letter to the attorney general's office, Margolin and Gips laid out their demands: "We suggest you assume that the expanded gaming to be conducted by the Tribe will consist of the identical types of gaming permitted by Connecticut's laws permitting operation of games of chance or 'Las Vegas nights.'" The letter addressed questions that had been raised at the meeting in Hartford about how Connecticut's "Las

Vegas nights" could qualify as Class III gambling under IGRA. After all, unlike the city of Las Vegas, the State of Connecticut did not allow cash prizes at these fund-raising events. Margolin and Gips wrote, "This distinction would be significant only if the Indian Gaming Regulatory Act intended tribal gaming operations would always be subject to state-imposed limits on wagers and prizes. . . . That was clearly not the intent of the Act. The Act requires good-faith negotiation on wagers and prize levels as part of the negotiation of a Tribal-State compact. . . . Congress intended that wagers and prizes be a subject of negotiations, not fixed by state law."

Connecticut's acting attorney general Clarine Nardi Riddle responded, "The fact that Connecticut permits the operation of games of chance (or 'Las Vegas Nights') to be conducted under license by charitable organizations for charitable purposes does not, under the provisions of the Indian Gaming Regulatory Act, compel the State of Connecticut to enter into negotiations with the Tribe for the ultimate purpose of the construction and operation of a casino on the reservation as you have proposed." Riddle didn't bother to present a countervailing legal theory as she thought it self-evident that Connecticut's "Las Vegas nights" bore no legal resemblance to IGRA's Class III casinos.

Skip was disappointed by Riddle's hard-line response, especially since he had courted Governor O'Neill assiduously for years, and O'Neill's support had been key to the success of the Pequots' federal recognition lobbying campaign on Capitol Hill. Skip had hoped O'Neill would be similarly helpful in getting the Pequots a casino. (Only later would Skip learn that O'Neill opposed a casino for the Pequots because he had already rejected a similar request from the Connecticut pari-mutuel industry—dog track owners—who were among his biggest financial backers.)

Riddle's letter wasn't hostile, however, which Margolin took as a good sign. Once again, Margolin felt his best chance was in court, so he decided to sue the State of Connecticut on behalf of the

Pequot tribe. His argument was that the Connecticut state government was not negotiating a gambling agreement in good faith as IGRA required. IGRA mandated that states negotiate within 180 days from the date a tribe first requested talks, a provision that up to this point had never been tested. Margolin was worried that the state might actually make minimal efforts to reach a compact, in which case a judge might rule negotiations were proceeding in good faith. Fortunately for Margolin, Riddle refused any further negotiations about casino gambling.

Before he could sue Margolin needed to ask the tribe's permission. They were about to sue the state that since 1973 had been their political ally. Up to this point, Margolin had not met the members of the tribe, having dealt exclusively with Skip. Now, he needed broader backing for what could be a bruising legal and political fight.

Margolin traveled down to Ledyard from Maine with Gips and Tureen. Margolin received a warmer than expected response from the tribal members, and made his case for litigation. He explained that the state had decided not to negotiate because it did not think the Pequots had a legal right to a casino. He explained he was prepared to file a lawsuit alleging that the state was not negotiating in good faith as IGRA required. "We want to find out whether you want to do it," he said. "The decision is yours. We are the lawyers, and we can figure out how to win, but you must first want to win." The Pequots wanted to know what the odds of winning were. He told them that it "was a tough case, that we [are] likely to get at least some remedy, but that it might simply be a series of negotiating meetings with the state," which did not necessarily mean they would get a casino.

On October 23, 1989, the tribal council directed Margolin and Gips to commence litigation. To avoid unduly annoying Governor O'Neill, Margolin asked Skip to tell the governor, who was named in the Pequot complaint, that the dispute was not personal and that the tribe would abide by whatever the courts decided.

"That was part of a conscious plan and strategy," Margolin recalled. "Because ultimately the most we could get was a court
order forcing the state to go back to the negotiating table with
us. That is all that the Indian Gaming Regulatory Act provided
for us. We were hoping for a court decision that forced both sides
to the table and provided cover for O'Neill to reach an agreement
with us."

On November 3, the Pequots filed their complaint against
the State of Connecticut in federal court. "More than six months
have expired since the Tribe's request that the State enter into
negotiations for a Tribal-State gaming compact," Margolin and
Gips wrote. "No compact has been entered into and despite the
Tribe's stated readiness to negotiate for the purpose of entering
into such a compact, no such negotiations have taken place. . . .
The State's failure to negotiate in good faith to conclude a Tribal-
State compact governing the conduct of gaming activities violates
the Indian Gaming Regulatory Act." The complaint asked the
court to order the state to negotiate a compact with the Pequots
within sixty days.

Their case was assigned to Judge Peter Dorsey, the same
magistrate who had ruled in their favor during the land-claim case.
In January 1990, Margolin asked Dorsey for summary judgment
to speed the process. In May, Dorsey ordered Connecticut to sit
down and negotiate a compact even as the state appealed his
summary judgment. Dorsey gave the state sixty days to conclude
a compact. The negotiations took place during the steamy summer of 1990 on the fourth floor of the ornate state capitol building overlooking Bushnell Park in downtown Hartford. Margolin
quickly deduced that the key state representative was O'Neill's
special counsel Howard Rifkin, a liberal Democratic lawyer. Rifkin
struck Margolin as a good guy who was not looking to be "an Indian fighter."

Margolin's pitch to Rifkin was simple: the Pequots wanted
a compact that would not be politically embarrassing to O'Neill,

who was on record as being opposed to gambling. Margolin promised confidentiality during the negotiations and proposed that once a compact was jointly arrived at, the Pequots would not insist on O'Neill's signature. Instead, the two sides would submit the compact to a mediator who would officially rule on the agreement. The mediator would then submit it to the Interior Department for its blessing, sparing O'Neill political embarrassment.

At the first meeting with Rifkin, Margolin put a detailed compact on the table, which included a substantial regulatory role for the state. Margolin knew the state wanted some control, fearing that a Pequot-regulated casino would open a back door for organized crime. Margolin proposed an eight-page regulatory model based on New Jersey's regulation of Atlantic City's casinos. Rifkin was pleased by this "concession," unaware that Skip desperately wanted some state police presence on the reservation. The Pequots had no police force and Skip recalled the days immediately after federal recognition when he had begged the state police to patrol the reservation.

The most crucial item in Margolin's draft compact was "video facsimile gaming"—slot machines—which in a typical casino generate about two-thirds of the revenues, and an even higher percentage of the profits. Rifkin replied that slots were a "deal killer." Connecticut's ultimatum created divisions within the Pequot camp. Margolin asked for patience, arguing with Skip and the tribal council that a casino without slots was better than no casino at all. They agreed, and Margolin went back to Rifkin, offering a "moratorium" on slots. The terms required that the Pequots get either a court ruling or the permission of the state before they could operate slots. Rifkin thought this settled the matter in Connecticut's favor.

Margolin saw things differently. He interpreted the moratorium clause as evidence that Connecticut had acknowledged it had the power under IGRA to allow slots, if it wanted to. How else could the state have agreed to a moratorium? The clause,

Margolin saw, was Connecticut's tacit acknowledgment that it had the authority to permit slots on the reservation even if it banned them elsewhere in the state.

On September 4, 1990, a federal appeals court upheld Judge Dorsey's ruling. The State of Connecticut declared it would appeal to the Supreme Court, but in private Rifkin and Margolin had already agreed on a draft compact. The state's appeal was mainly political posturing by Governor O'Neill to maintain the appearance of an antigambling stance. Since the two proposed compacts were nearly identical, it mattered little which one the mediator chose, and since the compact negotiations were confidential, the public was unaware of O'Neill's role. So when the mediator chose the state's proposed compact, the decision appeared to have been imposed on O'Neill. In October 1990 the compact was forwarded to Secretary of the Interior Manuel Lujan, Jr., for his review and approval.

14

WEICKER

I
n January 1991, Skip Hayward's old political ally Lowell Weicker was sworn in as Connecticut's new governor. Weicker was returning from the political wilderness, having been ousted from the U.S. Senate in 1988 by then–State Attorney General Joe Lieberman. Weicker blamed the loss on his own Republican party, especially the Reagan wing, which had failed to support him. He spent two years as head of a nonprofit organization that fostered medical research, which had seemed like a decent fit as his family fortune stemmed from the pharmaceutical business. Yet his heart was not in it. In 1989, Weicker's friend and former political ally Tom D'Amore approached him about a run for governor. "He was a guy who had spent his entire adult life in politics. A selectman in Greenwich. Then a state legislator. Then a congressman. And finally United States senator," recalled D'Amore. "He was clearly unhappy being out of politics and government."

In 1990, the Connecticut government was in fiscal crisis as the state fell into an economic recession. Real estate values plummeted, and unemployment soared. In addition, the end of the Cold War had devastated the defense industry, which Connecticut relied on for high-paying jobs. It was an ideal time for Weicker to come to Connecticut's rescue. The voters were tired of both major parties. With Tom D'Amore as campaign chairman, Weicker formed the independent Connecticut party and, running as an outsider, won in a close three-way race to replace O'Neill, who was retiring.

Weicker was in office but a few weeks when Skip Hayward showed up at the office of D'Amore, who had been named chief political aide to Weicker. Skip gave him a copy of *The Pequots in Southern New England: The Fall and Rise of an American Indian Nation*, an authorized history of the Pequots. The book was a public relations tool that portrayed the Pequots as victims of mistreatment by the state. Skip explained to D'Amore that high-stakes bingo had vastly improved the life of the tribe and that a casino would strengthen tribal unity even more.

"My impression was very favorable," D'Amore recalled. "Skip seemed a genuine guy who'd been pretty well screwed over. He talked to me about all the things he had done to try to keep the tribe alive. He hoped that he would have an opportunity to talk to Weicker and tell Weicker what their needs were. He was a very effective lobbyist. You could not help but feel that he was powerless and that if you were in a position of power, you should help him." Weicker, however, was in no hurry to meet with Skip. Connecticut faced a deficit of $2.4 billion on a proposed budget of $8 billion. The new governor was scrambling to balance the budget without slashing spending or raising taxes. The Pequots were not a high priority.

All that changed on April 22, 1991, when the Supreme Court declined to review *Mashantucket Pequot Tribe v. State of Connecticut*, which the state had appealed halfheartedly in the final days of the O'Neill administration. Weicker's administrative chief of staff, Stan Twardy, broke the news to the governor in his vast, second-floor office at the gold-domed state capitol in Hartford. "I don't want gambling in Connecticut," Weicker replied. "Gambling is not Connecticut. We have people who are qualified to perform much higher skill jobs than serving drinks in short skirts or serving as security guards in a casino. Tell me what this means and what you think we can do."

Twardy took the Pequot casino files home that night. As Weicker's closest aide, Twardy was staying with the governor and his family at the governor's mansion in Hartford. Twardy had been working for Weicker since graduating from the University of Virginia Law School; Weicker was Twardy's political mentor and was instrumental in Twardy's 1985 appointment as U.S. attorney in Connecticut. Reading the files, Twardy realized the courts had decided all the legal issues. "As I analyzed the decision by Judge Dorsey, who by the way rowed crew at Yale with Weicker," Twardy recalled, "I realized that the courts have decided that the Pequots are entitled to have a casino because Connecticut statutes provide for casino gaming, even though Connecticut statutes don't provide for high-stakes gaming. Las Vegas nights are not 'legalized gambling,' as most people understand that phrase, but Dorsey had decided that they are Class III gaming as IGRA defines it. And because Connecticut statutes allow Class III gaming, the Pequots are allowed to have it too. It is basically the concept of reciprocal sovereignty: if state law allows for it, then a sovereign Indian nation can do it too." Twardy decided that the state's only chance was to retry the case by repealing Connecticut's "Las Vegas nights" statute.

The next morning at the mansion, Weicker, who had just returned from an early morning swim at the Jewish Community Center in West Hartford, sat down with Twardy. "What do you think, Twardy?" he asked. "Is there anything we can do?

Twardy, still in his sweats, having just finished his morning run in a nearby park, said, "The best shot we have is repealing Las Vegas nights. The only way I can see out of this is if the state no longer allows Class III gaming—Las Vegas nights. Let's repeal Las Vegas nights."

"Is there any other way?" Weicker asked.

"There is no guarantee it will work, but it would give us an opportunity to go back to Judge Dorsey and relitigate the case."

"Let's talk more at the office," Weicker said.

Later that day, Weicker met with Twardy and a small group of his top aides. Weicker decided Twardy's idea of repealing the statute was the only possible solution. To keep the plan confidential, Twardy ran the operation out of Weicker's office; he spent the rest of the week evaluating the legal and political challenges of repealing the statute. Not only was there a question of whether such a repeal would hold up in court, there was also the challenge of getting legislation through the state legislature. Weicker, Twardy, and D'Amore banked on the solid support of culturally conservative Republicans from wealthier districts, but were less confident of Democratic members from blue-collar districts, where illegal gambling was more common and legalized gambling was seen as a way to create jobs.

In April, Weicker told his staff to invite Skip Hayward to Hartford. Skip, with Barry Margolin in tow, led a delegation into the governor's baronial office at the State House. They knew Weicker opposed gambling in Connecticut, as he had so stated publicly. What they didn't know was how Weicker planned to stop them. To convince Weicker that the Pequots planned to run a clean casino, Margolin brought along Michael (Mickey) Brown, a former New Jersey gambling regulator, and Al Luciani, the former president of the Golden Nugget casino in Atlantic City.

Weicker dominated the meeting of about a dozen people, arranging the seating by inviting Skip to sit beside him on a central sofa. "We have worked together before, Governor," Skip said, "and I'm looking forward to working with you on this." He explained the importance of the casino to the revival of the Pequots, and spoke about how important Weicker had been in the 1983 fight for federal recognition. He said that a casino was the only hope for rebuilding the tribe.

Weicker said, "I want you to know, Skip, that I'm going to be having a press conference later today announcing I will be introducing legislation to repeal Las Vegas nights. Skip, I love you, and we have worked together before, but if you get into gambling the mob will eat you alive." A casino, Weicker was certain, would be responsible for bringing more drugs and crime and prostitution into the state. Margolin jumped in and motioned to his experts Brown and Luciani. "I know all about your New Jersey operatives," Weicker replied dismissively.

Margolin then tried a different approach. He said that the state and the tribe already had a deal. That, he said, was why the Pequots had agreed to the state's version of the compact being submitted to the arbitrator. "We negotiated with the O'Neill administration in good faith, and they represented the state, and we are entitled to rely on them. The O'Neill administration did not see its goal as stopping the casino," Margolin insisted.

"I don't give a shit about all that," replied Weicker. "The state did an absolutely shitty job in negotiating."

To the surprise of the others in the governor's office, Skip began to tear up. Weicker said, "Sorry, Skip, but we have to fight you on this." On that note, the meeting ended, having lasted no more than fifteen minutes. Weicker recalled feeling that "it was not a good first meeting. [Skip] was emotional. I was emotional. I wanted to establish tough bargaining grounds. I don't think I was courteous, but I knew that I did not want to go ahead and see gambling expanded."

Outside the governor's office the press was waiting. Weicker announced that he intended to go immediately to the legislature and repeal the Las Vegas nights statute. He vowed that gambling was not going to be Connecticut's solution to its economic and fiscal plight. Following Weicker, Margolin and the other Pequot advisers pushed Skip before the press. "We really wanted to control the spin," recalled Charlie Duffy, a political lobbyist Margolin and Gips had retained for the Pequots. "The press was outside Weicker's office waiting. We knew that Skip had to be the voice. And Skip was actually pretty good. He was pretty calm and talked

about the message that we wanted to frame—the state was going
back on its word. Our view was that the only way we could win in
the State House was on the basis of Weicker 'reneging' on an
agreement Connecticut had already made. If the debate centered
on the substantive question of whether the state should legalize
the casino for the tribe, we would have very few votes. The question had to be, 'Would the state honor its word?'"

15

LAS VEGAS NIGHTS

The Pequots found themselves in yet another life-or-death political battle. They had to prevent Weicker from repealing the Las Vegas nights statute and amending Connecticut's antigambling law. The battleground would be the bicameral state legislature, where Weicker needed to get bills through both houses. Weicker had to introduce legislation right away to gain passage before the end of the comment period on the compact. Interior Secretary Lujan was on the verge of approving a compact.

Charlie Duffy and his business partner Keith Stover, two of the most effective lobbyists in Connecticut, led the battle in the State House. Margolin had found them for the Pequots through a fellow Harvard College SDS member named Miles Rappaport, a Democratic state representative from West Hartford. Like Margolin, Rappaport saw the Pequots as a minority group victimized by centuries of colonial oppression. Margolin hired Duffy and Stover to ensure political access and influence in the state legislature. Duffy's and Stover's services were retained for eight months of lobbying for $40,000.

Duffy had come to Connecticut in 1970 to coach Yale University's lightweight crew. A collegiate rower himself, the six-foot-seven Duffy had success at Yale, but the pay was small. So he joined the state government where he rose to become deputy commissioner in the Connecticut Department of Commerce during Ella Grasso's tenure. By the time Duffy met Margolin in 1990, he had been a lobbyist for ten years.

Duffy felt they could stop Weicker in the state legislature. Weicker was a political maverick to whom neither the Democratic nor the Republican party had loyalty. In addition, Weicker had the greater political challenge. To repeal the Las Vegas nights statute, he needed two bills passed, one in the Senate and another in the Assembly. Duffy had only to defeat Weicker in only one house. Duffy created an effective anti-Weicker coalition. He reached out to the Catholic Church, volunteer fire departments, and other charitable organizations that used Las Vegas nights to raise money. He spoke with the local chambers of commerce in eastern Connecticut to win business support. He encouraged these special interests to pressure their legislative representatives in Hartford to resist Weicker's repeal effort.

Meanwhile, Barry Margolin and Rob Gips ran a political war room from their hotel suite in the elegant Morgan Hotel in downtown Hartford. They spoke off the record with the press to explain the Pequot case—that the tribe had a deal with the state that Weicker was trying to break. They helped broker a deal between the Pequots and the construction unions, promising organized labor jobs in the building of the casino. At night, they wrote the position papers Duffy and Stover handed out when making their lobbying rounds at the State House, always emphasizing that the casino would be tightly regulated and well protected from organized crime. The lobbyists downplayed the size of the proposed casino, describing it as a modest 65,000-square-foot project. To ward off questions about the Pequots' authenticity, they brought in John Echohawk, executive director of the Native American Rights Fund, to vouch for them. Echohawk gave the Pequot lobbyists much-needed American Indian credibility, as some of Weicker's aides were making none too subtle references that the Pequots were fakes. Duffy also used Skip in the fight. "Doe-eyed and innocent," as Duffy recalled, Skip repeated a simple message to legislators: We have a compact with the state, and Connecticut is yet again trying to break its word to Indians.

Weicker's team fought back with Tom D'Amore as the point man in the Senate. "I needed every argument from the most substantive to utter bullshit," he recalled. "The most effective argument we could use was that we did not want gambling to change the culture of Connecticut. If the Pequots were allowed to have a casino, there would be enormous political pressure to have gambling legalized everywhere in the state, and we were going to see slot machines in 7-Elevens. Gambling would spread, and it could not be contained. There would be no way to stop it if we let the Pequots have it." Desperate to win his first legislative fight, Weicker was not above political horse trading. Weicker brought one Democratic legislator into his office and promised him a bridge for his district if he would support repeal. The Senate voted on May 9. When the clerk tallied the final vote, Weicker had won by a slender margin: 18 Yeas, 17 Neas, 1 Absent.

It was a short-lived victory. "The Senate vote was not indicative of what was happening in the House," D'Amore recalled. Weicker's repeal effort in the House got off to a bad start when chief of staff Stan Twardy was photographed by the *Hartford Courant* pumping his fist in victory on the floor of the state Senate after the vote. The photograph ran the next day on the front page. The appearance of a gloating Twardy did not sit well with legislators, and even less with Weicker. "First of all," he said, "you are not the governor. I am. Secondly, you should not be seen celebrating a win over the Indians."

Pequot lobbyist Duffy immediately exploited Twardy's gaffe. "The next morning, we cut the picture out and copied it and put it up in our offices to motivate ourselves and inspire us for the struggle to come." Duffy also had Twardy banned from the floor by the House leadership. "Charlie was essentially leading the

House by this point," D'Amore said later. "He was telling the House members, 'How can you let these independents tell you what to do? Who the hell are these independents to be putting down the poor Indians and telling you what to do? They're trying to tell you what to do. We all know what is right to do. They keep throwing up these unfair roadblocks to the poor tribe.'"

Duffy was increasingly confident of Weicker's defeat. "We had some people who were sympathetic to the Native American cause—liberal Democrats and Puerto Ricans and blacks," he said. "Then there was a core group of Republicans who were Weicker-haters. They blamed his third-party victory for denying Republicans the governorship. He had left their party. He had run against them. They were not going to help him. They did not want him to win any political victories."

Duffy also garnered support from companies that stood to gain if a casino was built. "I remember standing outside the floor of the House, and we had information sheets available to hand out that day. A young, clean-cut guy in a great three-piece suit is looking at our stuff. I ask him who he is. He says he's from IBM. 'My boss told me I should get up here and work on this. He wants to defeat the legislation too. IBM is the largest provider of information systems to casinos in the world. If the Pequots are going to do a casino, IBM wants to be a vendor.' I said, 'Great.' I grabbed him, and he spent the afternoon talking to House members from Fairfield County where IBM had a large presence. I would say, 'Here's a guy from IBM who's in favor of our position.' I think he was a sales guy from IBM. He was now a lobbyist. We used everything we had."

To lobby black and Puerto Rican members, Duffy made sure to bring in dark-skinned members of the tribe like Kenny Reels and other members of the Annie George Sebastian family. "We wanted a tribal face on the lobbying effort," Duffy said. "Kenny felt very close to these black legislators. He had been living in essentially African-American communities for many, many years.

What reverberated with these black and Puerto Rican politicians was that the tribe was another impoverished minority."

Tom D'Amore fought back with scare tactics. "We were saying that gambling would lead to rampant prostitution and AIDS and organized crime and that eastern Connecticut would become Atlantic City," he recalled. "I did not believe that was going to be the case. It was overkill because it made us look as if we were being unfair to the tribe. Why were we screwing these guys? Why were we opposed to gambling as a way to encourage economic development in a time of economic recession?" The argument backfired when an overzealous antigambling lobbyist distributed a position paper implying that if the Pequots built a casino, every woman in Ledyard would turn to prostitution. Duffy happily distributed this pamphlet himself to demonstrate the absurdity of Weicker's opposition to gambling.

With D'Amore floundering, Duffy and Margolin found an unlikely ally in Representative Kevin Rennie, a young conservative Republican member of the House from suburban South Windsor. "The part of the strategy that was most fun was recruiting conservative Republicans to take the point for us," recalled Margolin. "I remember Charlie and Keith Stover had cultivated a friendship with Rennie. He was wildly antigovernment and far more ideologically conservative than anyone I was used to dealing with. But the important point was that he and others like him hated Weicker. So he was a natural ally of ours. Through partisan dislike, he had persuaded himself that the casino was a noble fight. The speech he gave on the floor of the House before the final vote was great. He wrote it himself, but we could not have written it any better."

In the final debate before the vote, Rennie rose and said,

So this is Armageddon, where the world ends not with a bang but with the whirling of a roulette wheel. Is it plausible that the fate of our Shangri-la known as Connecticut rests on the

passage of something called Senate A? Do you believe that
the destiny of our entire state or even part of it hangs on our
willingness to smite the Pequot Indians? In a state that allows and promotes the Daily Number, Play Four, Instant
Lottery and its many variations, including one currently available at the Legislative Office Building called Blackjack,
LOTTO, off-track betting, Jai Alai, dog racing, and Casino
Nights? Can anyone claim that one more addition to that list
means the end of life as we know it, every virtue replaced
by a vice?

In this case, whatever rights the Indians have to conduct gaming activities derive from our state policy. The state
[under O'Neill] determined to ignore the law [IGRA], and
refused to negotiate with the Pequots. Judge [Peter] Dorsey
of the District Court of Connecticut sitting right here held
that the state was wrong. Not satisfied with his decision, the
state still refused to negotiate and appealed to the Second
Circuit where it lost again to the surprise of few. The
Supreme Court refused even to hear the case. . . . Suddenly,
faced with the consequences of our own policies, some
people want a wholesale change in our law, not because the
policies are bad . . . but because they want those Pequots
stopped. Well, where's the fairness? . . . In the 19th century,
which may seem like a long time ago, the trail of tears for
the American Indian led to Oklahoma and its reservations,
but today here in Connecticut it runs from the Senate to the
House of Representatives staining this building. Let it end
here, and let it end today. I urge you to reject Senate A.

Weicker's bill to repeal was defeated handily, with more than
twenty votes to spare.

16

THE MALAYSIANS

Even before their victory over Governor Weicker, Margolin and Gips were lining up financing for the planned casino. In the summer of 1990, they prepared a confidential business plan with economic projections for the Mashantucket Pequot Gaming Enterprise as a sales tool to convince lenders to finance the construction and operation of a Pequot casino. They were planning to borrow $60 million, nearly ten times the capital needed to get the bingo hall up and running. The intended footprint of the casino was similarly supersized—a 77,000-square-foot building containing a 42,000-square-foot casino, and 35,000 square feet of restaurants, bars, and other public spaces. The bingo hall's parking lot, which already fit 750 cars, was to be tripled in size.

The planning document reflected the confidence Margolin and Gips had in their ability to raise the money. "We were cockier than we should have been that we could raise the money in the conventional loan market," recalled Margolin. "We thought having the only casino in New England, located in Connecticut between Boston and New York, would be a bankable deal because the projected revenue and profit numbers were so good." In late summer of 1990, they even turned down a financing offer from a Malaysian-based gambling company controlled by an overseas Chinese family looking to expand into the United States market. The company, Genting Berhad, was led by Chairman Lim Goh

Tong, a Chinese entrepreneur living in Malaysia who had already made the *Forbes* magazine billionaire list through his ownership of the Genting Highlands casino in the hills above Kuala Lumpur. Genting Highlands was the largest casino and amusement park in the world, and the only legal gambling operation in Malaysia. Knowing firsthand the obscene profits to be squeezed from a gambling monopoly, Lim and his advisers appreciated the Pequots' potential business opportunity. He and his chief adviser, Colin Au, met Margolin and Gips in lower Manhattan. Au explained that they were looking for an American casino and that the Pequot project was the first thing they had seen that they really liked. He said they had access to billions of dollars in capital and that a project of this size would be no problem.

In exchange for financing, the Malaysians naturally wanted a piece of the action, specifically, a 50 percent ownership stake. Margolin was nonplussed. "We are very flattered that you want to be involved, but we are not interested," he said. "It's not legal for a non-Indian to own an Indian casino on a reservation. And even if it were, the tribe would never accept it." After the meeting, Margolin figured that was the last he would see of the Malaysians.

By late 1990, however, the U.S. economy had slumped dramatically and the financing environment had deteriorated. The banking system came under enormous financial stress, with borrowers defaulting on loans and federal banking regulators forcing higher lending standards on institutions. There was a credit crunch, and banks lent far less than they had six months earlier. Margolin and Gips sent the confidential financing document to every major bank in Connecticut, then expanded their search to include the Boston and New York City area. Twenty-three commercial and investment banks turned them down. The only lending institution that showed any interest was the Long Term Credit Bank of Japan. As a foreign bank, Long Term Credit was not subject to the heightened restrictions U.S. bank regulators had imposed on American institutions. The Japanese bankers said they were interested in lending, but that time was short. By November 1990, the tribe had already spent more than $1 million on land and tens of thousands of dollars for design drawings. The Pequots had voted at their annual meeting to build the casino. Skip had stood up in front of the two dozen tribal members at the meeting and said in support of the casino, "You are all going to become millionaires if you stick by me. We will all become rich."

With the Japanese hesitating to commit, Margolin and Gips decided they needed a backup lender, just in case. Margolin decided on a second meeting with the Malaysians. Margolin and Gips had in the interim devised a way for the Pequots to give the Malaysians a share of the Pequot profits without violating IGRA's prohibition against a nontribal entity owning part of a casino on a federal Indian reservation. The prohibition was intended to protect tribes from unscrupulous lawyers, lenders, suppliers, or managers. The history of American Indian negotiation is replete with tribes having been defrauded and exploited by non-Indian shysters. Margolin and Gips knew that any casino financing deal would have to be blessed not only by the Pequots but, more important, by the BIA. "Gips and I had found a way to give [the Malaysians] some premium over the conventional interest rate that we thought fell within the purview of the Indian Gaming Regulatory Act," recalled Margolin. "We decided we could give them some percentage of the casino's future income in addition to the interest rate on money borrowed." Margolin was confident he could convince the BIA that this percentage—which they dubbed "contingent interest"—was a reasonable commercial arrangement, consistent with prudent lending practices by banks when the borrower's credit is questionable.

The Malaysians had been tracking the Pequot project through Mickey Brown, the former New Jersey gambling regulator whom Margolin and Gips had hired to advise the Pequots on the casino project, and they too were eager for a second meeting. Margolin and

Gips used Brown as a go-between. A bluff Irish-American, Brown
had joined the New Jersey state attorney general's office and become head of the state's gaming enforcement division when casino
gambling was legalized in 1978. Brown later quit government service for the more lucrative business of advising the industry he
previously had regulated. Brown had met the Malaysians in 1983
when he was advising the Australian government on the regulation
of gambling, and they retained him as a U.S.-based scout. By 1990,
when Margolin and Gips hired Brown to advise them in the legislative battle against Weicker, Brown was already a member of the
board of directors of Genting.

Margolin met with Brown and the Malaysians at the restaurant of the Vista Hotel at the World Trade Center in lower Manhattan. Margolin updated the Malaysians on the status of legal
approvals required for the casino. The Malaysians again expressed
a desire to manage the casino for the Pequots in return for a management fee keyed to the casino's profitability. Margolin proposed
instead the "contingent interest" arrangement, explaining how
it would allow the Malaysians to share in the profit growth of the
casino. Margolin did not offer a management contract, as Skip opposed handing over managerial control to outsiders. Skip had no
plans to manage the casino himself, but he did want the managers to report directly to him. By the end of lunch, Margolin had
the Malaysians excited by the idea of a casino monopoly in New
England.

The next day, the Malaysians lunched with Brown in China-
town. They told him they wanted to see the reservation, so they
piled into Brown's Cadillac and drove to Mystic, where they stayed
at the Hilton Hotel. Skip picked them up at the hotel in his Lincoln Continental and drove them to the bingo hall. Margolin introduced them to Al Luciani, whom Skip was planning on hiring
to manage the casino. Luciani had worked previously as a senior
manager for gambling impresario Steve Wynn in Atlantic City. The
Malaysians were impressed, staying in Connecticut for several

days. By the end of their visit, the two sides had reached a preliminary financing agreement.

Skip and his tribal council authorized Margolin and Gips to approach the Malaysians with a formal financing proposal. The Pequots would pay an interest rate equal to the U.S. Treasury bond rate plus 2.5 percentage points. In addition, they would give the Malaysians 1 percent of the gross revenues of the casino and 7 percent of the net income (profits) for seven years. In the event the Pequots defaulted on the loan, the Malaysians would take over management of the casino and continue to receive 1 percent of the gross and 7 percent of the net. Allowing the Malaysians to take over management of the casino was a key point. If the Pequots defaulted on their loan obligation, this allowed the Malaysians to recover their money via management fees.

Margolin and Gips were now negotiating two deals—one with the Long Term Bank of Japan and another with the Malaysians. By the end of December 1990, Margolin wanted closure. On December 26, he and Gips went before the tribal council for a decision. Did the Pequots prefer the conventional bank loan offered by Long Term Credit or the unconventional "contingent interest" approach of the Malaysian deal? Long Term Credit would cost the tribe less because there was no profit sharing, but the Japanese might be slower to release the money for construction and more intrusive about how the money was spent. The Malaysians, on the other hand, would take more of the profits, but they would release the money sooner and allow the Pequots more autonomy. Margolin also explained that the Malaysians' desire to move quickly dovetailed nicely with his own strategy—that is, getting a casino built as soon as possible. Margolin worried that as the federal courts continued to interpret IGRA, they might limit its scope. He wanted to get the compact with Connecticut signed and the casino built before a court ruling in a future Indian gambling case defined more narrowly the rights of tribes under IGRA. At the meeting with the Pequot council, some members complained about giving the Malaysians a share in the profits. Skip, however, had learned during the bingo project that it was true that commercial bankers like Long Term Credit could be slow to release money. He didn't want anyone looking over his shoulder.

Margolin's and Skip's arguments carried the day. The tribal council authorized Margolin to offer the Malaysians a "commitment letter." The terms of the construction loan agreement had changed slightly since the November tribal council meeting. The interest rate was higher: a floating rate equal to the rate on the U.S. Treasury ten-year note plus 4.5 percentage points. The "contingent interest," or profit participation, was restructured as well: 9.99 percent of the net income for twenty-five years as opposed to the previous 7 percent of net income plus 1 percent of revenues for seven years. In addition, the Pequots waived their "sovereign immunity" from litigation. They agreed to resolve any legal disputes in the courts of Connecticut or New York or any federal courts in those two states. The Malaysians had asked for this provision to guarantee an impartial forum if they needed to sue the Pequots to get their money back. Indian tribes often refuse such requests. Tribes generally value self-rule above economic opportunity. Margolin explained to them, however, that without such a waiver of sovereignty the deal could fall through.

The loan closing was scheduled for February 25, 1991. One day before that date, the tribal council met on the reservation to approve the final terms of the construction loan, but they failed to reach agreement, despite Margolin's pleas. The next day, Skip and the other members of the five-person council flew down to New York City for the closing. The deal still looked like it might collapse. Not all the council members wanted to share profits with the Malaysians. Meanwhile, the law firm representing the Malaysians—Cleary, Gottlieb, Steen & Hamilton—doubted the enforceability of the clause stipulating resolution of a dispute in state or federal court.

When the Pequot tribal council and the Malaysians met face-to-face at Cleary, Gottlieb's offices, however, the two sides found that they liked each other. The Malaysians reassured the Pequots that while they retained Cleary, Gottlieb to ensure the legality of the contract, they cared more about the Pequots, shaking their hands and promising to pay them back. Skip and the rest of the council were moved by this last-minute appeal. They held a quick meeting and voted unanimously to sign the deal. By then Margolin had left. The "war chief," as he was referred to, was burnt out. The strain of a year of countless meetings with the unruly and often uncomprehending tribal council had finally gotten to him. When Skip put his name to the agreement at last, the architect of the agreement was fast asleep in his hotel room.

"We just borrowed sixty million dollars and I want to celebrate," Skip said. Mickey Brown was so excited he leaped down a full set of steps shouting, "We got us a casino! We got us a casino!" Skip told Brown to make a reservation at Windows on the World restaurant atop the World Trade Center. The champagne flowed like tap water. Skip invited his family to come down and party with him, along with the council and the Malaysians and the lawyers. His family could barely believe they were drinking Dom Perignon in the clouds above Manhattan. Skip toasted, "To the great future of the Pequot Tribe. To the partnership between the Lim family and the Pequots."

17

FOXWOODS

Within ninety days of the signing of the financing agreement, Skip gave builder Charlie Klewin the go-ahead to break ground on what was to become the largest casino in the world. Overseen by Al Luciani, Klewin and designer Kevin Tubridy, a pal of Klewin's, would design and build the casino in eight months. In typical fashion, Skip began the project without a contract. "Everything I did with Skip at that time was done on a handshake," recalled Klewin. "The entire casino that we opened in 1992 was built on a handshake. We had no contract. We got one at the end because the lawyers for the Malaysians needed a contract, but the building was built by the time the contract was signed."

This was the first casino Klewin had ever built. Designer Tubridy was likewise a casino rookie. One day he was showing Skip drawings for a planned expansion of the bingo hall when Skip asked, "Have you ever done a casino?"

"Skip, you know I've never done a casino."

"Neither have I. Let's go do one. This is going to be the biggest thing that has ever hit the area."

The casino was a low-slung, two-story, steel-reinforced cinderblock building akin to a supermarket in any suburban town in

America. Luciani, who was the only casino veteran, made sure Tubridy laid out the interior so that the casino would seem to flow efficiently. He showed Tubridy how to lay out the gambling rooms and where to place the counting room so that the armored trucks could get in and out of the building without taking the money through the public spaces. Tubridy spent much of his time on the interior design. There was a paucity of Pequot artifacts on which to base design details, so Skip encouraged Tubridy to turn to nature for inspiration. A naturalistic approach fit Skip's desire to open the building to the outdoors via windows and skylights. He wanted people to have a view of the reservation, rejecting the standard casino industry approach of intentionally closing gamblers off from the distractions of the outside world. Tubridy designed a main entrance with a soaring atrium and an artificial waterfall surrounded by potted trees, shrubs, and hanging plants. Luciani did not love the "natural" design approach, but he could work with it. He told the tribal council, "That can be what distinguishes us. We are not the glitzy casino. We are the casino in the woods."

Luciani planned to exploit the Pequots' public image as Indians for the marketing campaign. At his suggestion, the Pequots decided to install a statue of an Indian in the front lobby. Based on a smaller bronze by Chiricahua Apache sculptor Allan Houser titled *Sacred Rain Arrow*, the Pequot replica was twenty-five feet high, made of clear plastic resin, and renamed *The Rainmaker*. Mounted atop a rising platform of green foliage and illuminated by flashing red lights, the giant lucite Indian shot blue laser "arrows" into a darkened ceiling, which was followed by a "rainstorm," complete with "lightning" and taped "thunder" and "rain" via a sprinkler system concealed in the ceiling. A recorded narrator told the story of a brave warrior who could open the heavens with an arrow. Total cost: $1 million.

Skip and his sister Terry Bell invented a tribal logo to be installed at the casino's main entrance, featuring a black tree on a small hill representing the reservation, a white fox in the foreground symbolizing the original Pequots, and, below, the mark of Robin Cassasinnamon, the leader of the tribe after its defeat in 1637–1938. The logo was created from scraps of information gleaned from colonial and state histories and similar documents. The fox referred to a Pequot clan—the "fox people"—that the Haywards claimed to have descended from. Skip and his family began to introduce themselves to the media and the public as the "fox people." In late 1991, the Pequots took a vote and decided to name their casino Foxwoods.

Rushing to build Foxwoods, Luciani, Klewin, and Tubridy didn't see their families for days at a time. At the end of a typically high-pressured day, Skip would gather them all for dinner and drinking late into the night. They would invariably end up at two A.M. at Skip's house, where he would hold court until daybreak. The casino team eventually learned to invent excuses to get home to bed. Unlike Skip, who routinely slept until noon, they had to be back at work in the morning. At the drunken bull sessions, they brainstormed about the casino. (During one of these late-night sessions, Skip decided to color Foxwoods' roof teal, a kind of bright greenish blue, inside and out.) Talking about his anxieties of sudden wealth, Skip said, "I hope to God that I am not creating too much success, too much arrogance, too much greed."

Foxwoods opened for business on February 12, 1992, with a sneak preview for the region's heavy hitters, business and political leaders who were Skip's new best friends. Mayors, legislators, judges, and prosecutors rubbed shoulders with tribal members at the gaming tables. The VIPs were given play money to gamble with while cocktail waitresses costumed as Indian squaws in miniskirts served free drinks. The Pequots kicked off the party with a blessing. Skip imported a medicine man from the Wampanoag band in Massachusetts, since the Pequots didn't have one of their own, to offer a blessing. "We are on the verge of a major social and economic renaissance," Skip said in his welcoming speech. "We are going to be a major economic power in south-eastern Connecticut."

In 1992, two hundred and forty-five Pequots reaped an amazing jackpot—$148 million in revenues and $51 million in profits. Still, without slots, Foxwoods was not a full-service casino. The economics of a slot machine are stunningly brilliant. The machine costs about $5,000 to buy and install, an investment recouped usually within six months. The odds are rigged, of course. For every dollar the customer puts in, the average payout is, say, eighty-six cents. That is a 14 percent return on sales. Other than cigarettes, no legal enterprise in the United States has that kind of profit margin. Obscene profits are guaranteed. Slots generate about three-quarters of a typical casino's revenues and an even higher percentage of profits, a point not lost on Skip at the Foxwoods opening. "We're not yet a real casino, but someday I expect we will get slot machines."

Foxwoods' success did not go unnoticed. Steve Wynn, Al Luciani's old boss in Atlantic City, had already served notice that he intended to open a casino in the slums of Bridgeport, Connecticut, about an hour's drive closer to New York City than the Pequots' casino. At Wynn's behest, the Connecticut legislature established a task force to investigate the economic and fiscal potential of legalizing gambling throughout the state. It was a foregone conclusion that the task force would endorse some kind of casino legalization, given its enormous tax revenue potential at a time of budget deficits. In the fall of 1992, Charlie Duffy warned Skip and Barry Margolin that a bill legalizing non-Indian casinos might pass overwhelmingly in the next session. Weicker, who remained opposed to additional casinos, might not be able to stop it. "Once we saw that there was a threat that the legislature would pass a bill to open competing casinos, we concluded we had to come up with money for the state and for the legislature in particular," recalled Margolin. "The only way we could stop competition was to figure out a way that the state could get money off Foxwoods on some continuing basis."

With Foxwoods' profit potential on the line, Margolin and Rob Gips discussed how the Pequots might be able to preempt competition. Their idea was to compromise with the state over slot machines. If Connecticut let the Pequots have slots, the tribe would kick back to Hartford a percentage of the take. Margolin broached the idea to Skip during a trip to Malaysia that year paid for by the Pequots' Malaysian backers. The Malaysians wanted to show off their casino and resort in the hills above Kuala Lumpur. They hoped that upon seeing the vast complex of casinos, golf courses, and amusement parks, Skip and his advisers would begin to think about expanding Foxwoods far beyond its current size. With a claim on 9.9 percent of the casino's profits, the Malaysians stood to gain enormously if Foxwoods grew into a hybrid of Disney World and Atlantic City.

On the trip, Margolin suggested that Skip consider offering the State of Connecticut a guaranteed percentage of the slots winnings. Mickey Brown, who was traveling with them, was less enthusiastic. "It's crazy," Brown shouted. "We're not going to pay the state money to get slots. We can't give them a guarantee. It's too risky. What if we're wrong about the profitability of slots? We'd still be on the hook for the money. Nobody in the industry has ever done that." Brown calmed down after Margolin explained that a slots deal was their best chance of stalling Steve Wynn.

Governor Weicker was also worried about Wynn, fearing a statewide legalization of gambling. Chief of Staff Stan Twardy knew that Wynn had the political muscle to push a casino legalization bill through the state legislature over the governor's objections. Wynn had already stated publicly that he would spend $800 million on two casinos in Bridgeport and in Hartford and had launched an intensive lobbying campaign to that affect. Wynn had a powerful ally in Connecticut's Senate majority leader William DiBella. Senator DiBella told Twardy at a private meeting in the State House, "I know Steve Wynn. He would love to come here. He could do great things in Connecticut. We should go ahead and meet with him. The Indians are making a lot of money. We should be making some too. Hartford and Bridgeport are economically depressed. We should put in a casino."

At Twardy's suggestion, Weicker agreed to meet privately with Wynn. Wynn and DiBella arrived at Weicker's office with a promotional video of his casino properties, which Wynn described as "family entertainment." Weicker was impressed but remained unconvinced as they headed off to lunch together to one of DiBella's favorite restaurants, a steak and pasta place in the Italian neighborhood of the city. Weicker, Twardy, DiBella, and Wynn were seated at a corner table where they would not be disturbed. Wynn and DiBella made their pitch, describing their proposed casinos as part of an urban agenda to create jobs in areas of high unemployment and poverty.

"It's a great idea," Weicker said. "But how do we know we get the right jobs?"

"In Hartford, the construction jobs would be big-time," DiBella replied. "The waitressing jobs would be more than there is now. They're better than nothing, which is what we have now."

Wynn tried to allay Twardy's concern about the influence of organized crime. "We haven't had any scandals. We run a clean operation," he said, referring to his operations in Las Vegas and Atlantic City. Twardy was skeptical. Former colleagues in federal law enforcement had told him that the industry was not entirely clean. Weicker remained concerned about Mafia influence in the gambling business and wanted no part of that in Connecticut.

Riding back to the governor's office in his limousine after lunch, Weicker said to Twardy, "I don't like it. It just doesn't ring true. I'm not going to agree to support it. We have to start thinking about how we are going to defeat a bill."

* * *

In October 1992, Twardy drove down to Foxwoods for a meeting on casino regulatory issues, accompanied by Bob Werner, the young head of Connecticut's Division of Special Revenue. Special Revenue oversaw the state lottery and Foxwoods. Pequot lobbyist Charlie Duffy had told Twardy and Werner that the tribe had an idea they wanted to discuss in addition to regulation. Duffy had not gone into specifics, but Twardy and Werner expected it had to do with slots.

Werner was not surprised, therefore, when after the meeting he was asked to stay. He alone of the state's representatives met with a small group of Pequot advisers and Foxwoods executives in a windowless office in the basement of the casino. He and Barry Margolin were soon talking about a slots-for-money deal.

"Look, I think it makes a lot of sense on a lot of levels," said Werner. "Are you guys interested in revisiting it, or is it off the table? Are you happy with the table games you have? Are you going to make a legal challenge for slots?"

At this point, Skip showed up. He was in a sullen mood and looked hungover, according to people at the meeting. "We are here to talk about this deal but I want you to know that we are really entitled to them anyway," he said.

Margolin explained that the Pequots had a strong legal case in favor of slots and could win in court. But going to court meant time and money. He described how a compromise deal could work. "We would posture this deal as the settlement of the outstanding legal issue of slots. We will give you an as yet undetermined percentage of the gross revenues from slots. If Connecticut subsequently legalizes gambling, the money cuts off." Most important, Margolin explained, the governor could unilaterally agree to the legal settlement. No legislative consent was needed.

"This has real potential to solve a lot of problems," Werner said. "But the governor does not know about this conversation, and I will not take this to him until he has a deal he can't refuse. We need to make this deal so attractive that he will accept it."

The meeting ended with both sides agreeing to talk again soon. Werner briefed Twardy and advised him that if they did not cut a deal with the Pequots, the tribe might get slots anyway through a court battle. "We could end up with slot machines and no share in the revenue. I think these slot machines are going to be wildly successful and productive. If we can get a piece of that, we could get significant revenue for the state and God knows we could use it."

"If we go to the governor now, I don't think we are going to be allowed to do it," Twardy replied. "You go and see what you can do, and if at some point you have something worth bringing back to me, we will talk."

Twardy spoke to the governor the next day.

"Walk me through this," Weicker said. "How would it work?"

"I can't guarantee it's going to work this way," Twardy said, "but the way it could work is that we agree to settle the lawsuit that they brought against the state when O'Neill was governor. In exchange for our settling, they agree to pay us X dollars a year for several years and after than some percentage of the revenues from the slot machines."

"You have my blessing," Weicker replied. "But if you are doing this stuff and word gets out, I know nothing about this. You are on your own." If the existence of these negotiations leaked, it would be tantamount to Weicker conceding the legalization of gambling. Senator DiBella would press for gambling, and Weicker would be unable to stop him. "You have my blessing but not my knowledge of what is going on. Report back when you have something."

Twardy called Werner into his office. "Bob," he said. "Let's get this thing done."

Over the next several weeks, Werner and a small team at Special Revenue worked with the executives at Foxwoods to prepare estimates of the slots' revenue potential. Both sides agreed that because of the Pequot monopoly in New England, their slot machines would be 50 percent more "productive" than in Atlantic City. The average daily win per device in Atlantic City was $238; they reckoned Foxwoods could do $365 per day per machine. They planned to install three thousand machines by August 1993, which promised that by June 1994, the slots would gross $378.18 million.

Margolin met with Skip to decide what to offer the state. They very quickly reached the decision that the tribe would give 25 percent of the slot win to the state, enough money to cause people to say, "Holy fuck," a stunning number that would blow Wynn out of the water. At the meeting, Charlie Duffy suggested they consider giving Hartford a guaranteed dollar amount of the slots take that Weicker could plug into the next year's budget.

"That's no problem," Skip said. "We will guarantee $100 million, minimum." It was typical Hayward grandiosity: 25 percent of a potential $400 million take.

On October 27, Margolin faxed a memo to Werner containing the outlines of a deal. "We believe that we can assure the State of Connecticut $100 million in revenue through June 3, 1994, if we can reach agreement before January. These ideas remain subject to approval by the Tribal Council," Margolin continued. "My premise is that an agreement on the use of the gaming devices [slot machines] by the Tribe would be conditioned on a requirement that the Tribe contribute 25% of the gross win from the devices to the State on a monthly basis."

Margolin explained the political appeal of the deal. It created a choice between an assured level of state revenue from the Pequots' casino versus an unknown amount of potential revenue from many casinos. It also offered the state a monetary incentive to reach an agreement quickly. "If we can make the Agreement effective as of this January," Margolin wrote, "the Tribe could commit to a minimum contribution to the State of at least $100 million during the entire period ending June 30, 1994." Otherwise, he said, the tribe could commit to only $94 million.

As the negotiations progressed, so did the need for secrecy. The two sides decided to have their next meeting at an out-of-the-way inn in Old Wethersfield, Connecticut, called the Standish House. (Coincidentally, Wethersfield was one of the three colonial towns Pequot raiding parties had attacked in 1637, thus precipitating the Pequot War.) On November 19, Werner and the Pequot representatives met for dinner in an alcove off the upstairs dining room at the Standish House. Werner wondered whether the Pequots would still offer him 25 percent of their take from slots. "I'm thinking I want 25 percent," he said. "And I'm thinking that they'll offer somewhere around 10 percent. That's what I'm guessing because they will figure that $40 million [10 percent of $400 million] is a lot of money, and the state ought to be happy with that. That would be pretty close to the tax rates paid by the non-Indian casinos in Las Vegas and Atlantic City."

After some small talk, Mickey Brown said, "We've run our numbers. We have an idea of what we're willing to offer, and it's going to be very generous. There's going to be a lot of money here. We understand you can't bring a deal back to the governor unless it's a great deal. Here is what we are prepared to offer and don't start trying to negotiate this up. We will give the state 25 percent."

Werner was astonished. "Should I go for more?" he thought. "I could probably squeeze them for more. You know what? These guys are being straight. They've done the numbers. They're offering me a percentage of the gross. If they have underestimated the potential slot revenue, we could end up with a lot more than $100 million a year. They are sharing the upside with us. And their clients are really volatile, emotionally involved in this issue. Let's not press it."

Werner said, "I want to check with our analysts, but I think that number comes in around where we are. But I need some

kind of guaranteed minimum, some minimum dollar amount."
Brown mentioned Skip's already approved $100 million. Werner
walked out elated. He did not call Twardy yet with the news. "I
need a written document to know that this is real," he said to
himself.

On the first Monday of the new year, January 4, 1993, Werner
received the final draft of the memorandum of understanding
between the state and the tribe. He reviewed it in the Hartford
law offices of Robinson & Cole, where Charlie Duffy had an office. Werner now told Twardy he had the deal in writing.

Twardy told Weicker, who said, "Let's get the tribe up here
as soon as possible."

The following Monday, January 11, Margolin, Duffy, Twardy,
Werner, and Weicker met at the governor's mansion. Margolin and
Duffy did not bring Skip. They recalled the lambasting he'd received from Weicker the last time they met. "We didn't know
whether Weicker would say, 'Fuck you' or 'Thank you,'" Duffy
recalled. A state trooper in uniform served coffee.

Twardy asked Margolin to explain the substantive legal issue
to Weicker, which was that the gambling compact gave the governor alone the power to settle the issue of slots. "As it dawned on
Weicker what it was we were saying," recalled Margolin, "he got
this glint in his eye and said, 'You mean this is something I can
just do myself?' He loved it. As much as it was a way to succeed
at stopping Steve Wynn and making a deal with the tribe and
getting some money into the state budget, the sheer political
elegance of the move delighted the political animal in Weicker.
He understood that no one could stop him."

"Okay," said Weicker. "I don't think there is anything further to discuss or negotiate." He ordered Twardy to have the
memorandum of understanding quickly and quietly vetted by
Connecticut Attorney General Richard Blumenthal the next day.

The following day, Senate Majority Leader DiBella dropped by to see Twardy, who had decided to leave government service for private practice and a higher income.

"I understand you're leaving," said DiBella.

"Well, Bill," said Twardy, "I can't tell you I'm not."

"I really liked working with you," said DiBella. "But with you gone, we are going to get the casino now. We're going to win this session."

"We'll see," said Twardy.

The next day, January 13, 1993, Twardy called DiBella into his office. He said that in one hour Weicker would announce a slots deal with the Pequots, who were guaranteeing the state $100 million a year or 25 percent of their gross slot machine revenues, whichever was larger. DiBella's face fell. It was an offer Wynn would never be able to match.

At Weicker's press conference, Duffy said to his business partner Stover, "Keith, you know what? We should stop lobbying today because as long as we live we will never ever do another hundred-million-dollar deal for a client." In fact, it was far more than a $100 million deal for the Pequots. Duffy and Stover and Margolin and Gips were about to transform Foxwoods into a billion-dollar business. As Duffy recalled, the state might be getting "Holy fuck" money, but the Pequots were about to receive "more money than God."

18

ANNEXATION

Financed by a casino with slots, Skip Hayward planned a mammoth land grab in southeastern Connecticut. He wanted to expand the reservation, which was 2,200 acres per the 1983 settlement agreement, by thousands and thousands of acres, taking huge chunks of the three surrounding towns of Ledyard, North Stonington, and Stonington in the process. The Pequots' Malaysian partners, who wanted Skip to turn Foxwoods into a giant destination resort akin to theirs in Malaysia, encouraged Skip to aggressively buy land surrounding the reservation.

Not only were the towns unaware of Skip's plans, they were also uninformed of the process by which a federally recognized Indian tribe can incorporate land into a reservation. The towns assumed that the Pequot reservation boundary had been set in stone by the 1983 settlement. Skip knew better. Barry Margolin and Rob Gips had explained to him that the settlement had left open the possibility of dramatic expansion of the reservation.

The Indian Reorganization Act of 1934 allowed federally recognized tribes to buy land and petition the Department of the Interior to "take land into trust," in other words, transfer the land into federal hands for the benefit of a recognized tribe. The law was a progressive piece of legislation passed at the urging of Franklin D. Roosevelt. It had been intended to help western tribes in remote, rural locations buy land that previously had been part of a reservation. Roosevelt's chief adviser for Indian affairs, John Collier, believed tribes had a better chance of surviving culturally if reservations weren't chopped up by non-Indian land purchases. The law, of course, had not been passed with New England in mind, where a small band like the Pequots might live surrounded by middle-class suburbia. (At the time of the act's passage, almost all Indian groups in the Northeast—including the Pequots—were not recognized by the federal government.)

Skip quietly applied to have the federal government take into trust for the Pequots twenty-seven acres of land in Ledyard and North Stonington for an expanded Foxwoods parking lot, land that was outside the 1983 settlement area. The application went through the Department of the Interior's Bureau of Indian Affairs, which sent a routine notice to the towns of its intention to approve the Pequots' request, but the small-town officials did not understand its importance, and so did not respond during the comment period. The application was approved without any public discussion.

When, however, the towns were informed that the federal government had just taken the twenty-seven acres into trust, they were understandably furious. Ledyard's town planner added to their concerns by explaining to them that the Pequots had a legal right to buy yet more land outside the settlement boundary and annex it to the reservation. The twenty-seven-acre purchase was likely to be only the first of many. Ledyard officials could see out-of-control development, the whittling away of the town's geographic area, and perhaps most important, the erosion of its property tax base. Inadvertently adding fuel to this fire, Skip permitted Foxwoods to install massively brilliant lampposts on the new parking lot that would have been in violation of Ledyard regulations if the land were still part of the town. "The town went nuts," recalled attorney Jackson King, who by now was working for the tribe. "They got really pissed off, and I don't blame them. They called us before the zoning commission. I said that we were sorry that we did not get [their] permission and that Foxwoods management had not realized that lighting was a zoning issue. But the local people were really mad. The chairman of the zoning commission several times over the next few years referred to me as someone who was 'sticking light poles up their rear end.'"

Skip was about to drop a few more bombshells on the towns. He believed he could win BIA approval for larger parcels of land despite local opposition. The Interior's Bureau of Indian Affairs was, like most federal regulatory agencies, inclined to support its constituents—Indian tribes—in disputes with towns. The BIA's new head, Assistant Secretary of the Interior for Indian Affairs Ada Deer, liked Skip. A member of the Menominee tribe in Wisconsin, Deer had helped her tribe win federal recognition and identified with his efforts on behalf of the Pequots. Skip liked her as well. In 1990 the Pequot tribal council had authorized $700 to pay Deer's way to a meeting of the Native American Rights Fund board of directors of which Skip was also a member.

Skip was optimistic about political support from Congress for his land purchases. The Pequots had verbal assurances from two key Democratic members of Connecticut's congressional delegation—Senator Christopher Dodd and Representative Sam Gejdenson—that they would not oppose the Pequots' adding additional land to the reservation. Both Dodd and Gejdenson had accepted tens of thousands of dollars in campaign contributions from the Pequots and their business associates.

Barry Margolin was one of the few Pequot advisers to suggest that Skip seek a compromise with the towns. "I thought it was not possible for this issue to be resolved without a public resolution," Margolin recalled. "This basically needed a political deal and the tribe could not afford to try first to get it through BIA quietly. It would never happen. They needed a public initiative, a political deal crafted in such a way that local politicians could sell it to the surrounding population of voters. That meant putting everything that the tribe wanted to do on the table and making a deal with the towns and the state before they went to BIA."

Skip ignored Margolin's advice, petitioning the BIA in February 1993 to add another 247 acres of land across Route 2 from the reservation, land outside the 1983 settlement area. Skip followed that up with an additional request to have a 1,200-acre Boy Scout property called Lake of Isles taken into trust as well. The plan for Lake of Isles was to expand the reservation so that they could develop a golf resort on land that was beyond the reach of local tax and environmental officials. In response, officials from Ledyard, North Stonington, and Preston formed an alliance and hired high-priced attorneys from Washington to fight the Pequots and to lobby the BIA. By April 1993, the lawyers had convinced Secretary of the Interior Bruce Babbitt to delay a final decision on the Pequot petition until August 2.

That summer, the BIA regional administrator Bill Ott told Skip that he was under orders from Babbitt to broker a compromise between the Pequots and the towns. "You guys are going to sit down in a room and negotiate." As Skip's generous campaign contributions to the Democratic National Party in the 1992 elections seemed to be generating little political payoff, he had no choice but to try and negotiate with the three towns.

The meeting took place on July 25 at Hayward's favorite watering hole, the Mystic Hilton. The meeting did not get off to a good start. Skip and Kenny Reels, the Pequot representatives, were late and kept everyone else waiting for an hour. Ott was tired and annoyed that the two sides were asking his boss Babbitt to make the politically difficult decision. Ott lectured the two sides on what he wanted them to do. He told them it was their responsibility to work out their differences before the August 2 deadline. Skip agreed to meet with the town officials again and try to work something out.

Over the next few days, town officials met with Skip and his representatives on the reservation. Skip revealed for the first time just how much land he wanted to add to the reservation. In addition to the 247-acre parcel and the 1,200-acre Boy Scout property, he was dreaming of another 10,000 acres, a huge potential parcel of land in a small state like Connecticut. Skip told the three town officials that if the towns dropped their opposition to these future land acquisitions, the Pequots would pay the towns $15 million, $5 million per town. Skip provided them with a map showing them precisely the parcels of land he wanted. If the towns let the federal government take the land into trust for the Pequots—in other words, add it to the reservation—the Pequots would pay each town $1 million a year for five years plus an undisclosed amount of "impact aid" to compensate for lost property taxes. Skip signed the offer.

The town officials were not impressed. They saw the Pequot offer as a bribe, but before they could make up their minds, events outpaced them. The Pequots made the map public, and it was immediately published on the front page of the *New London Day* newspaper. It showed the existing reservation as a small green patch in the center. There was a blue strip representing the 247-acre parcel and a purple patch for the 1,200-acre Boy Scout property. The blue, green, and purple patches were as nothing, however, compared to a giant red zone representing Skip's dream—the additional 10,000 acres of land. The map illustrated that the Pequots wanted roughly 12 percent of Ledyard, 15 percent of North Stonington, and 5 percent of Preston. Nearly seven hundred houses and farms were located within the red zone.

When the map appeared on the front page of the *Day*, townspeople were up in arms. They called their elected leaders and demanded they reject Skip's proposal. Secretary of the Interior Bruce Babbitt made public that his agency would delay a decision on the 247-acres and urged the tribe to resolve the dispute.

Within weeks, a grassroots organization, Residents Against Annexation, was formed, demanding town leaders fight the tribe and refuse a compromise. Angry locals placed signs on Jackson King's front lawn in Ledyard saying, "Not One Acre." Such signs opposing annexation soon sprouted on lawns across the county. "Every political instinct told me that as soon as 'annexation' became the way it was talked about in the press, the battle was in big trouble," Margolin recalled. "I saw the problem as political, and it needed to be solved as a matter of political strategy. But Skip's sense of his own dignity did not allow that. He was relying on Jackson King for advice on this. Jackson was more sensitive to what Skip and Kenny and the council wanted to do, which was not to suck up to the towns."

Skip felt he could ultimately convince Babbitt and the BIA to approve the land-into-trust petition despite the fierce local opposition. Toward that end, he enlisted the political support of Representative Gejdenson, asking him to personally lobby Babbitt. At the local level, Gejdenson tried to convince the Ledyard Democrats that the town should cut a deal with the Pequots. Gejdenson told Ledyard Mayor Joe Lozier that the townspeople were "settlers," and reminded Preston First Selectman Parke Spicer that his ancestors had Pequot blood on their hands. (When word of this got back to the tribe, Jackson King said to Gejdenson, "Sam, even we don't call them 'settlers.'")

The Ledyard Democrats met in private with Gejdenson one evening. They asked him to remain neutral in the fight. They reminded him of their longtime support. Dave Holdridge, one of the original defendants in the 1976 land-claim suit, attended the meeting. "It was my impression that the 1983 land settlement had decided once and for all where there were legitimate land claims and where there were not," he said to Gejdenson. "That was why local, state, and federal government got involved and supported the 1983 bill, because of the threat to land values all over town. The motivation for government settlement was to clearly define where the tribe had legitimate claims and that would be the end of it. Now, with annexation, here are the same issues coming back. I am still alive, and I still remember what happened. It is clear in my mind that the reservation boundaries were defined by the settlement act. That was one of the key reasons why Congress passed this act."

Gejdenson countered that land annexation by the tribe was necessary for its economic development and argued that the language of the 1983 act did not say precisely that there could be no further land taken into trust for the tribe. He insisted it was murky and open to interpretation. The meeting quickly deteriorated into a shouting match, culminating in accusations involving campaign contributions Gejdenson had accepted from the Pequots. "Well, I guess we've said all we can," Gejdenson said, and left the meeting.

Skip continued his political lobbying campaign in Washington, sprinkling hundreds of thousands of dollars in campaign contributions into influential Democrats' coffers as well as to a few Republicans like Senator Robert Dole, to help sway the Interior. Many of the politicians took the money but did little to help the tribe. The former chief lobbyist for the Pequots in Washington recalled, "Skip trusted the Clinton administration to take some risks for them on the question of taking land into trust even if it was not popular in the region. I told Skip that if this issue ever came to a fight, the Clinton administration would not lift a finger to help them on issues that were overly controversial for the Democratic party."

With the lobbying campaign in Washington stalled, the towns took the tribe to court to stop the purchase of the 247-acre parcel across from Foxwoods. Skip remained confident he would win in the end.

19

DIVIDING THE SPOILS

Traditionally, American Indian tribes have distributed money among their tribal members on a per capita basis; in other words, everyone receives the same amount. The idea that one member deserved more than another was antithetical to the communal foundation of a tribe. Within the Pequot tribal council, however, Skip argued that "per capita systems" fostered "a welfare mentality," and thus would sap them of any incentive to work. Now that Foxwoods was famous, the tribe was growing fast, heading quickly toward three hundred members. Skip argued that the Pequots were already in danger of becoming "a bunch of idlers" held together only by the desire for money.

Skip asked Barry Margolin and Rob Gips to design a better system, an "incentive plan" in which the distribution of cash to tribal members would vary according to work effort and educational level. The plan was a market-oriented piece of social engineering that no Indian tribe had ever attempted. At first, everyone loved the idea. There were a few people who wanted per capita payments, but they were not vocal. Everyone thought that the incentive plan was worth a try. It was adopted unanimously.

The plan had several objectives—to provide older members with enough money on which to live comfortably, to pay members who worked or who went to school more than loafers, and to reward disproportionately those who had joined the tribe in the

1970s, most notably Skip's family. One of Skip's cousins who joined the tribe in the seventies said, "If you did not know the people behind the plan and some of the history, you would think that it was meant to incentivize people to get their education and to work for the tribe and be involved in the community. But the incentive program was also about rewarding those people who had been here since the early days. And that was largely the Elizabeth George family." A tribal anthropologist recalled, "It was always top-heavy toward the insiders. That's who was drawing up the plan."

By September 1992, Margolin and Gips had codified Skip's idea into a legal document, "The Mashantucket Pequot Tribal Incentive Ordinance." The ordinance established a Youth Scholarship and Education Incentive Program, creating a "scholarship account" for every tribal member under the age of twenty-one years old. The money was to be invested and withdrawn only for educational expenses such as tuition and room and board. The scholarship fund also paid any taxes on this educational benefit. If you turned twenty-one and there was still money in your scholarship account, the money became yours if you promised to join the career training program and work for the tribe for at least three years. If you took the money and failed to enter the training program, you were supposed to reimburse the tribe for prior withdrawals.

To encourage job training and employment for members over twenty-one years old, the incentive ordinance established a Career Development Incentive Program. Essentially, this program awarded extra incentive points to adults willing to get job training and work for the tribe. For members fifty-five years or older, the tribe created its own Social Security Program for adults with disabilities, provided they attended six tribal meetings a year.

Skip and the tribal council decided how big the pool of cash to be divvied up would be each year. Eighty percent of the incentive pool was to be distributed to members right away, and twenty percent was to be held pending appeals by members unhappy with how much they got. Complaints were to be reviewed by an Incentive Review Team, which included a representative from each of the families that made up the Pequots.

The calculation of each member's incentive payments was made by the tribal department of finance, which divided the total pool of money allocated by the council and further divided that figure by the total number of "incentive points" awarded to all members during the year. This computation generated a dollar value per incentive point. The more incentive points, the more money you received. Under the Scholarship Program, for example, a teenager would receive sixteen points if he or she enrolled in school but only twelve if the student dropped out. The student received twenty-five points for graduating from high school. Pequots aged eighteen to twenty received more—twenty points for going to high school, twenty-five points for graduating, twenty-eight points for part-time college work, and thirty points for full-time college.

Older members, who went to school under the aegis of the Career Development Program, did even better. If you were thirty-one to forty years old, you received sixty points for a high school degree or a Graduate Equivalency Diploma (GED), sixty-five for part-time college work, seventy-five for full-time enrollment, and eighty-five for a bachelor's degree. A master's degree was worth ninety points. If you were seventy-five or older and had at some point gotten your high school degree or a GED, you were automatically awarded 145 points.

No one ended up with more under the Career Development Program than the Haywards. The program was larded with "multipliers" that rewarded them disproportionately. Incentive point totals were increased, for example, by 1 percent for each year served on a tribal subcommittee since 1988, and by 3 percent for each year served in a "supervisory position" in the tribe since 1978. (A "supervisory position" was defined as managing "one or more employees.") And most important for the Haywards, who had sat on the tribal council from the early days, one's incentive point total was retrospectively goosed 5 percent for each year one had served on the tribal council since 1973. These multipliers meant that Skip and some others in his family were in line to receive three to four times the point totals of other members.

Between 1992 and 1994, the annual incentive pool ranged between $15 million and $20 million, and the tribal population averaged about 150. A per capita distribution system would have produced payments of about $100,000 to $125,000 a year per member. Under Skip's "incentive system," however, the range of payments was far wider. An incentive point was worth between $500 and $1,000. A few tribal members like Skip were earning hundreds of incentive points while others were not near that amount. Skip was earning about $500,000 a year while newer members might receive a scant $50,000 a year. By 1994 Skip had received well in excess of $1 million in incentive payments.

The inequality of incentive payments soon exacerbated underlying racial tensions within the tribe. Black newcomers began to learn of the vast sums being deposited to the bank and brokerage accounts of Skip, his family, and other light-skinned Pequots. "We give points by how long a person's been here, by their education, by this and that," recalled Phyllis Monroe. "And what has happened is that the people who have come here to do the hard work, the menial work, to dig in the dirt, are not the ones getting the money. It's the ones with the education that are getting it. They're the ones reaping the harvest of what other people have worked for and that is wrong."

At one tribal council meeting, several black Pequots stood up and shouted at Skip and the council members, asking where their money was. Where was their promised million dollars? A nontribal attendee at the meeting recalled, "Their message was just that they were as entitled to the money as Skip was. They did not see why they had to work for the money. Their basic message to the tribal council was, 'You invited me to join the tribe. I'm here. I'm as legitimate as you are. Where's my money?'"

By December 1992, Jackson King had decided to join the Pequots full-time as general counsel. It seemed to him a natural progression from opponent during the land-claim suit to employee now that the tribe was the largest business enterprise in the region. Not long after federal recognition in 1983, the tribe had begun employing King as local counsel for real estate transactions and other minor matters. As the business grew with bingo and gambling, the business relationship grew as well. By 1992 there was so much legal work that Skip felt the need for an in-house lawyer, and he offered the job to King. The evening before he was to start as general counsel, King dropped by the reservation to speak with Skip in his office. They were talking when a recently arrived black female tribal member burst into Skip's office with two tough-looking black men, one of whom carried a long, thick wooden bat. She was entitled to money from the incentive plan's Scholarship Program, but the tribal finance department was refusing to give her the money. She yelled at Skip, "I am going to school and I'm entitled to my money. I am here for my fucking money."

King, who had been deeply involved in the crafting of the incentive plan, listened to her story and said, "Wait a minute. The ordinance does not allow you to qualify."

"Bullshit," the young woman said. "I want my money, and I'm entitled to my fucking money."

At this point, one of her male companions came forward and showed Skip and King a bullet scar on his body, saying, "I got shot in New York and I'm not afraid to die. I can take you guys out with me. Do what my sister wants. She works her ass off and she's going to school. You better get her some money." Looking at King, he said, "You get the fuck out of here." He then threw a cup of coffee in King's face and pressed the wooden bat so close to the lawyer's face that King could feel it against his eyelashes.

Two Connecticut state troopers soon arrived accompanied by the chief of the tribal police, Clifford Sebastian, a recent transplant from New York City, where he had been a transit cop. Sebastian suggested they all go outside and talk. Sebastian led the young man out first, and when the young man was outside the door, the police chief locked him out. Enraged, the man punched his fist through the door. The state police officers asked Skip if he wanted them to make an arrest. Skip declined, instead giving the angry young man a job on the tribal road crew the very next day. He later became a tribal member.

By now it was clear to Skip that there would be more violence if the incentive ordinance wasn't liberalized. He tweaked the Youth Scholarship and Education Incentive Program to make it easier for blacks to get more money. Skip and the tribal council lowered the age at which a high school dropout could get money from his "scholarship" account. Education incentive points were dramatically increased. High school enrollment became worth forty points versus the prior twenty points. College enrollment earned one hundred points versus the prior thirty points. A hairdresser's license earned a tribal member as many incentive points as a college degree.

The liberalization of the point system went even further. The Pequots abandoned the residency requirement, along with the requirement to work to qualify for points. Attendance at six tribal meetings a year was all that was required. New point categories were created. Tribal members who received honorary college degrees received bonus incentive points. The honorary degree became a way for tribal leaders—the most likely to receive such perks—to pad their incentive payments. By 1994, Skip had earned three honorary degrees from local universities—the University of Connecticut, Eastern Connecticut State University, and Roger Williams College in Rhode Island—which added tens of thousands of dollars to his annual income.

In 1995, the incentive pool was increased to $35 million. Over the next five years, the Pequots paid themselves about $300 million in incentive payments. Take, for example, one black twenty-year-old female member who dropped out of high school in the mid-1990s (she declined to be identified). She received $6,000 a month in incentive payments, or about $72,000 a year. In addition, she was assigned a clerical job that paid her between $50,000 and $75,000 a year. She also received tens of thousands of dollars a year in medical, housing, and other benefits. In total, she received from $125,000 to $150,000 a year, but she felt cheated. "I got my $6,000 a month but those Haywards were getting $12,000 to $13,000 a month. What am I? A second-class Pequot?"

After Foxwoods opened, many poor or working-class African-Americans joined the tribe. Three-quarters of the tribe's adult population joined after 1994—that is, after the establishment of Foxwoods and the introduction of slots. They were, of course, attracted by the money. Another reason for the sudden increase in membership was that it became easier to attain. In 1991, the tribe had lowered the required blood quantum from one-eighth to one-sixteenth. Not long after, they did away with the blood quantum altogether. Anyone related to a person who had been listed on either the 1900 or the 1910 census was eligible to become a Pequot. This easing of the entrance requirement made practical sense within the tribe. White members ensured their children and grandchildren membership, and black members could enroll more of their extended families.

Between 1991 and 1993, Pequot membership more than doubled from about 125 to 275. It would double again in the next few years to between 500 and 600 members. According to one Pequot leader, a former tribal council member who declined to be identified, "We are the first Indian tribe to come together for money." Clifford Sebastian, for example, was asked after he joined the tribe how it felt to be back on the reservation. He replied, "How does it feel to be *back*? I'm a Puerto Rican from the Bronx. All of the sudden my grandmother was an Indian, and now I am going to become police chief."

Like Sebastian, most of the new members had no prior contact with the Pequots. Theresa Casanova, a descendant of Mabel George, a sister of Eliza and Annie George, was born in 1980 to a black mother and a Puerto Rican father. She was raised in a series of ghettos in New York City and Florida. "We had been living in New York City and then Florida," she recalled. "We would move every year to a different place. We were on and off welfare. . . . One day [her mother] told me that we were moving to Connecticut. She told me that we were Indian. I asked her what tribe. She said the Mashantucket Pequot. I could not pronounce it. She told us that we were Native American. I never knew about that. At school, I told everyone that I was Puerto Rican. She said that now that there was a casino we were going to live there. And she said that we might be rich. At that time, we were poor.

"We did not have any place to live, so the tribe set us up with an apartment in Groton, Connecticut," she recalled. "They gave us vouchers to go food shopping. And we got some new clothes. We went to a store and we had never bought so many clothes in our whole life. And they gave us vouchers to get furniture. They gave my mother a job. A couple of months later, we got a house, even though we wasn't enrolled yet as members. They helped us buy a new car. We had this old beat-up station wagon we had driven from Florida. . . . We bought a brand-new purple van. I look back at it now and I think how ugly it was. But to us at the time, it was really nice. It was new."

When asked why her family became Pequot, she said, "The only reason why a lot of people are here is for the money. That is the only reason my family is here. Because of the money. We would not have come here without the money. We did not need to come here to feel that we had some Indian identity. We could have that same feeling in Florida. We came back for the money. I don't know if we deserved it or not. Maybe we were just lucky. But we deserved the money just as much as anyone else who the tribe said were Pequot."

In 1992 a twenty-nine-year-old black man from the urban ghettos of southern California named Antonio M. Beltran joined the tribe. A member of the Sebastian family, he had been incarcerated in prison for several crimes, including a stabbing that left his victim paralyzed from the waist down. "I wanted a better life," he recalled. "My brother encouraged me to return to the reservation. That is not correct. I should not say 'return' because I had never actually been to the reservation." Beltran quickly made a name for himself as one of the most confrontational Pequots. "When I first came here I would attend membership meetings and voice my opinions," he said. "I began studying Pequot history and I noticed that one of the common themes throughout was that we were considered an aggressive and warlike people. I said to myself, 'Aha, now I know where I get my personality.'"

Other tribal members remembered Beltran as a frightening figure. "He was very vocal in saying that the whites were getting everything and the blacks nothing," said a former tribal council member who declined to be identified. "He was a scary guy." A female historian who worked for the tribe in the 1990s recalled an unpleasant incident involving Beltran. "I happened to run into Tony Beltran in a parking lot at night after a meeting.

I was working on a project he opposed, a project on the history of the Pequots. He had just arrived and his attitude was, 'Where is my money? I want my money now.' He saw our project as competition for the money from Foxwoods that should be put into the pockets of tribal members like him. That night he had been drinking. I remember he said to me, 'I'm paying your fucking mortgage. Don't think you are kidding me.' I was really scared. He got into his car and I thought he was going to run me over."

Little did she know that Beltran had a record of violent crime. He had been convicted of attempted manslaughter for the stabbing in California and served time in San Quentin prison. Late one night in 1980, Beltran was cruising with friends north of Los Angeles when he spotted a white teenage boy walking alone down a deserted street. Beltran told the driver of the car to pull over. He got out and attacked the young man, whom he did not know, from behind. Beltran had told his friends in the car before the attack that he wanted to "kill a white boy." Beltran recalled it differently after his arrest. He said, "I was going to stab someone. That was it. I was angry at the world, about my upbringing and poverty." At his sentencing hearing, which the victim and his family attended, Beltran was sentenced to seven years in prison. Leaving the courtroom, he turned to his victim and said, "You may be smiling, but at least I'm walking." Beltran served four years in prison before being released. In 1991 he was convicted as a felon of possession of a firearm following a fight in a bar. In 1994, by then a Pequot, Beltran pleaded guilty to breach of the peace after being stopped for a traffic violation and calling the arresting policeman "a nigger selling out to the white man," adding that he "wasn't Rodney King and would kick this officer's ass," and, shouting at bystanders, "A nigger is about to get beat up."

Blacks weren't the only ones to join the tribe after Foxwoods opened. Whites from middle-class suburbs came as well, largely for the same reasons—to better their material lives. Bill Guevre-mont, a grandson of one of Eliza's half sisters, was one. Born in the early 1960s, Guevremont was raised primarily outside of the United States. "I marked off 'White' or 'Caucasian' on forms," he recalled. "I never had any real consciousness about being Pequot. My association with Pequot was that it was just part of my family background." He had no contact with the tribe until 1994, when he paid a visit to see Foxwoods and the reservation. An aunt, who had already moved to the reservation, gave him a tour. "The first thing I saw was the housing, which was fairly impressive. I thought, 'Wow, this is nice for a reservation.' Then I saw the community center and that was really nice too. I'm thinking, 'There's some real cash flow here.' Then I see the casino, Foxwoods. It really was impressive. I started asking more questions. She asked me if I had put in my paperwork to become a member." He hadn't. So he went straight to the tribal clerk's office and spent the rest of the day filling out forms. He left the next day to return to his home in Oregon. "We didn't stay very long at all," he recalled. He had seen enough. When the tribe offered him a job, he moved his fam-ily to Connecticut.

As one of the few tribal members with professional skills and a college degree—he was an architect—Guevremont was assigned a managerial job. But after nine months he had yet to be officially accepted as a tribal member, which meant he wasn't eligible for incentive payments. Then one of his cousins, who was already a member, approached him one day with a piece of paper and said, "You need to see this." It was the tribal roll submitted to the BIA with the preliminary federal recognition petition. There were fifty-five names on the list and Guevremont's was one. This is how he discovered that Skip had used his name to inflate the tribal roll during the federal recognition process.

Guevremont went immediately to see Jackson King. "Jack-son, is this list for real?"

Jackson said, "Skip needs to see this."

"Yeah, because I'm still not a tribal member."

Presented with the list, Skip went to the tribal council the next day with a resolution acknowledging that Guevremont had been a member of the tribe since 1983: because his name had been used for the federal recognition process, he was therefore legally entitled to be compensated as having been an active tribal member since 1983. He stood to receive hundreds of thousands of dollars in retroactive incentive payments.

20

SPENDING SPREE

ozens of sparkling new BMWs, Mercedes-Benzs, and SUVs were double-parked outside the tribe's new $50 million community center, which looked like the largest, most modern Adirondack stone-and-timber lodge ever built. Rap music was blasting from every car. Tony Beltran checked his gleaming BMW roadster for nicks while an aide sat in the front passenger seat reading the business section of the newspaper and checking the stock quotes. It was Friday, and they were waiting for their money—their salaries and incentive payments.

By 1995 the Pequots were drowning in money from Foxwoods, which that year generated $236 million in income to the tribe, about $750,000 per Pequot member. Bruce Kirchner, a former tribal council member, recalled, "There was so much money flowing from Foxwoods, hundreds of millions a year. There was so much money being distributed via the incentive plan. There were so many high-paying jobs handed out to tribal members. People were suddenly getting all this money, anywhere from $150,000 a year to several million dollars. It all led to a desire for instant gratification and huge spending and buying at both the tribal and the personal level. It simply reinforced everyone's sense of entitlement. I have heard people say, 'Foxwoods is there for me to get whatever I want.' The notion grew that because we were 'Pequot,' we were entitled to whatever we wanted."

Skip embarked on a spending spree unrivaled in American Indian history. Hiring, which had started slowly in the 1980s after the bingo hall opened, exploded with the money generated by the casino. Foxwoods employed about 11,000 people, and the tribal government employed another 1,030 whose sole job was to provide governmental services to the tribe's 372 members. (The ratio of government workers to Pequots was about three-to-one.) The total payroll topped 12,000. The number of tribal government departments grew to forty-five. (The Pequots had their own "Department of the Interior," responsible for decorating and cleaning the interiors of tribal buildings.) By 1997 the Pequots were budgeting close to $80 million a year for their government alone, and that did not include the $30 million to $35 million in annual incentive payments they lavished on themselves. By 1998 the tribal government's budget had risen to around $100 million to provide social services and security for the approximately 500 tribal members. (In contrast, the combined budgets for the three towns surrounding the reservation— Ledyard, Preston, and North Stonington—totaled $25 million, and their combined population was about 25,000.)

Skip felt there was nothing the Pequots could not afford. On December 11, 1996, for instance, the tribal council approved a $452.6 million capital spending program for the next two years. Skip's budget included a $335 million hotel, a $200 million museum, a $50 million monorail for the reservation, $92 million in land purchases, a $12 million police and fire station, a $10 million child development center for tribal youth, and $39 million for "Other Projects." The budget forecast $1.7 billion to be spent on capital projects over the next five years.

Skip's tribal council accounted for roughly 50 percent of the tribe's government spending in the 1990s. In one year alone, he and the other six councillors—they had expanded from five to seven members at the behest of the Sebastians—spent close to $30 million, a far cry from the early days when the council was a volunteer operation. Salaries accounted for much of the money. Skip was paid more than $1 million a year in salary and bonuses, excluding incentive payments. All told, he was taking home $2 million to $3 million a year, and paying only federal income taxes on that amount. (He declared the reservation as his official residence and thus avoided state and local taxes.) Skip insisted that no one should make more money than he, not even the chief executive officer of Foxwoods. The way Skip saw it, he was CEO of the Pequots.

Skip spent more on travel and entertainment than any other tribal member. A former senior manager in the tribal government who declined to be identified said, "Skip would charter a plane or a helicopter to fly to New York City from Groton, Connecticut. This is very, very expensive stuff. He showed no concern for tribal expenses. He had his own tribal council expense account. Occasionally, he would overspend, and they would come to me and say, 'You have this big budget. We want you to pay for this expense.' Skip paid for very little of his travel and entertaining personally. I can't imagine that he paid for anything personally. I suppose he made the argument that he had no personal life."

A tribal member who oversaw one of the tribe's governmental departments recalled, "I had a $395,000 annual budget. It was to do monorail research. One day I noticed that there was $110,000 missing from the budget. Gone. My assistant asked me, 'What's this expense here?' It was for $110,000. I said, 'I don't know. Go find out.' She comes back to me. [One of Skip's aides] had told her, 'Don't worry about it. It's none of your concern.' It turned out that Skip had gone on a trip to Bermuda. He came back and said to [his aide], 'Take care of this.' They went into the money allocated to the monorail budget and called Skip's trip 'monorail research.'"

Skip's fellow tribal council members were paid less than he— in the range of $500,000 to $1 million a year—but they compensated by assembling huge staffs to wait on them hand and foot. By the late 1990s, the typical council member spent about

$3 million on staff and other expenses. The council's chief of staff—A. Searle Field—was paid more than $500,000 a year. (Like Jackson King, Field was a former adversary, an ex-aide to Lowell Weicker, who Skip hired for his legal and political experience.) Field created a cabinet of highly paid aides to service the tribal council, who in turn hired dozens of legal and financial advisers and consultants. In 1995, for instance, Jackson King's law firm, Brown, Jacobson, was paid about $1.5 million by the tribe.

Skip and his fellow council members lived like princes. They routinely rented private jets, traveled first class on airlines, rode in chauffeured stretch limousines, and slept in presidential suites at the finest hotels. "I know council members have paid as much as $9,000 a night for suites," said a former council member. On a trip to Saint Croix, ostensibly to investigate the possibility of establishing a Pequot casino on the Caribbean island, they rented a DC-9 to take them, according to Mickey Brown, who was CEO of Foxwoods for several years in the 1990s. "They probably took fifty people," he recalled. "They went down for seven days. They stayed at a first-class resort. They may have met a few times in a conference room at the hotel. But mainly they partied and went fishing. And they did not all come back together. So they got a smaller jet, a Citation, to ferry them back to Connecticut. I bet the tribe spent more than $300,000 on that trip alone."

When tribal members did work for the tribe, they came in at, or near, the top of the pay scale. They codified their privileges in the "Mashantucket Pequot Tribe Indian Preference and Affirmative Action Plan." According to the confidential plan, tribal members received a preference in four areas—jobs and promotion, the procurement of goods and services for tribal businesses, construction services, and the provision of professional services. No job was to be posted externally unless tribal members had already declined the position. No Pequot was required "to possess higher qualifications than the lowest qualified" person already in a job. "They all wanted supervisors' jobs," recalled Mickey Brown. "This was a very complicated situation for us [nontribal managers]. We were dealing with people with limited education. Most of these people had a high school equivalency degree or less. Most of these people came from poor inner-city minority neighborhoods. We tried to encourage a structured training schedule. If you had never had a job before, if you had been unemployed or on welfare all your adult life, we brought the tribal member in at the entry level. After they showed they could do that job, we would make them trainees for first-line supervisor jobs. Then, we would promote them to a manager's job and ultimately a director's job. The tribal members didn't like this approach. They didn't want to begin as an employee. . . . They felt they should have the right to participate in upper management right away. . . . A brand-new tribal member would show up in my office at the casino and say, 'Hi, I want to be director of entertainment.'"

Brown continued, "In response to pressure from the tribal council, we tried to create a summer intern program for tribal youth to learn jobs in the casino. It was a program for teenagers to work four hours in the afternoon at the casino Monday, Wednesday, and Friday. . . . They would sit beside a cashier. They would work with one of the guys who drive the forklift in the warehouse. . . . So twenty kids came down. They're all given assignments. Only five of them agreed to work the assignments. Fifteen of the kids say, 'I'm not going to do that.' I get phone calls from the different department heads who say, 'I have Jimmy and Billy and Mary here, and they don't want to do these jobs. They wanna be managers.' I said, 'If these kids don't want to work, put them back on the bus and send them back to the community center.' I start getting complaining calls within one hour from parents and the tribal youth coordinator. 'What in the hell are you doing to these kids? Don't you understand these are the future leaders of the Mashantucket Pequot Tribal

Nation?'" I said, 'I'm sending them back because they refused to work.'"

Many black tribal members believed they were being discriminated against by Brown and his team of nontribal managers at Foxwoods. The managers denied the allegations and countered that, in truth, they were afraid of being fired if they didn't hire and promote unqualified tribal members. By 1996, only thirteen tribal members worked at the casino. Foxwoods was a demanding work environment that required night shifts and diplomacy when dealing with unhappy customers. Tribal members migrated away from Foxwoods and toward the tribal government, where there was little or no accountability. Tribal members knew that a nontribal manager in the Pequot government offices would not dare give them an unsatisfactory job rating—that is, if the manager valued his job. In contrast to Foxwoods, where managers reported to nontribal executives, managers in the Pequot government reported directly to the tribal council.

Managers in the tribal government offices had as their mandate boosting the number of Pequots in top jobs. As a result, they often encouraged tribal members to seek supervisory jobs far beyond their capabilities. One twenty-year-old female tribal member explained, "I had one year of college before I dropped out, and I said I was thinking of majoring in environmental science when I went back. So they suggested that I go into the tribe Natural Resources department, and they would put me into the highest position not filled by a tribal member. They wanted me to become a manager. First of all, I have one year of college. I have no experience at all in environmental science. I wouldn't know what I was doing. I have nothing under my belt. I'm not qualified. They don't care. They are taking their orders from the tribe and the orders are to put tribal members in top positions no matter what. It was like, 'Do you want this position? You can have it.'" At the time, the average minimum wage for Pequots was $50,000 to $60,000 a year. Managers were paid in excess of $100,000.

The lack of accountability for Pequots in the tribal government led many to abuse the system. Tribal members worked twenty hours a week when they were supposed to work thirty-five, and nothing was said in reprimand. One female tribal member recalled, "When my sisters and I went to work, we would say, 'It's time to play executive.' That's what we called it—'playing executive.'" Other tribal members did not bother to show up for work at all.

A former senior manager in the tribal public affairs office—not a tribal member—offered a typical example. "I had one fellow who worked for me who was thirty-eight years old. He had neither a high school nor a college education. In three months, I might see him one-third of the time. He just did not show up. He got paid $120,000 a year. And then he got his incentive payments. He probably received $400,000 a year. Now you tell me, if you were a tribal member and you're getting $400,000 a year, and you have a BMW and you have a million-dollar home and you have a whole bunch of skilled people like me to do the work, would you clock in every day? I don't think so. There's not a lot of incentive. You can't be fired from the job. You can't lose the money. It's a done deal before you even show up to work."

A former manager in the tribe's education unit attributed the no-shows to tribal member insecurity. She said, "They are like people who have been asked to perform brain surgery and don't know how and so don't show up to do the operation. They have put themselves in positions where they cannot do the jobs they are supposed to be doing, so they don't show up. . . . They suffer from 'imposture syndrome.' . . . We have people here who are the directors of departments and make $125,000 a year and can't even read or write."

Despite all the preferences and advantages available to tribal members, many remained unhappy about their rate of career advancement. In their view, too few tribal members were being named directors of tribal government departments. The former senior manager in the Pequot public affairs office recalled, "The tribal members who worked in my department were hostile and resentful about having to work for a nontribal member. They would show up to work for a while and then they would stop showing up. Of course, they were getting paid whether or not they showed up. The big scam was the career development department. You would get a call saying you were getting Skip's nephew or niece for training to become the director of your department. They meant for that to happen within months, not years. So the tribal member would typically come in as 'assistant director' and you were supposed to train that tribal member to take your place. The guy would arrive and want a big office and start spending a lot of money. Typically, the tribal member had absolutely no experience in the area. No college degree. Often not even high school degree. He would be driving a BMW. You would see him once a month.

"I wanted to have a professional organization," the manager continued. "Anybody who wanted to work, I was happy to have . . . but I was not going to put up with the scams. Not only would I have to pay them out of my budget, but also they would expense all kinds of personal things to the department. The tribal member who ran my department before me, the brother of a tribal council member, disappeared for months at a time. He had a major drug problem, and he was running up these incredible American Express bills. The only way we knew he was around was when we would get his American Express bills. He spent over a hundred thousand dollars personally before we cut it off. He was ordering Dom Perignon champagne. He would expense his trips to strip joints. The ethic of these people was, 'I want to be the director. I want to run the show. But I'm not doing work that is beneath me.' In my experience, the tribal members were strictly no-show.

"I am a member of a minority group myself," the manager said. "So I support the idea of affirmative action, but it didn't take long for me to realize that tribal members with no experience at all who worked for me felt that I worked for them. That created conflict. Occasionally, I had to tell them what needed to be done. They would say, 'I don't agree with you. I am not following your orders.' And soon I would hear from a tribal councillor, 'Stop leaning on people.' So I would fudge their performance evaluations. If they had been working for me at my former employer, I would have transferred them out of the department or fired them."

As both Foxwoods and the Pequot tribal government grew at an incredible pace, new construction projects created a cornucopia of business opportunities for tribal member–owned businesses. Foxwoods and the tribal government bought hundreds of millions of dollars of construction materials and services: steel, stone, wood, carpentry, plumbing, drywall, ceramic tile, flooring and carpeting, electrical wiring, insurance, even paper cups. The more entrepreneurial tribal members set up side businesses in order to provide these materials and services to the tribe.

When awarding business contracts, the tribe had a "15 percent" preference for tribal member–owned companies. These companies could win a bid to supply goods and services to the tribe as long as the bid was no more than 15 percent above the lowest nontribal bid. A tribal member who later investigated the preference system for the tribe explained, "It worked like this. An outside nontribal contractor, say, an electrical or plumbing guy, would say to a tribal member he knew, 'Come partner with me. You will own 51 percent of the company. I will own 49 percent. I will do all the work, and you will see to it that we win the bid.' And the tribal member, not knowing anything about construction or contracting, would say, 'Sounds good.' And the tribal member would be the front man. The problem was that competition arrived. Other, more experienced contractors would show up and offer lower bids than the member-owned companies. Tribal members would come back to the tribal council and say, 'Wait a minute. We are not getting our fair share of the business. We are applying for these contracts at Foxwoods, and we are not winning bids.' So the council passed a resolution saying that if the bids came in and if the tribal member's bid was within 15 percent of the lowest outside bid, the tribal member would get the contract."

With the 15 percent rule in place, the tribal council issued instructions stating that if a tribal member's bid was not the lowest in the first round of bidding, he should be given one more opportunity to bid. Additionally, tribal member–owned companies were able to learn of the best nontribal bid before making their final offer.

Perhaps the most successful exploitation of tribal preference involved members of Skip's and Kenny Reels's families. The partners included one of Skip's nephews, a half brother of Kenny Reels, and two of Kenny's cousins. Atlantic Industries, as it was known, was in the business of crushing rocks, normally a low-margin business. The tribe needed gravel for its various construction projects. The tribe's Sand & Gravel department, effectively run by Reels's family, provided rocks to Atlantic for free, along with tribal-owned dump trucks to carry the rock from the reservation to Atlantic's crusher. Atlantic then sold the gravel back to the tribe or to contractors working for the tribe. By the late 1990s, the tribe was the proud owner of about 400,000 cubic yards of unused gravel. "It had to be the most profitable member-owned company," said the tribal member who subsequently reviewed Atlantic's operations for the tribe. "Sand & Gravel was losing $5 to $10 million a year at that time, and I think much of those losses were little more than the flip side of the money Atlantic was making." He estimated that the tribe paid Atlantic Industries in the range of $25 million.

Tribal council members, aware of the questionable relationship between Atlantic and Sand & Gravel, acted to shut it down only after the Occupational Safety and Health Administration (OSHA) and the Internal Revenue Service began investigating

Atlantic for possible worker safety and tax law violations. Mickey Brown said, "Skip had a fine line to walk in terms of tribal politics. He had bigger fish to worry about than this. If he caused too much of a ruckus over issues like this, he would have caused problems for himself politically. I don't know that he allowed other people to take money as much as he felt he could not afford to stop it."

21

SCHEMITZUN

The richer the new Pequots became, the more the paucity of Pequot culture came under public scrutiny. The absence of Pequot culture—for example, language, dance, rituals, religion, or other shared values and customs—led to some awkward moments when the Pequots were invited to display their cultural identity. In the early 1990s, a group of tribal members stopped over in Hawaii on a visit to see their Malaysian business partners. They were invited to the Polynesian Cultural Center, a courtesy often extended to visiting aboriginal groups. They were asked if they would sing a traditional Pequot song. The only problem was that they had no such song. Instead, they sang "You Are My Sunshine." It was the only song everyone knew. "It was so embarrassing," recalled one tribal member who sang along.

It became evident to the leaders of the tribe that they needed some public displays of Pequot culture to deflect skepticism about their legitimacy and heritage. In the late 1970s, Skip and his family had made a few halfhearted tries at Pequot powwows as a fundraising tool for the then nascent tribe. As Bruce Kirchner recalled, "We brought in a dancer and a drummer. It was very amateur, very low-key. There were no Pequot dances or songs or anything. We just worked behind the scenes cooking hamburgers and making chowder and organizing the event." But by 1992 Skip and his family needed, and via Foxwoods could afford, to put on a powwow with

Indians from across North America performing traditional dances and songs. Skip's sister Terry Bell led the way. She asked, "Skip, can we have that powwow we always wanted? We have land now."

"Yeah. Put a budget together, and we'll put one together."

Bell began the historical research to find an authentic-sounding Indian name for a Pequot powwow. She came across an Algonquian word in a book, "Schemitzun," which meant "green corn festival." The new Pequot festival was born.

The first Schemitzun was held on October 23, 1992. Bell described Schemitzun to reporters as a "revival" of a traditional Pequot corn harvest festival. The Pequots erected three large tents next to Foxwoods for entertainment, crafts, and food catered by Foxwoods, and the third tent offering T-shirts and playing cards. From a public relations point of view, the first Schemitzun was less than successful. Fewer than three hundred people came to the opening day. One local newspaper article was headlined "Crowds Small at Foxwoods Indian Festival," and did not mention the Pequots until the fourth paragraph. Few, if any, Pequots participated in the dancing, drumming, or singing.

The next year, the Pequots revamped Schemitzun and promoted it as the "World Championship of Native American Music and Dance," offering significant cash prizes to attract twelve hundred dancers and drummers from across the continent. They moved the show out of the shadow of Foxwoods and into the Hartford Civic Center. It was a public relations hit. By 1995, Schemitzun had become an extravaganza with more than $750,000 offered in prize money and some four thousand dancers and fifty drumming groups. The Pequots gave away 20,000 free tickets to local schools and advertised that children would have an "opportunity to experience Native American culture firsthand."

By then, however, many tribal members wanted little to do with Schemitzun. They found it embarrassing to pretend that they had a traditional culture. Anthropologist James Wherry explained, "The whole Indian thing was not really part of their experience.

It does not mean that they looked down on dancing and drumming and singing. They don't think it's silly, but they did not feel comfortable doing it themselves. You have to remember that they did not grow up in any kind of native community. The Pequots by the time of Eliza were not involved in the powwow scene."

Black tribal members became Schemitzun's most enthusiastic supporters. Wherry recalled, "You had some of the new members who joined the tribe and took a great interest in cultural aspects of Native Americans. Not necessarily Pequot, but Native American. I think it has to do with their upbringing and race. A lot of the members today come from an urban background. Black. They tend to be more outgoing. They tend to be more demonstrative. Schemitzun offers them a way to demonstrate and legitimize their Indian identity."

Regrettably, other Indians attending Schemitzun did not always welcome the Pequots who participated in the festival. "I used to compete in the dances," said a niece of Kenny Reels. "But the judges are from other tribes, and they pick the winner based on who looks Indian. And other tribes look more Indian than I do. I never won anything. I got sick of competing and losing. It is bad enough when you go to other tribes and always lose but then you have your tribe's powwow, Schemitzun, and we lose there too. My uncle paid this lady a lot of money to come and give us Indian dancing lessons. I competed but people kept saying that I was black and not an Indian." A member of a Western Indian tribe who worked for the Pequots for many years recalled, "It's obvious to us that the Pequots have no tribal traditions. They come out on the first day of Schemitzun and do this grand entrance dance that is like a Caribbean rumba. The Indian dancers from other tribes can barely contain themselves not to laugh because it is so clear that the Pequots are making up their traditions as they go along. They look as if they are trying to learn how to be Indians."

An internal Pequot tribal government memo from 1992 noted, "It has been reported to the Committee that ugly and extremely derisive and jeering comments have been heard from individuals stating that the Mashantucket Pequots must hire western Indians to promote their Indian culture." The Pequot response, according to the memo, was to redouble efforts to teach tribal members how to become Indians. The proposed efforts included dance classes, arts and crafts classes, a regalia-making class, and programs to teach tribal children Pequot history. In addition, the memo called for more workshops for tribal employees to enrich their understanding of Pequot culture so they could better instruct the Pequots in how to become more authentic Indians. Finally, the memo suggested more time and money be spent promoting the tribe to the public as well as to other Indian tribes.

22

MUSEUM

Pequot museum had figured in Skip Hayward's plans for years. Since federal recognition in 1983, he had talked about it with his advisers. Using government grants, Skip hired University of Connecticut archaeologist Kevin McBride to discover and acquire as many artifacts as possible for a planned museum. McBride, who was later hired to head the Mashantucket Pequot Ethnohistory Project, explained, "Skip saw the archaeology I was doing as something that would ultimately contribute to the exhibits in a museum. Skip kept saying, 'Let's wait to build the museum. Let's wait. If we wait, we will have more money, more artifacts, and we can build a better museum, a world-class institution." By 1990, with Foxwoods on the horizon, Skip assembled a board of nontribal directors—mainly friends of the Pequots in the federal recognition fight—to help him plan the museum. At one of the early director meetings, Skip unveiled a scale model of the casino complete with landscaping.

Sandy Cadwalader of the Indian Rights Association, who had helped finance the tribe in the early days, was a director and asked Skip, "What is that?"

"The casino," Skip replied.

Cadwalader recalled later, "He presented it to us to make the point that one purpose of the casino was to finance this museum. It goes back to Eliza and her desire to keep the memory of the Pequots alive. Skip has a very finely tuned sense of the injustice and persecution of the Pequots. The museum was a way to enshrine the memory handed to him by Eliza."

Initially, Skip had asked that anthropologist Jack Campisi and archaeologist McBride oversee the museum project. As a trial run, he decided to install a 2,000-square-foot gallery of Pequot history in the basement of Foxwoods. Campisi rounded up several exhibit designers. The Pequots chose as their designer Mike Hanke, a young man with an easy, unpretentious manner. Hanke came aboard after the Pequots had already contracted with a company to provide a turnkey gallery for Foxwoods. He was asked to take the Pequot story and create an exhibition to fit the prefab design in ninety days. "We want to tell our story," Skip told Hanke. "We do not want to have to say that we were like the Narragansett or the Eastern Niantic or the Wampanoag. We want to say, 'These are the Pequots and this is their story.'"

At Skip's suggestion, Hanke focused on the Pequot War, as so few artifacts or tribal documents existed to support a full exhibit of the 350-year period since 1638. Under the deadline pressure imposed by the scheduled opening of the casino, Hanke relied entirely on secondary sources, in particular a twenty-five-page tribal history written by Jack Campisi and paid for by the tribe. The result focused almost exclusively on the Pequot War, save for a few nineteenth- and twentieth-century woven baskets said to have been made by Pequot women. Skip and his family loved it. They referred with pride to the little basement gallery as "the museum."

Several months after the basement gallery opened, Hanke was asked to propose a design for a full-fledged, stand-alone museum. Foxwoods was successful beyond anyone's expectations, and Skip decided that the Pequots could afford a museum sooner than expected. An added impetus was the discovery by McBride of the remains of a late-seventeenth-century Pequot encampment on the reservation. McBride considered it a major find that would yield a trove of Pequot artifacts. Skip signed Hanke to design for approximately 20,000 square feet of exhibit space.

Skip took charge of the museum project, appointing his sister Terry "tribal representative." Less inclined toward compromise than her older brother, Bell used her position to exclude non-Haywards from the project. "Terry did not make a legitimate effort to reach out to other families," recalled one of the senior museum designers who worked with Hanke. "She liked it that way. We could try to forge some bonds with other tribal members, but the Hayward family controlled the whole thing. . . . Everyone in the tribe knew that."

Campisi served as Bell's first lieutenant, wholeheartedly endorsing her exclusion of other tribal members from the decision-making process. The designer said, "Jack was the Haywards' representative. It did not matter to him whether other tribal members disliked him. He did not like most of the tribal members. He made no secret of that. He thought they were buffoons. Stupid. Badly educated. He looked down his nose at them. He used to refer to one tribal member who showed up for some of the initial meetings as 'Chief Horse's Ass.' "

As the museum effort gathered steam, most Pequots stayed out of the process. The museum designer recalled, "The notion that they should now come to more meetings with more white people to talk about a museum which would be run by the Haywards just did not wash. We tried so hard to get them involved in their museum. We would announce that on the first Monday of every month we would be making a presentation to everyone in the tribe interested in participating. No one would show up. There certainly was a strong thread in the tribe of 'Who gives a fuck about this cultural bullshit? I am here because I am getting tons of money, and I have a new car, and I have it made.' We would be there with models and sketches and ideas in hand, and finally, maybe Terry Bell would show up and call a couple of her sisters and their kids to come and we would talk to the Hayward family."

Hanke's team presented the final exhibit design to the Pequots using a thirteen-foot scale model. About forty tribal members including the tribal council showed up for the presentation. Before the presentation, Campisi gave Hanke a tip on how to approach his audience. "You will probably do better if you refer to the Pequots as 'your people.' They need to hear you recognize them explicitly as 'the Pequots,' not as 'descendants of the Pequots.'" Hanke obliged and was wholeheartedly embraced.

After the design was approved, Skip became more involved in the process. He typically met with the design team in the evenings over dinner and drinks at the Hilton Hotel in nearby Mystic, which the tribe had bought not long after Foxwoods got its slot machines. Skip held court over long boozy feasts that included both people involved in the museum project and visitors. Skip would sit at the head of the table. He would be surrounded by whomever the most important guests were, sometimes out-of-town Indians who had put on their best clothes and were being wined and dined beyond their wildest dreams. They ate when Skip decided to eat, after lots of cocktails. When their main course arrived they would all be tipsy and ravenous.

Skip chose the architects for the museum well after he had picked Hanke as exhibit designer. Hanke had suggested Polshek & Partners, a well-known New York firm headed by James Polshek, former head of the architecture school at Columbia University. The Pequots also contacted Kevin Roche, an architect known for his work for New York's Metropolitan Museum of Art and the National Gallery in Washington. Roche would have seemed the odds-on favorite given his museum experience. "The work he showed us was great," said McBride. "The problem was that when you go to see the Pequots, you just don't go in with three white men. You just don't do that. You're really asking for it. He essentially came in and said, 'Here we are. We are white men. We're all middle aged. We wear three-piece suits. And here is what we will do.' He had the most sympathetic design to what the tribe wanted. And he had the most thoughtful approach. But he seemed unbending, and the Pequots do not like working with people who are not willing to bend to them, especially not well-educated white men."

In contrast, architect Polshek presented with a team of associates McBride called "the rainbow coalition." Polshek had a woman as project architect, an elderly man as landscape architect, and an American Indian to work on the interiors. Polshek also had the gift of "contextualizing" his buildings, explaining how they fit in with the history of the neighborhood, town, or in this case, the reservation. He happily took questions and shared the stage with his subordinates. He got the job.

By mid-1993, Polshek had a design for the museum building. He presented it to several dozen tribal members at the former Boy Scout camp across Route 2 from Foxwoods that the tribe had bought. Polshek told the tribal members, who had been promised dinner after the presentation, that he would keep it short. Referring diplomatically to his design as "your museum," he emphasized that it was in an early phase and that he was open to any changes the Pequots might want to make. "This building has to reestablish and recapture the history of the Mashantucket Pequots forever," Polshek said. "Not just for you but for your children and your grandchildren and your great-grandchildren." A preliminary sketch of the building pictured a long rectangular structure, with one side gently curved like a seashell and a tower at one end. Polshek emphasized a central feature, a windowed atrium called the "Gathering Space," designed to hold up to a thousand people for dinner. He also said that the tower would offer museum visitors a "clear view" of the site of the 1637 Pequot fort at Mystic. (It later turned out that the tower wasn't tall enough to see quite that far.) He emphasized that the design elements of the building represented the historical importance to the Pequots of "the land, the water, and the sacred center which unites land and water."

After about fifteen minutes, Polshek began to lose his audience. He cut directly to his scale model of the museum and fielded questions from the audience. Speaking with an elderly woman who asked about the tower, Polshek suggested the tribe might want to limit access exclusively to tribal members, an idea she liked. A glaring Tony Beltran, wearing a big-shouldered, black satin varsity jacket, pointed at the Gathering Space portion of the scale model and demanded of Polshek, "What do you need that for?" Polshek explained the symbolic meaning of a place where the tribe could gather to view the Great Cedar Swamp. "We'll see about that," replied Beltran, and turning to several other tribal members, added, "You want to know where your money goes?" He pointed accusingly at Polshek and the museum model.

Over the next few years, Skip expanded dramatically the scope and scale of the museum. He would be shown an exhibit idea and say, "I love it. Make it bigger." A member of the project team remembered, "We started with 20,000 square feet of exhibition space and ended up with 85,000. We felt that was way too big. Nobody builds a museum that big for a tribe this small. It was silly. There simply was no need for that except Skip's desire." The expanded plans included a research library, an archaeology laboratory, a bookstore and gift shop, a café, conservation laboratories, and a movie theater. The cost of the project grew in excess of $100 million, making it the largest museum project undertaken in the United States since the Getty Museum. By 1996, the budget had hit $135 million; $25 million was spent on the exhibits alone.

As the museum budget skyrocketed, it became increasingly necessary to justify the expenditures to other, especially non-Hayward, members of the tribe. Like Beltran, many of the dark-skinned members felt money should instead be spent on member services or paid out in cash via the incentive plan. Some members of the museum project team told tribal members that the museum would break even in spite of the fact that subsidies are financial necessities for all museums. Skip believed that attendance would cover operating costs, envisioning the museum as a cross between the American Museum of Natural History, the 1964 World's Fair, and, in particular, Disney World. Skip wanted cars within which visitors could ride through the exhibits. He researched rides at various amusement parks, taking his sister Terry Bell, Jack Campisi, Kevin McBride, and others with him to Disney World. They stayed in suites at the luxurious Michael Graves–designed Dolphin Hotel and dined in a private room. "Anyone want a Caesar salad?" Skip would ask. "I don't see it on the menu but let's have it anyway. Caesar salad for everybody." He also liked the hotel's house wine, a $90-a-bottle California cabernet, so much that he asked the Mystic Hilton in Connecticut to stock it for him.

When Skip wasn't eating and drinking, he spent most of his time on the rides at Disney's Epcot Center, home to the theme park's "edutainment" rides. Skip envisioned a museum exhibit of the Ice Age, where visitors could descend through a fake glacier. A member of the project team who went on the Disney trip recalled, "When we realized that we might have people moving through Skip's glacier, we tried to figure out some way to make it work within the existing exhibition design. We needed to bring people from the top level of the building down to the lower level of the building. We needed to build an escalator anyway, so we decided, 'Why don't we just surround the escalator with this glacier.' We referred to it as the 'glaciator.'"

Skip pushed the idea one step further. "I woke up last night," he said. "I was thinking about this glacier, and I realized I don't like it anymore. It's just not enough. It should be a ride. People should get in giant ice cubes and travel through this glacier and maybe at some point it would go down like a flume ride and splash through some water and they would get wet and that would be wild."

The designers said they would look into the possibility. They did not design amusement park rides but they knew people who did and they would get in touch with those experts. Skip was happy. But when the museum team did the legwork, they found there was no way to fit a motorized ice cube ride into the museum as conceived.

Skip's "World of Ice" exhibit showing how the glaciers shaped the reservation at Mashantucket was to be followed by an exhibit called "The Arrival of the People," dramatizing the movement of humans into the region. The idea was to suggest that when the glaciers retreated, the Pequots had moved in. Here, the exhibit designers ran into a hitch. The Pequots had no creation story that explained when they might have come to the region. Unlike most Indian tribes, they possessed no lore that had been passed down through the centuries to explain where they had come from or when. The earliest signs of Pequot life dated back only to the late sixteenth and early seventeenth centuries. Archaeologist McBride had found signs of habitation on the reservation dating back thousands of years, but it hadn't been determined if those people were Pequots, ancestors of the Pequots, or perhaps an unrelated, extinct people.

Skip believed the ancestors of the Pequots had arrived after the glaciers receded. Some members of the Sebastian family, however—notably Kenny Reels and his brother Wayne—believed the Pequots had always lived in the area and objected to the notion that they had ever lived anywhere else. Wayne therefore opposed having a glacier exhibit as part of the museum. He believed its presence would imply the absence of the Pequots and raise questions about whether the Pequots had always been here.

Other tribal members tried to reconcile the notion of Pequot permanence and the glacial period by saying that perhaps the Pequots had lived on the edge of the glaciers. In truth, the project team had no evidence from any tribal members of a shared Pequot creation story.

Terry Bell said that if there had been a Pequot creation story, her grandmother Eliza would have certainly told Skip. Since she had not, such a story never existed. Bell insisted that the exhibit skirt the issue of Pequot origination. To paper over the omission, the museum team decided to present the origin stories of other tribes. They hired Indian filmmakers to shoot storytellers from other tribes telling creation stories in their own languages.

Other gaps in the Pequot story posed additional challenges for the museum team when designing the next exhibit, "Life in a Cold Place." This exhibit intended to show how people lived at Mashantucket 11,000 years ago. The centerpiece was a domed diorama eighty feet in diameter of a group of Pequot hunters in caribou-skin clothing killing and slaughtering reindeer. The problem for the museum team was that there was no evidence that anyone had ever done such a thing, let alone that they had been Pequot. "The caribou diorama was not any of our favorites," said one of the senior exhibition designers. "We felt that the evidence supporting that was pretty shaky. Not that there wasn't somebody here doing something. But was it 11,000 years ago? Were they wearing caribou skin? We didn't have any assemblage of prehistoric tools that indicated what was going on at the time. We had no Pequot artifacts to support this diorama. What we show there are reproductions from other tribes. We don't even know if the people back then were Pequots or ancestors of the Pequots. The only support we have for anything Pequot prior to contact with Europeans is about 1600. This exhibit was really a desire by the tribe to push habitation at Mashantucket as far back in time as they could."

While the caribou exhibit did not make any explicit claims about the people presented, the implication is that these are Pequot ancestors. The designer added, "I wish we could've been a little more clear with visitors about this. It would have been better if we could have simply said, 'We don't know who these people were.' The implication that these were Pequots is slippery."

The most important exhibit in the museum to Skip was the "Pequot Village," a 22,000-square-foot re-creation of a Pequot encampment circa 1600. The idea was to walk the visitor through a sixteenth-century Pequot village to experience the sights and sounds and even smells of daily life.

Pequot Village intended to show Pequot culture at the moment before the tribe was conquered by the English colonists— a prosperous tribe living peacefully in idyllic Eastern woodlands. Skip wanted to have present-day tribal members play the parts of the original Pequots, interacting with museum visitors. His idea was nixed because too many tribal members did not look the part. They were either too white or too black. The exhibit designers solved this problem by using brown-skinned costumed mannequins and "acoustiguides" to answer questions. Based on artifacts from other tribes, the Pequot Village exhibit was essentially a collage of Northeastern Indian history. The senior exhibit designer said, "Those of us who were part of the team always understood that while the tribe wanted a museum about Pequot life, we were developing a museum about Northeastern Indian life. Most of the stories and exhibits in this museum are not unique to the Pequots. . . . It just so happened that the Pequots are the ones who had the money to build it."

Originally, the museum team conceived of a Pequot War movie as a short documentary using historical artifacts and scholarly observations. Terry Bell, however, wanted a docudrama, not a documentary, complete with invented characters and scenes. Bell hired a movie producer who agreed that a full-length, semifictional reenactment of the Pequot War was just what the museum needed. The producer, who brought in her own directors, had experience with large-screen IMAX movies. Terry and Skip wanted something big, and IMAX films are nothing if not big. Some of the museum team members told the tribal council that Bell's movie could be an embarrassment to the museum. They argued that museum visitors with young children might not want to see butchery and blood on the screen. The tribal council members disagreed, saying that you would not believe the stuff you see on TV these days. Skip said, "People want to see heads being blown off." He and his fellow tribal council members regaled each other with the gory details of TV programs and videos they had recently enjoyed.

A "Pequot Village" movie set was built in rural Tennessee for the film's climactic massacre scene. Campisi and Bell went down for the filming. As if reprising Elizabeth George's final photo shoot of herself as an Indian, her granddaughter Bell was costumed as a "Pequot princess" and appeared in the thirty-minute vanity production, which cost $7 million.

For the museum designers, the most sensitive exhibits related to the ethnic and racial evolution of the Pequots since the Pequot War. In the intervening 350 years, Pequots had been cohabiting significantly with African slaves and their African-American descendants, not too surprising given that the two groups shared the bottom of the social ladder in southern New England. Unfortunately, Skip's family did not want to acknowledge this historical fact in the museum. "They did not want to handle race," said a senior member of the project team. "We tried very hard in the eighteenth-century section of the exhibition—'Life on the Reservation'—to show intermarriage between native people and black people. This is before the American Revolution. So it is of long-standing importance if you want to understand the Pequot story. New London County during the colonial period had the highest concentration of African-American slaves of any place outside of the South. But Jack [Campisi] followed Terry's orders and personally cut out the discussion of intermarriage. He said, 'I don't think we need to address this issue at all.' This was considered 'dirty laundry,' not to be aired in public."

Bell and Campisi opposed discussing the issue of race because the racial issue had yet to be resolved within the tribe itself. A member of the exhibition design team said, "I think the main reason they didn't want the whole black intermarriage thing discussed is that it raises the whole question of blood quantum for all of them, white or black. I mean, let's be candid. These people are mainly something other than Pequot. And some of them may not be Pequot at all. Who knows? The genealogical records are very confusing. So the Pequots are very sensitive about the fact that they don't have much Pequot blood in them. They didn't want to highlight that in their museum. When you start asking about their blood quantum, they hear you as suggesting that they don't exist."

The museum exhibition was designed to end with a gallery of large photographs of the new Pequots with tape recordings of tribal members talking about the meaning of being Pequot. The idea was to assert that, although the new Pequots may not look the part, they were Indians. The problem was getting enough good material from tribal members to support the exhibit.

This was a typical exchange between a tribal member of African-American descent, and an oral historian.

> Interviewer: "So, as you were growing up, you really didn't have any contact with the Pequot side of your family?"
> Tribal Member: "No. When I was growing up basically the contact that I had wasn't on the Pequot side. . . . My [Indian] background lies in Narragansett. . . ."
> Interviewer: "Did you ever come to the reservation here, the Western Pequot?"

Tribal Member: "No. I never visited the Western Pequot
until I was grown when I came back. That was the first
time. As a matter of fact, I really didn't know much
about the Pequots."

Interviewer: "Tell me about coming back here in terms of
learning more about your Pequot heritage. What have
you learned here, and what value has that had for you?"

Tribal Member: "I feel coming back here to this tribe. . . .
I've learned that this is a tribe within a tribe, meaning
that this tribe consists of more than just one culture or
one tribal identity, meaning that we're also Narragansett, Pequot, Afro-American, German, whatever."

Most of the interviews, which numbered about one hundred,
were never used.

The Pequot museum opened on August 10, 1998. The building
had metastasized into 308,000 square feet, costing close to $225
million. The Pequot public relations department in its press
release described the ribbon-cutting ceremony as both "traditional" and "private." It was neither. More than a thousand
guests and reporters gathered outside the massive concrete
building. President Bill Clinton, to whom the tribe had given
hundreds of thousands of dollars in political campaign contributions, sent videotaped congratulations. Skip, in a dark Armani
suit, cut a huge purple ribbon with a pair of giant orange scis-
sors, and the crowd surged into the Gathering Space to the
pounding of tom-tom drums.

At the podium set up for the event, Terry Bell stated that
the museum was "as true to the facts as best we know them." She
wiped away tears when she gave special thanks to her grandmother
Eliza. Skip spoke next. "For those of you who haven't see the exhibits," he said, "you're in for a treat." Another of the Hayward
sisters, Susan Penrose, stepped up to the microphone wearing a
white cowboy hat and sang a country and western song she had

written for the occasion. Kenny Reels followed Penrose and delivered a short tribute to Skip, comparing him to Geronimo and Chief Joseph. He said in a tribute that sounded more like a eulogy that Skip had done a great job, and it was now time for him to rest. The director of the Smithsonian's National Museum of the American Indian, Richard West—whose brother had written the "West Report" on racial relations in the tribe—presented Skip with a war club and thanked him for pledging $10 million to a new Indian museum to be built on the Mall in Washington, D.C. After many tributes, the bar and buffet were opened for champagne, caviar, shrimp, and filet mignon.

Many tribal members did not attend the opening, however. Some had felt excluded by the Haywards, and others simply did not care enough about the museum to begin with. A niece of Kenny Reels said, "That museum was talked about since I was a girl. And you know what, I've not even been inside it yet. I don't even want to go now. They put too much money into it. It is so expensive. They did not need to spend all of that money to tell our history."

Are the Pequots cynical about their museum? Do they hold it up to the world as their story while knowing that the truth is far more complex and messy and raises questions about their cultural authenticity? "Of course," said a professor of anthropology at a college in New England who is an expert in the tribes of the Northeast, and who declined to be identified because she has received grant money from the Pequots. "Is that good psychologically for them? No. It would be better if they could be more candid about who they really are and where they really come from. But they cannot do that because at the moment that their link with the Pequots of the past is severed, we would all hit on that lack of connection, and they might lose their legal status as a tribe, and they might lose Foxwoods."

23

GROWING PAINS

By 1998 Foxwoods was generating $1 billion in revenue and $152 million in net income for the tribe. The tribal roll tribal roll had grown to about six hundred members, many averaging from $250,000 to $500,000 a year in salary, incentive payments, and other financial benefits. The rattletrap tribal office trailers had been replaced by the lavish Adirondack-style community center with a teak-paneled tribal council chamber, indoor and outdoor swimming pools, a vast gymnasium complete with fitness club, and large dining room. The HUD houses had been gutted and expanded beyond recognition. Skip spent close to $500,000 rebuilding his own home. He turned it into a 4,000-square-foot McMansion with expanded rooms, a finished basement, and a wine cellar.

Despite all the money Skip poured into the house, he no longer lived on the reservation. With his millions from Foxwoods, he had bought two adjacent waterfront properties looking out on exclusive Fisher's Island, where Eliza had once worked as a maid. Skip had not lived in the house on the reservation for years, using it only for public receptions. "I think what happened was that he was moving on," said Mickey Brown. "He moves from project to project. He was less interested in what was going on in the tribe and on the reservation. He held the other tribal members in such low regard, their complete lack of work ethic. He didn't want to be around them."

Skip would disappear from the reservation for weeks at a time. Skip's disappearances became known within his inner circle as "walkabouts." The former head of the tribe's public affairs and marketing department explained, "Where was he when he was away? He was just walking about. He might be in Florida fishing. He might be in England hanging around the British Museum. He might be at his place on the water. A lot of the time, these trips were just boondoggles. Sometimes, he was simply too hungover to come to work." Mickey Brown said, "Skip's whole life was a binge. What was a typical day like for Skip? I don't think he slept much. He just napped. He had no normal schedule. I know sometimes he got up after noon but I also know that sometimes he went to bed at noon. I doubt he slept more than three or four hours a night."

In his efforts to avoid the reservation and the tribe he had helped create and lead, Skip increasingly played the role of the lone entrepreneur—working obsessively on Foxwoods and a few other ventures to the exclusion of internal tribal matters. He spent more and more time in a 20,000-square-foot brick factory building in Mystic he called his "war room." Skip wanted a place away from the interruptions of the reservation where he could lay out all the charts and maps and sit there with his planners brainstorming and coming up with massive plans. He modeled the war room after the underground control center he had seen at Disney World in Orlando. No one was allowed in except by invitation. Surrounded by planners and project personnel who reported directly to him, Skip worked on one crazy idea after another. He spent well over a year trying to win a federal government grant to finance a $350 million high-speed rail system from Connecticut Interstate 95 to the Foxwoods casino. He also planned the Pequot River Shipworks, a quixotic attempt to reestablish boat building along the Thames River in Groton.

Skip spent weeks at a time in Washington, D.C. Ever since the federal recognition debates, he had loved the behind-the-scenes politics of the nation's capital. From 1996 to 1998, Skip authorized about $1 million in campaign contributions to the two major political parties—nearly $800,000 of it to the Democratic party. He raised hundreds of thousands more at Foxwoods fund-raisers from vendors and employees of the casino. The campaign contributions, like the $10 million pledge to the Smithsonian's Museum of the American Indian, were intended to buy influence in Congress, the White House, and the BIA. He feared that a political reaction in Congress against new, rich tribes like the Pequots might limit growth at Foxwoods. After all, the Pequots were subject primarily to federal law and regulation, not state or local restrictions. Skip took pride each time he was introduced in Washington as "chairman of the Mashantucket Pequot Tribal Nation." He retold the story of the new Pequots to everyone and anyone who would listen. And because Skip had such a fat wallet, politicians were lining up to be his friend. Skip became one of Bill Clinton's favorite Indian chiefs, allowed to sleep in the Lincoln bedroom like other top Democratic party contributors.

Skip also gave money to mainstream American Indian organizations. He used money and personal charm to overcome the skepticism of western tribes about the sudden emergence of the Pequots. He hired Indians from western tribes to run the Pequot lobbying effort in Washington and established an office in the capital the likes of which Indian country had never seen. Skip authorized a $1,550,000 annual budget. He paid his chief representative $231,000 a year and another special adviser $173,000. Skip rented them 5,000 square feet of prime office space between the White House and Capitol Hill. He decorated the office with $190,000 worth of American Indian sculpture and an additional $110,000 on decorating a conference room.

Skip's Washington office had one basic mission: to protect the gambling franchise. A key goal was to prevent federal taxation of

Foxwoods. To ensure this, the Washington office forged ties to more established Indian tribes. "The argument we needed to make," said the former head of the Washington office, "was that gambling was the only way for tribes to achieve economic success and that the Pequots were just another victimized tribe. But this argument did not wash with some people in Washington when the Pequots made it. They carried a lot of political baggage being so new and so money-oriented. That is why it was so important for the Pequots to maintain alliances with other tribes. The other tribes could make that statement, and it was more believable. They didn't come across as quite so greedy."

Managing the Pequot relationship with other tribes was not simple. Skip would boast about the Pequots' financial success and about how much money he was making. "Skip thought that was fine," said the former head of the Washington office. "Steve Wynn could brag about how much money he made off his casinos. Why couldn't Skip Hayward brag about how much money he had made off Foxwoods? He didn't seem to realize that being a tribal leader is different from being a businessman. Being a tribal leader is more than that. The other tribal leaders felt diminished by Skip's bragging about all the money he made. The president of the Navajo nation, for example, earned $50,000 a year. That is less than the lowliest Pequot. And the leader of the Navajo tribe, or any of the major tribes, has a far larger tribe and many more problems to deal with. So if Skip comes to a national meeting and implies that he's making millions of dollars a year to a crowd of tribal leaders, it does not play well. I told Skip, 'You better not be so revealing about stuff like this. People don't like it.' He said, 'We make this money. We should let people know how well we are doing.'"

While Skip was becoming a minor celebrity—he made the cover of *Forbes* magazine—by 1996 he was also coming in for direct criticism at tribal council meetings. Led by Kenny Reels, the Annie

George Sebastian family was pushing to take over the tribe Skip and his family had founded. Skip was well aware of the threat. His mother Theresa, who had opposed letting in blacks in the early days, had warned him that they posed a permanent threat to Hayward family control. But Skip had done nothing to stem the tide of new black members, not even using his power as chairman to cap enrollment. He still believed he could control the tribe through sheer will and personal prestige, no matter the racial and family demographics.

As the Sebastian family became a majority of the tribe, however, Skip was forced into an informal power-sharing arrangement with Kenny Reels: Skip would remain chairman, but Kenny and his fellow Sebastian family members would hold a majority on the tribal council. To ensure this balance of power, Skip even dissuaded white Pequots from running for tribal council seats held by members of the Sebastian family. One light-skinned tribal member recalled, "I ran for council in 1996. Kenny Reels and Pedro Johnson [another dark-skinned tribal council member] were up for reelection. I was running against them. Skip called me into his office one day. And he had never called me into his office before. He says, 'I don't want you to run for council this time.' I said, 'Excuse me?' And he said to me that this was not the time for me. He was not asking me. He was telling me. I didn't understand why until the next year's election when both Kenny and Pedro actively supported Skip. That was how the quid pro quo worked."

Within the tribal council, Skip let Kenny advance his family's agenda. Essentially, this translated to Kenny controlling the enrollment process while Skip managed the expansion of Foxwoods, other tribal business ventures, and the museum. "To some degree, Skip would let them do what they wanted on certain issues, and they would let him do what he wanted on issues important to him," observed James Wherry. "But if Skip was not there, Kenny would downgrade and delay a lot of things that Skip wanted. And

Skip would come back, and he would say to me, 'They never listen to me.'"

As his power eroded, Skip became increasingly truculent in tribal council. He would filibuster their proposals by reading the newspaper to them for hours at a time at council meetings. One former senior aide to the council said, "By 1996, I would be summoned to council, and Skip would read word-for-word news clips from the *New London Day,* and this could take an hour and a half because he was commenting and making editorial remarks. When Skip was reading, the rest of the tribal council would sit there and shake their heads. It drove them crazy. But they wouldn't stop him. Skip would say, 'This is the chairman's hour, and I want to read the newspaper to you.'"

When delay failed, tempers flared. By 1997 the arguing had reached such a pitch that visitors in the waiting room outside the council chambers could hear it reverberate through the closed doors. Tribal member John Guevremont recalled a day when, over Skip's objections, the tribal council voted to authorize an audit of the twenty-story hotel addition under construction at Foxwoods. The hotel budget was spiraling out of control, and the other council members worried that the tribe was being cheated by the contractors. Skip stood up and shouted, "If you find any money [via the audit], I will kiss your ass," and then he stormed out. The audit went ahead.

By the end of 1997, Skip had essentially stopped attending tribal council meetings. Kenny Reels filled the vacuum. "Skip was so busy with stuff away from the reservation that who do you think most tribal members went to to have their problems addressed? Kenny," Guevremont said. "He was the guy all the new members got to know. There were many members who had never even met Skip. Most of the newer tribal members hardly knew who Skip was."

Reels by now had enough votes to elect whomever the Sebastian family wanted to tribal council. In 1997, three members of the family, including ex-cons Tony Beltran and Michael Thomas, who had been on probation for a drug-dealing conviction in Rhode Island, were elected from a field of eleven candidates. No white Pequot tallied more than thirty-eight votes, and one of Skip's sisters received only twenty-one votes. The 1997 vote was a watershed for the tribe. The Sebastians now held five of the seven council seats.

Reels had not directly challenged Skip for the chairmanship since 1992. But in 1998, Skip's three-year term on council was up. In November, he faced a two-step election to remain chairman—first he needed to be reelected to the council and then reelected chairman, in both instances by a direct vote of the entire tribe. Reels had promised Skip that he would not run for the chairmanship without giving him notice. Reels told Skip in the weeks leading up to the election, "I don't think you should be the chairman much longer, but I will not run against you." In private, however, Reels continued to wrestle with the idea of taking a run at Skip. He held meetings with other members of the Sebastian clan. Family matriarch Phyllis Monroe urged Reels to take a shot at Skip's chairmanship.

The morning of the vote, Reels arrived at the community center and saw supporters putting up banners and posters saying, "Vote for Kenny." He made his decision on the spot without informing Skip. A light-skinned tribal member who supported Reels's decision recalled, "He had an agreement with Skip not to run and all of the sudden he pops up and runs. I think Kenny does not think things through that well. I think a lot of people in his family were trying to convince him to run. I also think tribal members from other families went to him as well. It was a combination of the Sebastians and other black families getting together. They approached Kenny with different arguments. Many of the less educated members of the tribe said to him, 'Kenny, you're interested in us. Skip is not attending to the tribe. He is off in la-la land.' The more educated people said, 'If we keep Skip, he will just keep on finding more money-losing projects to waste our money on. He is going to waste our jackpot.'"

Skip arrived at the community center and saw the front doors plastered with the "Vote for Kenny" posters. Skip was taken by surprise. A longtime adviser to Skip remembered, "He took Kenny's promise not to run seriously. Before the election, he had asked Kenny directly, 'Are you running?' Kenny said, 'No.' Skip is really quite principled when someone tells him something. He wants to believe it is true."

In the first vote that day, Skip was reelected to council. In the second vote for tribal chairman, Reels won almost three-quarters of the votes. When the results were announced, there was stunned silence. People could hardly believe it.

Gracious in defeat, Skip spoke to the tribe from the stage in the large gymnasium. He acknowledged that the membership had spoken and offered Reels his support. He left the stage surrounded by family members, some of them crying. The "royal family," as the Haywards were known within the tribe, was for the first time in twenty-five years not in charge of the tribe they had invented. Skip remained on council—albeit as vice chairman—while the rest of the Haywards were in line to have their special privileges revoked immediately. Skip knew Reels was going to replace many of them with his own family entourage. After Skip's defeat, his sisters blamed Reels for having betrayed Skip. One of his nephews talked about shooting Reels; the young man was escorted off the reservation until he cooled off.

Skip fled to his home overlooking Fisher's Island Sound. "I just can't believe it," he said to friends like Mickey Brown. "I can't believe they did this to me." The next day he flew to Fort Lauderdale where he kept his yacht and checked into the presidential suite at the Hyatt Hotel overlooking the marina where his sleek forty-five-foot Hatteras was docked. Friends called and urged him to take a run at Kenny in 1999 when the new chairman would be up for reelection, but Skip was too shattered to consider that then. From Florida, he flew to Hawaii for two more weeks of rest and relaxation. All he wanted to do was go fishing.

Bruce Kirchner, a tribal member who had been especially close to Skip in the early days of the tribe, said, "Here is his family, Liza's family. She had held on to the land for decades. Her family then gets rid of the state. They get rid of the towns. They get sovereignty. They get money. They get power. Skip committed his life to this. He did this. And then he gets pushed aside and with him his family. At the end of the day, the real enemy turned out not to be the state or the towns, but the people Liza had tried to keep off the reservation all those years."

24

CRISIS

Skip Hayward, former chairman of the Mashantucket Pequot Tribal Nation, sat hunched in front of a cockpit of computer screens, the kind of setup you might see on a Wall Street trading desk. It was the middle of the night in late 1999 at the height of the technology stock bubble, and he was picking stocks. He liked chip-maker National Semiconductor, wireless phone service provider Nextel, and all the NASDAQ high-fliers. He had millions in the stock market and a high-net-worth broker at Paine Webber who was having a party for his best customers the following week. Skip couldn't wait. Skip was worth millions, traded stocks like a pro, fished with wealthy friends on his yacht, and garnered the occasional honorarium from pan-Indian organizations to whom the Pequots had given money. A full year after his ouster by the Sebastian family, however, he remained a wounded, lonely man. Skip had stopped attending tribal council meetings altogether. No one saw him on the reservation.

The year 1999 was not a bad time to be away. Profits at Foxwoods had peaked in 1995 at $236 million a year and had declined to the $150 million range. The nearby Mohegan tribe had opened a competing casino in 1996—the Mohegan Sun—six miles away on the western bank of the Thames River, and closer to the interstate.

Mohegan Sun was growing and capturing market share from Fox-woods, and top executives at the casino foresaw the day when the Mohegan Sun would overtake Foxwoods in size and profitability. Meanwhile, the Pequot tribe was saddled with $1.2 billion in debt taken on to finance Foxwoods and the outsized welfare state they had created for themselves. The debt was not a financial crisis in and of itself, for Foxwoods generated more than enough cash each year to service the $1.2 billion in debt and was likely to do so for the foreseeable future. Foxwoods' cash flow, however, was insuf-ficient to service the debt, provide the Pequots with their incen-tive payments, and also subsidize the many money-losing tribal businesses Skip had started up.

The tribal council had for years been warned by their finan-cial advisers of looming shortfall. A former council member and longtime tribal member recalled, "But basically any adviser who made too much of a stink got fired. I have seen it time and time again. They have a financial officer who says to them, 'Guys, this is the situation. You'd better do this. You better do that.' And they say, 'We don't like what you are saying. Get out of here.' They have fired several financial officers for bringing bad news."

Over a period of three years, tribal debt had soared from between $50 million and $60 million in 1993 to about $550 mil-lion in 1996 and was projected to jump to $750 million in the next few years. A confidential report to the tribal council ex-plained, "The earnings forecast for fiscal 1996 represents a de-terioration from the prior year . . . and a significant reduction from the previous projections. This trend will have a substan-tial negative impact on cash flow in future years. . . . The tribe will need to reach a debt level of over $985 million if they are to complete the capital project schedule through fiscal year 2000. We recommend that the tribe not exceed a prudent debt level of $700 million."

Before his ouster, Skip had ignored such warnings from those he labeled "doom-and-gloomers." As far back as 1996, the tribe's financial advisers had suggested that council cut incentive payments and government spending, which had more than doubled during the previous three years. Skip replied, "You're pushing the alarm button too soon. All companies take on debt. That is how you grow." The only council member who appeared upset by the dire warnings was treasurer Pedro Johnson. Upon hearing the dismal financial analysis, Pedro grabbed his heart and said, "I can't believe this. I can't believe this."

Under Skip, the council took only minor cost-cutting measures. They cut Foxwoods' free meal program for employees to one hot meal a day to save $2.3 million a year. They lowered medical benefits and raised the cost of the benefit package to employees at Foxwoods to save several million more. Yet those cuts were utterly insufficient when compared to the astronomical growth in spending on tribal members and on imprudent business investments.

In 1997, the tribe hired a new chief financial officer, Susan Tohbe, an African-American with considerable experience in the private sector. Once she understood the extent of the tribe's fiscal crisis, she briefed the council. She updated the prior warnings, and as the financial problem had grown larger, her proposed budget cuts were more draconian. Skip and the council told her that they had heard this before and that the situation was not as bad as she believed. At first, Tohbe could not understand their reaction. She wondered if they were listening. Was this how they normally operated? With the council in no mood to cut, Tohbe did what any sensible CFO would do. She refinanced the tribe's debt at lower interest rates and stretched the maturity date of the obligations. Five- and ten-year debt was exchanged for twenty- to twenty-five-year paper, which temporarily alleviated some of the immediate financial pressure.

Nonetheless, by 1999, she had stretched the debt payments as far into the future as was prudent. The tribe owed close to $1.2 billion. The roughly $150 million to $200 million a year in profits from Foxwoods was now inadequate to cover all the spending and debt service. Council members began fighting with one another over whether or not to trim incentive payments or trim the luxury hotel tower being built at Foxwoods. Before his defeat, Skip had argued that the new hotel was critical to fending off the expanding Mohegan Sun casino, which would soon build its own luxury hotel. In contrast, Kenny Reels had countered that incentive payments to the membership should be the highest priority. They complained bitterly that Skip had promised that the hotel tower would cost only $200 million and earn a profit; in fact, it looked like it would end up costing $500 million.

After Reels's election, Tohbe received a slightly better reception from the council. "You can do whatever you want to do, but here is the situation," she said. "These cuts are intended to avoid problems with the lenders, to avoid default on the debt, to protect the enterprise [i.e., Foxwoods]." Nevertheless, in Kenny's initial days as chairman, he remained afraid of the political damage he'd incur if he bit the financial bullet. He faced reelection in 1999. When should he break the bad news to the tribe, and how was he going to resolve the fiscal deficit? Some councillors argued that he wait until after the 1999 elections, while others such as Michael Thomas suggested they find a way to sell a larger ownership interest in Foxwoods to the Malaysians to raise cash to pay down the debt.

The debt crisis was such, however, that Reels could not wait until after the elections. If the Pequots borrowed more money, they risked violating loan covenants that would trigger accelerated principle repayments. Reels delivered the bad news at a membership meeting in the spring of 1999. He told the various families that the $70 million incentive pool had to be cut. The reaction was predictable. Pequots jumped up to rail at the inequity of having to sacrifice "when we are paying all these 'suits,'" a reference to the nontribal executives who managed Foxwoods and the Pequot government and its welfare state.

Tohbe pressured Reels to accept a package of austerity measures and propose it to the members after Labor Day. Following a council retreat to the Oneida tribe's casino in central New York State, Reels notified the members of an all-day meeting to be held in the gymnasium at the community center in early September. There would be a presentation by Tohbe and changes in the incentive ordinance would be discussed.

The meeting in the gymnasium started off with an appearance from Skip, the first time he had attended a tribal meeting in many months. He was puffy-eyed and looked hungover. Some tribal members smelled alcohol on his breath. Before Tohbe could begin her presentation, Skip declared loudly that the meeting should not be allowed to proceed. He declared that the public notice of the meeting had not specifically stated that Tohbe was going to make a financial presentation and that therefore the meeting violated tribal rules. Given Skip's history of calling and canceling tribal meetings according to his whims, tribal members ignored his objection. Some felt he was grandstanding to curry favor with tribal members before the November election, positioning himself as the only council member willing to save their incentive payments.

Reels cut Skip off. He said they were going to hold the meeting. Skip said he would not participate and stormed out, trailed by several of his sisters and aunts. His family members followed him to his office on the second floor of the community center. There they accused him of cowardice, each trying to convince him that if he ever wanted to become chairman again, he must return to the meeting and show people that he cared. He told them plaintively, "I care. I care too much." They urged him to return to the meeting. Skip said he would, but instead he slipped out and left the reservation.

Tohbe made her presentation. She explained that the tribe's annual income from Foxwoods was about $50 million short of that needed to pay for government services, incentive payments, and debt obligations. They were spending about $70 million a year on incentive payments. Government expenditures were another $100 million a year. And the interest expense on the $1.2 billion of debt was running at about $80 million annually. That added up to about $250 million a year, while Foxwoods netted them about $200 million, thus a $50 million a year shortfall. The tribe had been borrowing money to make up the difference and was scheduled to repay $200 million in bank debt. Drastic cuts had to be made right away. The longer the Pequots waited to make the cuts, Tohbe explained, the heavier the debt burden would become as interest charges compounded year after year.

In an afternoon session, Tohbe presented the council's proposed austerity plan: slash incentive payments and government programs. The incentive pool was to be cut from $70 million to $40 million. Council also proposed a radical change in the incentive plan's structure, which was to scrap it. Reels and other members of the Sebastian family had always hated the incentive system, and the financial crisis was the perfect excuse to eliminate it. Reels wanted to replace it with a "per capita" system in which everyone within a certain age group would be paid the same regardless of length of membership or work effort. Everyone would get a "base payment" of $25,000 a year for those aged eighteen to thirty years old, $50,000 for those thirty to fifty-five, and $100,000 for those over fifty-five. If you worked for the tribe, you could double your base payment, the only incentive multiplier. This payment did not include their tribal salary and other benefits. Skip and many members of his family were now looking at their incentive payments being cut in half.

Tohbe wasn't finished. She outlined another $30 million or so of cuts from the $100 million tribal government budget. Cuts of that magnitude meant substantial layoffs, perhaps as many as four hundred of the government's twelve hundred employees. Even though Tohbe made it clear that no Pequots would be laid off, there remained the question: Who was going to provide services to the members if so many people were fired? Tribal members had little appetite for doing the work themselves. Worse, firings implied deep cuts in programs for the members. There was talk of cutting the Pequots' education department, a $12 million per year unit that paid tuition and other schooling services for Pequots. Tohbe proposed that from now on tribal members pay for school costs using the educational trust funds the tribe had set up for them. Tribal members had not previously applied the trust funds to educational purposes, instead using them as general purpose savings accounts to be tapped as soon as a child turned eighteen and dropped out of school. In many cases, these trust funds held in excess of $100,000.

Commenting on the tribe's reaction to Tohbe, a former senior aide to the tribal council asserted, "If you can say anything about Pequot culture, it is that they believe that the genie in the lamp will always bring more money and that all they have to do is rub the lamp correctly to have it happen. That has been their consciousness for so long. The phrase 'prudent fiscal policy' is beyond their understanding. Their basic understanding is, 'I want the money, and I want it now. It's mine.' It has nothing to do with seven generations of the tribe into the future. Tribal members are thinking, 'I have to make payments on two houses. I have to make payments on a Mercedes and a BMW. You cannot cut my incentive by one-third or one half.' That's what was going on in people's minds when Tohbe was talking."

Barbara Kirchner, a former tribal council member and later chief of staff to the council, said, "It was just a complete shock to membership. You have to remember that this September meeting was taking place shortly before the annual incentive payments were due to be distributed. Our fiscal year begins in October. A lot of people had already spent in anticipation of their checks. They were in no mood to hear that they might not be getting all the money they had planned on."

After the stunned silence, tribal members verbally attacked Tohbe and the tribal council, employing a standing microphone in the audience. They accused the council of having mismanaged their money. They wanted to know how much the council members were paid, whether they flew first class. Others decried the revised incentive ordinance's preferential treatment of elderly tribal members, complaining that the elders did nothing but take expensive, tribally financed trips. Why should they get more money under the proposed budget than younger Pequots?

The Hayward family, who had the most to lose from the planned cutting of the incentive payments, was furious. One of Skip's nieces stood up and berated the tribal council. "How can you cut back on our incentive payments? We were always led to believe that these payments would be a regular thing. We went out and we bought houses and cars and furniture, and we're in debt. Now, you're cutting us back, and we're in jeopardy. How can you do that to us? You should cut back on your salary and your staff. Why do we have all these people in tribal government? What do we pay outrageous money to all these nontribal members who work in the tribal government?" Hayward family members shouted that this would never have happened if Skip were still in charge.

Fatima Dames, a young dark-skinned member of the Sebastian family who had joined the tribe in the 1990s, was so outraged by the austerity plan that the next day she organized a protest march, complete with placards and a picket line, in front of the community center where the council met. Dames invited the local media onto the reservation to cover the event. The protest began with a rally in the gym, where about fifty angry Pequots showed up. Dames and her Sebastian family supporters railed against scrapping the incentive system so close to the annual distribution. She called for incentive distributions for all members, even to tribal members who were incarcerated, of which there were always a few.

Dames and her followers carried placards plastered with the *Forbes* magazine cover photo of Skip. Under Skip's picture, they had written, "Where are the other 599 [millionaires]?" Dames screamed, "Why is he the only millionaire?" Others carried placards that read, "Where's the Money?" and "Impeach Our Council."

Half the people at the protest, however, were Skip's relations, who were hoping to fuel a draft movement for Skip that might allow him to defeat Reels in the coming election. Some of the Haywards carried signs reading, "Time For a Change: Not Our Incentives, But on Council." After a joint picket outside the tribal council chamber, Kenny Reels came down from a balcony where he had been watching to speak with the protesters. His gesture mollified Fatima Dames and her group of black Pequots, who then decided to end their protest. The Haywards continued their picketing, marching out to the reservation's main entrance along state highway 214, or old Indiantown Road, as Eliza would have known it, to protest before the assembled television cameras and newspaper photographers. A tribal member who did not participate in the demonstration said, "They might as well have stood out there and held up placards that said, 'I am an asshole.' I saw one person out there jumping up and down and waving a protest sign who I know had just applied for a total disability qualification from the state, which means that she is claiming she is unable to work because of a physical disability. I saw another tribal member out there crying poverty who had just built a $700,000 house in Ledyard near the reservation." The head of one department of the tribal government recalled, "There were pictures of all these well-fed people who don't even look like Indians demanding more money. I was embarrassed for them. It was so ridiculous. They played right into the outside world's perceptions of them as greedy, wasteful people who are not real Indians. It was hee-haw Indian style."

Most tribal members, however, thought the public protest was appropriate and not at all embarrassing. Tribal member Theresa Casanova said, "I don't see why that should surprise or embarrass anybody. This tribe was brought together by money. People put us down saying we should not protest because of money. Money is what this tribe is about. Let's face it. That is reality. We are here because of the money. I am here because of the money. My family came here because of the money. That is what this tribe is about."

25

ABUSE

By 2000, a cash crunch was not the only problem facing the Pequots. Tribal members were becoming increasingly worried about crime, violence, and general mayhem on the reservation. Tribal members were showing up in the local police reports with disturbing frequency. More than 200 tribal members had been arrested since 1984, according to police records, a period of time when the total tribal population averaged only 400. Increasingly, Pequots were afraid of other Pequots. One tribal member, who declined to be identified, said, "I have lived in Los Angeles, and I have lived in Washington, D.C., and I can say that Mashantucket has more in common with Watts than Chevy Chase. Some of it is cultural; a lot of people who live here come from the black urban culture. But what really bothers me is the behavior I see on the reservation from all sorts of people. There's just too high a percentage of unwed mothers, teen pregnancy, drug abuse, domestic violence, absentee fathers."

Marijuana and cocaine use by tribal members had been rampant on the reservation for years. Even current and former council members smoked pot. Two social workers, who worked for the tribe for years, estimated that close to half the adult population smoked dope. "They do it in front of their kids," said one of the social workers.

Anti-drug laws had always been weakly enforced by tribal police officers, who learned to go easy on tribal members if they valued their jobs. One tribal member said, "The last policeman who really took any aggressive action was a detective. In 1996, one of the tribal members was driving through the reservation with some of his buddies, and the tribal police stopped them. They searched the car and found illegal drugs in the car. So this detective reported them to the state police. Tribal council got wind of this and went ballistic. They said that this detective had violated tribal sovereignty, had overstepped his authority, and they fired him. Nothing happened to the kid who was arrested despite the fact that he had prior arrests for drugs. The tribe did not want to press charges, and so the state police did not pursue it. The case never went anywhere." A female tribal member whose husband was a small-time drug dealer said, "Tribal members think of the tribal police as security guards, rent-a-cops. When the tribal police force was first established, it was overstaffed. They ended up harassing some tribal members. There were a couple of gung-ho cops on our force who went overboard. They were fired."

State and local police were kept out as a matter of tribal policy. The exclusion of outside law enforcement was deemed essential to tribal sovereignty. A senior state police officer who has dealt extensively with the Pequots said, "It is very, very difficult to get these people to talk to us. Without that information, it is very difficult to investigate. This is a closed society where everyone is related to everyone else. They don't talk to us, even when they know there has been a crime. Sometimes, they will not even press charges when we present them with evidence. We are aware of the drug problem on the reservation. We are aware of the high incidence of other crimes on the reservation. However, the tribe rarely calls us in, so our hands are tied. We are not looking for a political controversy. If we went busting in there, you know they would be screaming about tribal sovereignty to the governor.

Beyond that, we have limited resources. We are already stretched thin. If they don't want us on the reservation, we have a lot of other communities in our area that do."

Other social ills were spreading by 2000 as well. Men beating their wives or girlfriends was not uncommon. The husband of the one-time head of the tribe's "family services unit" beat her, according to two of her former colleagues in the unit. One said, "When [her husband] is high on drugs, he is wacko." A tribal elder complained that her young granddaughter was routinely beaten by her husband.

Child neglect also became more common. Parents who had been out late the night before and could not get up in the morning hired limousines to take the children to school. Others left their children alone at home for days, provided only with a wad of cash. The children would be seen wandering the reservation and hanging around the community center until it closed.

Child abuse was a continuing problem. A confidential tribal memo from the mid-1990s documented a report by a social worker alerted to a case where a ten-year-old tribal child was found with severe bruises on his body. The memo reported that the mother's "boyfriend had beat the boy and left bruises on him. Now, according to the mother and the child, the mother is the only one who beats the boy. The mother states that she cannot handle [the boy] because he has behavior problems. The mother stated that she was not going to stop beating him. She admits to beating him with her hand and a belt."

Children were sexually abused as well. Dozens of adult tribal members had been molested as children, and a few saw it as part of family life. "You have both a lot of molesters and molestees in this tribe," said one former tribal social worker. "We had some girls who had been sexually abused by their grandfather. I was told by the mother and aunts of the children that the grandfather had said that it was customary, a part of their culture, for the grandfather to sleep with the grandchildren when they were young. He had evidently slept with the mothers when they were girls. The amazing thing to me was that some of these adult women still thought that this kind of incest was part of their culture and that it was acceptable. They had it done to them, and they allowed it to be done to their children. Thank God, the grandfather is no longer alive to molest any more kids."

The sexual abuse problem was so great that the tribe created a "safe house" for children. A place was needed on the reservation where they could protect the children. The safe house was a six-bedroom colonial-style house in a residential development adjacent to the reservation that the tribe had bought and added to reservation lands. The house was staffed by a full-time team of social workers and operated at its peak in the late 1990s with a $1 million budget.

Tribal youth had been a problem on the reservation for years. As far back as 1995 adult members were complaining about tribal children who were, according to a confidential tribal memo, "angry, aggressive, abusive and disrespectful." Security at the tribal community center had asked for something to be done. The same children were being expelled all the time. The nine- to twelve-year-olds ran aimlessly through the halls. Many of the children were almost vagabonds, wandering from house to house, relative to relative. Pequot teenagers were dropping out of high school at a rapidly rising rate, collecting $100,000 in annual payments from the tribe and getting into trouble. As one teenage Pequot girl wrote Skip in 1996, "I want the members of the [Tribal] Council to understand that I am truly concerned about the future of our tribe as we approach the twenty-first century. I see such a lack of motivation among my peers and I do not foresee them prospering in the future. This fact alone scares me because we are the future of our tribe."

In the 1990s, Pequot teens were increasingly in trouble with the police. In 1993, for example, Kenny Reels's nephew Ernest Reels was convicted of sexually assaulting a fourteen-year-old girl behind Ledyard High School. After release from prison, he was transferred to a drug rehabilitation facility, where the eighteen-year-old was indicted in 1996 for raping another fourteen-year-old. In November 1998, a tribal teen and his half brother kidnapped another young tribal member at gunpoint in a dispute over a stolen gun, striking the victim several times on the side of the head, causing him to bleed and forcing him into a closet before he escaped. In April 1999, another tribal youth fired shots at a young Pequot only a hundred yards from the community center with a handgun he kept in the glove compartment of his silver Lexus. In June of that year a tribal member, who was cashing his paycheck at a local savings bank, got into a fight with a drug dealer who complained he had not been paid, and the two smashed each other's car windows. A gunman fired shots in November 1999 at a group of young Pequots standing outside a tribal-owned house near the reservation. Luckily, no one was hurt in the incident.

The increase in crimes and violence resulted in more tribal members abandoning the reservation. They worried that criminal activity would increase over the next several years as the population of teenagers and other children increased to total more than half the reservation population. "I'm moving out of here," said one middle-aged member, who had lived on the reservation since moving into one of the original HUD houses in 1982. "There are shootings on the reservation. It's just a matter of time before someone gets hit. The tribal kids don't have the best upbringing. They're misguided and have far too much income. Combine those two things, and they are out of control. I'm tired of seeing tribal teenagers cruising my street late at night in their BMWs with gang members from who knows where. I don't want my kids around these people, and I don't want myself around it either. I don't like what I see happening on the reservation. . . . A lot of people have essentially moved off and that includes Skip. Hardly any of the tribal council members live on the reservation."

New members increasingly decided not to move onto the reservation. A light-skinned Pequot explained why he chose a waterfront enclave in Groton Long Point instead of the reservation: "When we moved here, we considered living on the reservation to get the tax savings." (Tribal members who live on the reservation pay neither state nor local taxes.) His wife added, "My daughter knows that tribal youth are not a group we like her hanging around with. She can invite them down to our house, but we don't like her hanging around the reservation and the community center. We don't spend much time with these kids' parents and we don't want her spending too much time with the children."

A few Pequots abandoned not only the reservation but also the tribe and most of the financial rewards that came with it. They gave up high-paying sinecures with the tribal government for the simple reason that they did not want their families and children living in what Jean Swift, a black tribal member, called "a high-class welfare system. That is the society that they have created. You have all kinds of allowances for therapy and programs, which is not a bad thing, but it has gone to the extreme. There is such a high level of dysfunctionality in so many of the tribal members now with all of this wealth and opulence. People have neglected their marriages, their children. They expect everything to be done for them. Their sense of entitlement is breathtaking. I want no part of that."

Swift first came to the reservation in 1994 with her husband and their newborn daughter. She was college-educated with a graduate degree in accounting. She was disappointed with what she found on the reservation. "I found people whose entire lives were consumed by money. It was like they had gone crazy," she recalled. Once, at a membership meeting, she was asked by Skip why she had not yet enrolled her young child in the tribe. Didn't she know that if she did they could begin accumulating money in the scholarship accounts?

She replied, "When and if my children wish to be enrolled when they get older, that is their decision to make."

Skip said, "Well, they could be having scholarship accounts."

She responded, "I'm not interested."

Hayward was taken aback. He was not used to tribal members saying no to free money.

By 1999, Swift had decided to leave, moving back to the Midwest. "I decided that my husband and children were far more important than the money I get from the tribe," she explained. "The tribal council takes the social problems very seriously. But the council is almost like the parent who does not know how to handle its kid. They care deeply but they don't know how to address the problem. It is really sad because they do want to fix the social problems. They want the tribe to be successful and healthy. But it is just not happening."

Twenty-five years after the Pequots' reinvention by the Haywards, they had yet to become a tribe in more than name and legal standing. "They are a tribe according to federal law," said Shepard Krech III, a Brown University anthropologist. "But I don't assume that means anything about communal life or about their sense of themselves as a people." Tribal members agreed. "I don't think Skip gave any real thought to what kind of community this would be, what kind of tribe it would be if people did come back," said tribal member Bruce Kirchner. "I don't think he even thought about it." Skip himself had admitted as much, saying, "Repatriation has been extremely tough. My mission from day one has been to create housing and jobs for people. Perhaps I should have concentrated more on other things as well."

26

THE DREAM

O n February 26, 2002, Kenny Reels and his tribal council ended the Pequots' nine-year attempt to annex hundreds, if not thousands, of acres of land to the reservation. (Federal courts had whittled the original 247-acre request down to 165 acres—86 in Ledyard and 79 in North Stonington.) Throughout the 1990s, the Pequots had waged a behind-the-scenes lobbying campaign inside the Interior Department's Bureau of Indian Affairs. At times, it looked as if the lobbying was paying off—for instance, at a meeting in Washington on June 5, 1997, when BIA Deputy Commissioner Hilda Manuel and Bill Wakole, head of the Eastern Area Office, privately assured Pequot lobbyists that Washington would approve Pequot annexation of the land.

The 2000 election of Republican George W. Bush as president, however, led to a reconsideration of the matter. Bush appointees at the Interior Department and its Bureau of Indian Affairs made clear their intention to review and revise the land-into-trust process to give towns and states more voice in these matters.

On the day of the Pequot withdrawal, Reels warned the towns in a terse press release that the Pequots would be back. "Nearly 10 years have passed since this initial application," he wrote. "And we may apply for this or other land to be taken into trust outside the settlement boundaries in the future. If and when we do, we will do so according to current and future needs, priorities and plans of the Tribal Nation."

Kenny's threat was not idle. Barry Margolin explained, "Even if they have to wait another generation, they think they are going to be there. So taking this land into trust right now is not a life-or-death issue. The way they see it, the question is not if they get the land but when." This has been the Pequots' attitude from the beginning. In a private letter to Dave Holdridge in May 1993, Jackson King wrote, "Even if the petition were denied for some reason (and I know of no reason why it should be), it would surely be resubmitted at a later date."

The land annexation was never about economic survival. Barry Margolin recalled, "This is not a make-or-break issue for them like the land-claim settlement or the casino battle or slots. Those were decisions where if the tribe won it would become rich and powerful, and if they lost they would end up back where they started in the 1970s. Today, they fight because they are rich and powerful and can do what they like."

There has been considerable public skepticism about the genealogical authenticity of today's Pequots. Writers have alleged that none of them descend from the original Pequots. This question cannot be answered with complete certainty without an independent genealogical investigation, and today's tribe will not allow such an inquiry for both political and privacy reasons. It is undeniable, however, that today's Pequots have only the most attenuated genealogical connections to the Pequots of yore. Skip Hayward, who claims to be "one-eighth Pequot," can make such an assertion only by assuming that his maternal great-grandparents, Martha Hoxie and Cyrus George, were full-blooded Pequots. They were not, however, according to confidential Connecticut state genealogical records, which indicate they were likely one-quarter Pequot. In that case, Eliza George Plouffe and Annie George Sebastian were at most one-eighth Pequot, which means that Skip is at most one-thirty-second, and that most of today's tribe is one-sixty-fourth or one-one-hundredth-and-twenty-eighth Pequot. In short, this is a tribe where most members, by ancestry, are at least 63/64th something other than Pequot.

Were the Pequots an Indian tribe in 1975 when Skip met Tom Tureen? "That question was never dealt with," Tureen said. "We were able to avoid dealing with that because the State of Connecticut decided to recognize them as a tribe, whether they were or not." Are the Pequots an Indian tribe even today? Can a family corporation become a tribe simply via federal recognition and gambling riches? Does it matter that the Pequots themselves admit they have no authentic culture or traditions? The State of Connecticut will soon have the opportunity to answer these questions. Two other state-recognized Indian bands financed by gambling interests are seeking federal recognition.

What would happen if the money ran out? Tim Love, a former leader of the Penobscots who has lobbied for the Pequots and run tour buses for them over the years, said, "If [the Pequots] suddenly did not have all this money, there would be a lot of people who might not have the desire to stay. What is the motive to be a member if you did not want to be a member before Foxwoods? It was really the money that gave them the opportunity to pull the tribe back together."

Tribal members agree. Bruce Kirchner declared, "We are the first tribe in American history to be formed around money." Another former tribal council member said, "If the money spigot stops, the members will in large part drift away in different directions. There will be a core of people left, but a lot of people will decide to go elsewhere." Another Pequot said, "If the money holds out, maybe we will become a tribe. Talk to me in 2040."

*   *   *

If you ever visit Foxwoods, wander away from the casino, the museum, and the neatly paved suburban development of McMansions. Try and find your way to the southeast corner of the reservation as defined by Route 214, or Indiantown Road, as Eliza knew it. Just a hundred feet in off the road, in a glade surrounded by maple and dogwood and apple trees, sits a small, abandoned wood-frame house with boarded-up windows and a sagging roof. The cedar-shake shingles on the sides are mottled with age. Abandoned toys and an ancient Frigidaire icebox litter the lawn around the old farmhouse. This was Eliza George Plouffe's house.

The Hayward family would rather see the house collapse than allow the tribe to fix it up. The Haywards reject any notion that the house is tribal property. They may have told the BIA in their preliminary federal acknowledgment petition that the "Homestead" symbolized tribal continuity, but it actually symbolized the continuity of just one family. Anthropologist James Wherry explained, "The basic stance of the Haywards toward the homestead was, 'It's our home. You're not touching it.' Terry Bell has told me that her grandmother told her before she died, 'Burn it to the ground. Don't let anyone touch it. To the ground.'" Tribal member Bruce Kirchner agreed, saying, "The Haywards do not want to live there, and they do not want anyone else in the house. They do not view it as a tribal house but as their family house. In their view, that is Elizabeth George's house, and no one is to enter but her family."

For the Haywards, coming to the reservation was never really about forming a tribe. A tribe and tribal members were little more than practical necessities for Eliza's family to move onto the reservation, build themselves houses, and, later, achieve wealth. The true goal of the Pequots has always been to acquire what so many other Americans want—jobs, homes, wealth, social status. In short, the American dream. When asked what it means to him to be Pequot, Skip answered the question with another question, asking, "What does it mean to be an American?"

What makes the new Pequots so remarkable is that they have achieved the American dream by redefining themselves as an American Indian tribe. Led by talented lawyers, they managed to leverage the barest trace of Indian descent into a fortune akin to the Rockefeller family. "My only regret," concluded Tom Tureen, "is that the rewards fell so disproportionately on so few people. The Pequots are the luckiest tribe in history." Eliza would be proud. She more than anyone would appreciate the irony of her children and grandchildren becoming American millionaires by becoming American Indians.

ACKNOWLEDGMENTS

I would first like to thank those members and employees of the Mashantucket Pequot tribe who spoke with me, both on the record and not for attribution. (It is always best to get the story directly from the inside rather than to rely solely on outsiders and critics.) They also provided me unparalleled access to thousands of pages of tribal and government documents invaluable to my understanding of this remarkable story. People can, and do, reinvent the past. Documents do not.

Charles Loxton provided able research assistance and was a great help.

Thanks to my former editor at the *Washington Post*, David Ignatius, who allowed me to step away from the financial news beat and investigate the Pequot story. Rich Leiby, then Sunday editor for the Style section, commissioned my first piece on the Pequots and got me started in the right direction. *Post* copy editor Denny McAuliffe generously explained other tribes' views of the Pequots. In Connecticut, Morgan McGinley, Maura Casey, Gregory Stone, Dave Collins, and Karen Florin of the *New London Day*, and Ray Hackett of the *Norwich Bulletin* shared their insights into the Pequots. Former *Washington Post* colleague Betsy Corcoran and her husband George Anders of the *Wall Street Journal* kindly read the manuscript and helped improve it. Thanks also to Seth Klarman for taking the time to review an early version.

In addition, I would like to thank attorneys David Wienir and Kevin W. Goering of Coudert Brothers for their close reading of the manuscript.

Many other friends and relations encouraged me in the process of writing this book. Thanks to John and Myra Appleton, Ted Caplow, David and Peri Clark, Javier Ergueta, Bill and Charlotte Ford, Rene Goodale, Lenny and Yasmin Groopman, Whitney and Tizzy Hatch, David Kirkpatrick, Chris Knowlton, Ralph Mason, Rich and Martha McDermott, Tom McLellan, Nick Nicholas, Charlie and Pam Perkins, Roy Pfeil and Topsy Post, George and Linda Post, Rosemary Ripley, Chris and Inez Scholz, Bill and Susan Sheeline, Paula Spann, Jim Tisch, John Train, and Robert Wilson.

This book would not exist, of course, without the support of my publisher, Morgan Entrekin. Morgan showed great patience and had the inspiration to assign editor Brando Skyhorse to this book. Brando gave me a wonderful edit and improved the book immeasurably.

Every writer needs a place to write and for this book mine was the New York Society Library. Many thanks to head librarian Mark Piel and his staff, who were unfailingly helpful.

Closer to the home front, my dad and Sandy consistently encouraged me. So too, my sister, Michele, and brothers, Mike and Tim, also cheered me on when needed.

My greatest thanks go to my wife, Carmel Snow Wilson, and our intrepid son, James. Living with a writer is never easy. They showed forbearance, kindness, and love, all of which I will try to repay in the years ahead.

SOURCES

Interviews

Mikki Aganstata
Jo Allyn Archambault
Bob Bee
Theresa Darnice Bell
Tony Beltran
Ralph Bergman
Bob Birmingham
John Bodinger
Bonnie Bostrom
Ken Brown
Mickey Brown
Kim Burgess
Sandy Cadwalader
Jack Campisi
Dave Cannon
Theresa Casanova
Maura Casey
Gregory Chester
Joan Cohn
Bob Congdon
Paul Costa
Janet Courtenay
Dave Crosby

Jim Cunha
Tom D'Amore
Ed Danielczuk
Steve Dennin
Bob DeSalvio
Charlie Duffy
Michael Dutton
Terry Dzilinski
Melissa Fawcett
Lee Fleming
Karen Florin
Ray Geer
Rob Gips
Robert Goodman
Larry Greene
Bill Guevremont
John Guevremont
Erin Guyot-Thomas
Ray Hackett
Laurie Halderman
Mike Hanke
Suzanne Harjo
Barbara Hartwell

Larry Hauptman
Alan Hayes
Richard (Skip) Hayward
Arthur Henick
John Herman
Dave Holahan
John Holder
Dave Holdridge
Joanne Isaac
Leon Jacobs
Wesley Johnson
Kevin Kane
Brendan Keleher
Alice Kirchner
Bruce Kirchner
Jackson King
Charlie Klewin
Shepard Krech
Vincent Laudone
Tim Love
Barry Margolin
Denny McAuliffe
Kevin McBride
Bruce McDonald
Morgan McGinley
Ann McMullen
Chris McNeil

Joanne Melish
Cheryl Metoyer
Dennis Montgomery
Don Peppard
Byron Quann
Harry Raucher
Trudie Lamb Richmond
Ed Sarabia
Nancy Shoemaker
Lucille Showalter
Gregory Stone
Ralph Sturges
Jean Swift
Bill Tallman
Lois Tefft
Michael Thomas
John Tobin
Kevin Tubridy
Tom Tureen
Stan Twardy
Lowell Weicker
Robert Werner
Richard West
Jim Wherry
Howard Wilson
Jeff Wosencroft

Unpublished Sources

American Express Travel Related Services Co., "Travel, Meals, Entertainment and Charge Card Policy for Members and Employees of Mashantucket Pequot Tribal Nation," January 1996.

Bayer, Aaron S., "Memo to Twardy and Blumenthal," May 28, 1991.

Bear Stearns & Co., "Confidential Offering Memorandum for Mashantucket (Western) Pequot Tribe, Special Revenue Bonds, 1996 Series A, $200,000,000.," September 1996.

Boyd, Arline, "Letter to Brendan Keleher," January 9,1975.

Blumenthal, Richard, "Letter to Sec. of Interior Lujan," January 28, 1991.

————, "Letter to Conn. Senate Leadership," May 1, 1991.

Brend, Alice, "Letter to Irving Harris," CIAC, November 4, 1976.

Brown, G. Michael, "Foxwoods Interim Cost Savings Report to Tribal Council," May 30, 1996.

Burgess, Kim D., "The Ethnic Identity of the Mashantucket Pequots: An Investigation Into the Effects of African Slavery and Cape Verdean Immigration on the Tribe," October 1994.

Butler, Eva, "Notebooks on Connecticut Indians," The Indian and Colonial Research Center, Old Mystic, Connecticut.

Campisi, Jack, "Preliminary Petition for Federal Acknowledgement Submitted by the Mashantucket Pequot Tribe to the United States Department of the Interior," 1982.

Chester, Gregory, "Personal Correspondence with Amos George et al., 1975–1985."

Connecticut Indian Affairs Council, "Western Pequot Reservation Development Plan," (draft), 1975.

————, "A Brief Summary of Key Aspects of the Regulations of the CIAC as they Relate to the Western Pequot Tribe," June 27, 1975.

————, "Minutes of Regular CIAC Meetings, 1974–1982."

Connecticut State Park and Forest Commission, "Minutes of Monthly Meetings and other Records," 1925–1939.

————, "The Pequot Indians," 1937.

Connecticut Welfare Department, "Genealogical Records of George Family," undated.

————, "Confidential Records of Significant Events on State Indian Reservations," 1929, 1935, 1969.

————, "Notes on Western Pequot Genealogies," 1936–1944.

————, "Memo from Clayton Squires to Marvin Barrett Regarding Aid to Eliza George Plouffe," November 14–26, 1941.

————, "Case Summary on Eliza Plouffe," 1942–1950.

————, "Data on Indian Reservations," 1946–1959.

————, "Letter to Elizabeth Plouffe Re: Gas Bill Payment," January 11, 1961.

————, "List of Indians on Reservations," June 15, 1961, June 23, 1967, July 10, 1968.

————, "Letter to Elizabeth Plouffe Re: Daughter's Desire to Move Onto Reservation," March 19, 1968.

230   BRETT DUVAL FROMSON

————, "Letter to Ledyard First Selectman Granting Permission to Burn Flower Shack on Reservation," April 30, 1968.

————, "Memo Re: Western & Eastern Pequot Reservation," May 2, 1968.

————, "Memo Re: Bathroom Addition for Elizabeth Plouffe Etc," July 3, 1968.

————, "Memo Re: Elizabeth Plouffe," February 4, 1969.

————, "Inspection Report on Eastern and Western Pequot Reservations," March 29, 1969.

————, "Memo Re: Residents of Western Pequot Reservation," July 15, 1969.

————, "Annual Report of Indians In Residence," July 9, 1970.

————, "Memo Re: Elizabeth Plouffe's Residence," October 20, 1972.

————, "Memo Re: Transfer of Reservation to Department of Environmental Protection," August 20, 1973.

————, "Listing of Residents of the Four Indian Reservations," September 30, 1973.

Coopers & Lybrand, "Confidential Report to Tribal Council Re: Gaming Enterprise," May 22, 1995.

Crosby, David C., "Memo to File, Pine Tree Legal Assistance, Inc.," October 17, 1974.

————, "Legal Opinion for Conn. Tribes Re: Title to Reservation Lands," June 10, 1976.

Dames, Fatima, "Agenda Items for Special Meeting of Citizens for Equality, Inc. Board of Directors," March 7, 1999.

Danielczuk, Edward A., "Letter to Irving Harris," March 26, 1971.

Dautrich, Kenneth, and Carl Van Horn,"Mashantucket Pequot Survey: Attitudes of Connecticut, Eastern Connecticut and Rhode Island Residents," April 1997.

DeTora, Alice E., "Memo from Robinson & Cole to Pequot Tribal Manager Re: Benefits for Tribal Member Students," March 10, 1997.

Dobrzynski, Judith H., "Profits from Casino Help an Indian Tribe Reclaim Its History," September 1, 1997.

Dube, Leonard F., "Letter to Kenneth Wood," September 20, 1973.

Field, Searle, "Memo to Tribal Council Re: Hiring of Susan Tohbe and Her Career Summary," September 23, 1997.

Foxwoods Resort Casino, "Confidential Financial Statements," July and August 1996, and July 1997.

————, "Confidential Income Analysis," July 15, 1997.

Grasso, Ella, "Letter Certifying Pequots for Federal Revenue Sharing Program," March 3, 1976.

Harris, Irving A., "Letter to Edward Danielczuk," March 24, 1971.

————, "Letter to Conn. Dept. of Environmental Protection," April 24, 1974.

Hayward, Richard A., "Letter to B. Keleher," January 12, 1975.

————, "Letter to Tribal Members Re: IRS Audit of Members' Tax Returns for 1994 and Previous Years," May 2, 1995.

————, "Letter to BIA Head Ada Deer Asking for Exemption from Proposed Local Notification Rules," July 11, 1996.

Joy, Kristyn K., "Redefining Themselves: The Mashantucket Pequots' Return to a Reservation Community," Undergraduate Honors Thesis, Amherst College, 1988.

Keleher, Brendan S., "Letter to David Crosby," April 5,1974.

————, "Memo Re: Purchase of Vehicle with Western Pequot Funds," January 22, 1976.

King, Jackson, "Letter to David Holdridge," May 7, 1993.

————, "Memo to Tribal Council Regarding State Police Protocol," August 15, 1996.

————, "Memorandum to Tribal Council," November 4, 1996.

————, "Memos and Correspondence Relating to State Income Tax Exemptions for Tribal Businesses and Members," October 1996 and September 1997.

————, "Memo to Tribal Council Re: IRS Audit of Tribal Members' Individual Tax Returns," May 23, 1997.

KPMG Strategic Services, "Centralization Project Study for Tribal Council," c. 1990s.

Langevin, Martha, "Letter to Mrs. Alice Guevremont," 1927.

————, "Letter to Mrs. Alice Guevremont," December 1, 1929.

Lewis, Larry, and Cindy Lewis, "Memorandum to Phyllis Monroe," February 12, 1994.

Louziotis, Demetrios, "Letter to Mickey Brown Re: Slots," June 26, 1992.

Margolin, Barry A., "Letter to H. Naruk," September 28, 1990.

————, "Letter to Richard M. Sheridan," October 1, 1990.

————, "Letter to John B. Larson," April 30, 1991.

————, "Letter to S. Twardy and R. Blumenthal," May 31, 1991.

Mashantucket Pequot Economic Development and Planning Committee, "Confidential Minutes," April 1996–February 1997.

Mashantucket Pequot Judicial Committee, "Recommendation to Enact the Child Protection and Family Preservation Ordinance," June 8, 1995.

Mashantucket Pequot Museum Oral History Project Papers, "Transcripts of Interviews with Tribal Members," 1988–1996.

Mashantucket Pequot Museum Project, "Museum Plan," Undated.

Mashantucket Pequot Tribal Council, "Minutes of Council Meetings," August 18, 1974–February 24, 1999.

————, "Real Property Report," December 31, 1984.

————, "Opinions of Counsel Concerning the Mashantucket Pequot Tribe with Related Papers," May 13, 1982–May 8, 1986.

————, "Confidential Minutes of Tribal Council for Calendar Year 1987."

————, "Annual Report Prepared for Annual Membership Meeting," November 6, 1988.

————, "Annual Report Prepared for Annual Membership Meeting," November 5, 1989.

————, "Environmental Assessment of Bingo Hall Expansion," June 1990.

————, "Annual Report Prepared for the Annual Membership Meeting," November 3, 1991.

————, "Proposal Regarding the Placement of Land Owned by the Mashantucket Pequot Tribe Outside of the Settlement Area Into Trust," July 29, 1993.

————, "Resolutions and Memorandum of Understanding Re: Preference for Tribal Member–Owned Business," August, September, and November 1994.

————, "Council Resolution and Budget Package for: Washington Office," April 2, 1996.

————, "Resolution to Print Book about Pequots for PR at a Cost of $80,000," April 2, 1996.

————, "Letter from Skip Hayward to Smithsonian Regarding Terms and Conditions of $10 Million Pledge," June 13, 1996.

————, "Memo to Director of Cultural Resources Department," June 24, 1996.

————, "E-Mail Invitation to Pequot Fundraiser for Rep. Gejdenson," October 17, 1996.

————, "Memo to Tribal Council Members from Tribal Secretary Gary Carter Re: Amendments to the Tribe's Constitution," December 16, 1996.

————, "E-Mail to Council Regarding Conversations with Sen. Ben Nighthorse Campbell and Campaign Contributions," January 10, 1997.

————, "Memo to Council Regarding Relationship with Pres. Clinton, DNC and RNC," May 2, 1997.

————, "Resolution for Revised Budget for Foxwoods Phase VIB," May 21, 1997.

————, "E-Mail to Tribal Council Regarding Press Coverage and Public Image of Tribe," September 9, 1997.

Mashantucket Pequot Tribal Nation, "Annual Reports," 1994–2000.

————, "Confidential Executive Management Reports," June, August, November, and December 1996.

Mashantucket Pequot Tribal Nation Historical and Cultural Preservation Committee, "Meeting Minutes," June 10, 1996.

Mashantucket Pequot Tribal Nation Office of Facilities Management, "Real Estate Property Development Strategy," September 4, 1998.

Mashantucket Pequot Tribal Nation Tribal Clerk's Office, "Tribal Council Election Results," November 4, 1997.

Mashantucket Pequot Tribal Planning Committee, "Mashantucket Pequot Tribal Nation Ten Year Comprehensive Plan," August 2, 1999.

Mashantucket Pequot Tribe, "Constitution," February 20, 1977.

————, "Indian Preference and Affirmative Action Policies and Procedures," 1994.

————, "Incentive Ordinance," September 29, 1992, with revisions through September 17, 1998.

————, "Memorandum on Incentive Accounts and Income," July 24, 1997.

McMullen, Ann, "Culture By Design: Native Identity, Historiography, and the Reclamation of Tradition in Twentieth-Century Southeastern New England," submitted in partial fulfillment of the requirements for the degree of Doctor of Philosophy in the Department of Anthropology at Brown University, May 1996.

Menihan, Annette, "Memorandum on Child Protection Team, with Child Abuse Protocols," February 12, 1994.

Morgan Stanley Dean Witter, "Confidential Offering Memorandum for Mashantucket (Western) Pequot Tribe Subordinated Special Revenue Bonds," January 21, 1999.

New England Design, "Memorandum on Foxwoods Resort and Architectural Drawings," January 6, 1998.

Old Mystic Baptist Church, "A Funeral Service for Theresa Victoria Hayward," August 10, 1928–March 7, 1996.

Pearson, Alan, "Letter to Welfare Dept. Asking for Money for Elizabeth Plouffe," January 10, 1956.

Pearson, Christopher, "Letter to Tribal Membership," November 1999.

Plouffe, Elizabeth, "Letter to Welfare Department," May 13, 1959.

Reels, Kenneth M., "Chairman's Annual Report," November 7, 1999.

Tantaquidgeon, Gladys, "The New England Indians," U.S. Department of the Interior Office of Indian Affairs, December 6, 1934.

Torres, Jennie, "Letter to Skip Hayward," May 23, 1996.

Wallace, Kathleen, "Hold Onto Your Land: Elizabeth George, Martha Langevin, and the Survival of the Pequots," senior essay, Yale University, New Haven, Connecticut, April 10, 1995.

West, James L., "Report to Mashantucket Pequot in Regards to Analysis of Factors Dividing Reservation Population," May 14, 1986.

Wherry, James, "Memorandum to Jackson King," June 5, 1997.

Williams, J. R., "Notebook from Files of Connecticut State Parks and Forest Commission," undated.

Articles

Allen, Mike, "Casino Riches Build an Indian Museum with 'Everything,'" *New York Times*, August 10, 1998.

Associated Press, "Indians Look to Connecticut for Beano," *Bangor Daily News*, November 4, 1983.

————, "An Ex-Convict Sits on Pequot Tribal Council," *New London Day*, October 26, 1998.

————, "Tribal Museum a One-Sided Exhibit, Some Say," December 27, 1998.

Barnes, Julian, "Lobbies with Wolves: Indian Casinos are Becoming Political Players," *U.S. News & World Report*, November 10, 1997.

Battista, Carolyn, "Pequot Indians Plan Museum on History of Ancestral Land," *New York Times*, October 5, 1986.

Beinart, Peter, "Lost Tribes," *Lingua Franca*, May 1999.

Belanger, Gregory, "Lobby Talk," *Connecticut Law Journal*, May 13, 1991.

Bishop, Gerald, "A Progressive Hand Leads Tribe," *New London Day*, February 16, 1986.

Bixby, Lyn, "A Record of Violence," *Hartford Courant*, October 25, 1998.

————, "Angry Pequots Back Ouster of Tribal Leaders," September 10, 1999.

Blumenthal, Richard, "Opinion No. 91-015," May 1, 1991.

Bradshaw, Harold Clayton, "The Indians of Connecticut," Connecticut, 1935.

Burgard, Matt, "Probationer Charged in 2 Sex Assaults," *New London Day*, May 23, 1996.

————, "Sebastian No Longer Directing Tribe Police," *New London Day*, June 2, 1996.

Butler, Eva, "The Mashantucket Home of the Pequot Indians," *Ledyard Directory*, 1956.

————, "New England Colonial News," vol. XXXVII, no. 4, Mystic, Connecticut, *Colonial Research Associates*, undated.

Collins, Clare, "Ledyard Tribe Looking Ahead with High Hopes," *New London Day*, September 23, 1984.

Collins, David, "State, Pequots Agree to Slot Machine Deal," *New London Day*, January 14, 1993.

————, "The Possibilities Are Endless," *New London Day*, May 1, 1993.

————, "Haywards Buy Cottage in Noank," *New London Day*, October 30, 1993.

————, "Mashantuckets Owe their Riches to an Unpretentious 'Visionary,'" *New London Day*, November 19, 1993.

————, "Tribal Fortunes Rise in Washington," *New London Day*, April 30, 1994.

————, "Thomas Elected to Tribal Council While on Probation for Drug Charges," *New London Day*, January 12, 1996.

————, "Tribe to Buy Hilton for $18 Million," *New London Day*, December 14, 1996.

Connecticut Indian Affairs Council, "American Indians in Connecticut," 1977, 1979.

Connecticut House, "Vote Tabulation on Repeal of Las Vegas Nights Legislation," May 16, 1991.

Connecticut Senate, "Vote Tabulation on Repeal of Las Vegas Nights Legislation," May 9, 1991.

Connery, Tom, "Pequots Have Visions for Land . . . ," *New London Day*, June 25, 1977.

Conway, Jack, "Land of the Pequots," *Waterbury Republican*, July 10, 1966.

Cross Paths, Commemorative Issue, vol. 1, issue 3, Summer 1998.

Cusick, Martha, "Pequots Initiate Court Fight to Acquire Ledyard Property," *Norwich Bulletin*, January 8, 1976.

————, "Mashantucket Reservation Called Ideal for Solar Experiment," *Norwich Bulletin*, November 18, 1976.

————, "Courtroom Powwows—Viable Force for Indians," February 6, 1977.

DeCoster, Stan, "Field's Back on His Feet. After Financial Trouble, He Rejoins Weicker's Team," *New London Day*, March 8, 1992.

————, "Mashantuckets Solidify Children's Place in Tribe: Tribal Members OK Revisions in Bloodline Requirements," *New London Day*, December 17, 1996.

DeCoster, Stan, and Lisa Hayden, "Field Conflict of Interest Denied," *New London Day*, March 18, 1995.

Dufresne, Bethe, "A Tribe's Identity in One Woman's Face," *New London Day*, August 10, 1998.

Edgecomb, Kathleen, "Judge Refuses to Dismiss Assault Case on Jurisdictional Claim," *New London Day*, December 20, 1997.

Farragher, Thomas, "Veto of Mashantucket Land Bill Draws Ire," *New London Day*, April 6, 1983.

Feinberg, Margie, "Mashantucket Dream Bears Fruit," August 31, 1981.

Florin, Karen, "Shots Fired," *New London Day*, July 17, 1999.

————, "Man Fires Shot at People in Front of Ledyard Home," *New London Day*, November 9, 1999.

————, "Mashantuckets Withdraw Land-Trust Bid," *New London Day*, February 2, 2002.

Foley, John, "Theresa Hayward, Mother of Tribal Chairman, Dies," *New London Day,* March 8, 1996.

Freedman, Samuel G., "Indian Land Conflict Rekindled in Connecticut," *New York Times,* April 11, 1983.

Fromson, Brett Duval, "The Pequot Uprising," *Washington Post,* June 21, 1998.

————, "The Pequots' Latest Gamble," *Washington Post,* August 30, 1998.

Giago, Tim, "Indian Sovereignty in Question. Mashantuckets Find the Casino Runs Them," *New London Day,* August 13, 1995.

Gladwell, Malcolm, "Traditional Yankees Wary of Gambling on Looser Land Rules for Pequot Tribe," *Washington Post,* November 12, 1993.

Green, Rick, "Boundless Intrigue Over Missing Map," *Hartford Courant,* March 1, 2002.

Groark, Virginia, "Tribe's $193 Million Museum is Ready to Open to the Public," *New London Day,* August 11, 1998.

————, "Hayward Ousted as Mashantucket Chairman in Upset," November 2, 1998.

————, "A Rambler Among Gamblers," November 22, 1998.

————, "Dissent in Mashantucket: Smaller Cuts of Casino Pie Spark Protest," *New London Day,* September 10, 1999.

Guillette, Mary E., "American Indians in Connecticut, Past to Present," CIAC, 1979.

Hartford Courant, "Connecticut's Indians: Most have intermarried with other groups and only a few remain on the state's four reservations, which may soon be scrapped," January 22, 1956.

————, "Return of the Natives," May 22–29, 1994.

Haygood, Will, "Mashantuckets Face the Challenge of Wealth," *Boston Globe,* August 18, 1995.

————, "Tribe's Riches Create Divisions Among Some," *Boston Globe,* August 19, 1995.

Hayward, Richard A., "The White Man Has Tried to Destroy Our Heritage," *Norwich Bulletin,* May 23, 1977.

Hileman, Maria, "Mashantucket Ready to Build Two Schools, Concern About Youths Prompts Tribe's Move," *New London Day,* December 10, 1995.

————, "Senator Questions Pequots' Donations," *New London Day,* November 13, 1997.

————, "For Researchers, Pequots' Family Tree has Posed a Knotty Problem," *New London Day,* July 2, 2000.

Indian Rights Association, *Indian Truth,* vols. 232, 241, 247, 251, 252, 254, June 1980–December 1983.

Johnson, Kirk, "Weicker to Block Indian Casino, Seeks Repeal of Charity Gambling," *New York Times,* May 1, 1991.

————, "Connecticut Clears Way for Indian Casino," *New York Times*, May 16, 1991.

————, "Pequot Casino Faces Challenges of Success," *New York Times*, May 3, 1992.

Katz, Ian, "The Tribe That Found a Fortune," *The Guardian*, July 29, 1995.

Kemper, Steve, "Whose Land? Indians and Settlers in Connecticut," *Yankee Magazine*, December 1, 1998.

Larson, Kay, "Tribal Windfall: A Chance to Reopen History," *New York Times*, July 26, 1998.

Lender, John, "Senate Passes Ban on Vegas Nights," *Hartford Courant*, May 10, 1991.

Liberman, Ellen, "Pequots Admit 100 New Members, Enlarge Tribe," *New London Day*, November 9, 1993.

Liburd, Sondra, "CETA Funds Fan Embers of Hope for Ledyard's Indian Reservation," *Norwich Bulletin*, December 20, 1978.

Lightman, David, "Draft Report Concludes Pequots Used Donations to Buy Access," *Hartford Courant*, February 11, 1998.

McMullen, Ann, "Soapbox Discourse: Tribal Historiography, Indian–White Relations, and Southeastern New England Powwows," *The Public Historian*, vol. 18, no. 4 (Fall 1996).

McNamara, Eileen, "BIA Had its Doubts About Legitimacy of Mashantuckets," *New London Day*, May 3, 2000.

Nalder, Eric, Deborah Nelson, and Alex Tizon, "The Pequots: How a Wealthy Tribe Got Federal Aid it Didn't Need," *Seattle Times*, December 4, 1996.

Naruk, Henry J., "Proposal of the State of Connecticut for a Tribal–State Compact Between the Mashantucket Pequot Tribe and the State of Connecticut," 1991.

New London Day, "Pequot Indian Murdered," October 1898.

————, "Unmarried Mother of Nine Arrested by State Police," August 16, 1930.

————, "70 Members Now in Two Pequot Indian Tribes," June 30, 1931.

————, "Victory in Pequot War Saved Early Connecticut," January 27, 1934.

————, "Bill to Abolish Indian Reservations Set for Opposition at Hearing," March 14, 1953.

————, "State's Four Indian Reservations Have Population Totaling Only 32," August 29, 1957.

————, "Amos George Obituary," January 18, 1967.

————, "Dog License Dispute: Indian Woman Challenges State," April 4, 1968.

————, "Legislation Would Improve Indians' Status," December 15, 1981.

————, "Ledyard Man Accused in Shooting Incident," April 1, 1989.

————, "Three People Charged with Assault After Drug Raid," October 8, 1995.

————, "Lake Spears Charged in Domestic Incident," July 19, 1997.

————, "Tribal Member Charged with Assault at Casino," January 7, 1998.

————, "From the Dream to the Reality," August 9, 1998.

————, "Mighty Museum in the Woods," August 23, 1998.

New York Times, "Pequot Tribe Tops List of Political Donors," June 29, 1997.

Norwich Bulletin, "State Report on Ledyard Tribe," June 8, 1933.

————, "Mashantuckets Move to Increase Their Tribal Membership," April 2, 1977.

————, "Beano Game Raises Larger Issue," November 7, 1983.

————, "Youth Imprisoned for Rape," September 1, 1994.

————, "Police Report," January 11, 1997.

————, "Timeline for Pequots," May 23, 2002.

Pequot Times, Mashantucket Pequot Tribal Nation Public Relations, 1992–present.

Pequot Times Drum Beat, "Message to Pequot Membership from Kenneth M. Reels," November 6, 1998.

Ravo, Nick, "High Court Clears Way for Indian Casino," *New York Times*, April 23, 1991.

Reels, Kenneth, "Running Water's News," vol. 1, issue 1, April 1999.

Richard, Randall, and Peter Phipps, "The Deal that Built Foxwoods," *Providence Journal*, September 19, 1999.

Richards, Margaret, "Who's Sovereign Here Anyhow?" Connecticut Consortium for Law and Citizenship Education, Inc., 1994.

Ringle, Ken, "The Casino on Sacred Ground," *Washington Post*, February 15, 1992.

Roberge, Martha M., "The Legal Status of Connecticut Indians," CIAC, May 1985.

Ryan, Bill, "Profile of a Vanishing American: Pequots Still Dislike 'White Eyes,'" *Hartford Times*, September 29, 1969.

Speck, Frank G., "Native Tribes and Dialects of Connecticut," Report of the Bureau of American Ethnology, 1928.

Specter, Michael, "In This Corner: Connecticut Governor Lowell Weicker," *New York Times Magazine*, December 15, 1991.

Stanley, William A., "Her Dying Words Were, 'Hold the Land,'" *New London Day*, August 30, 1980.

Stets, Dan, "Indians Sue to Obtain 800 Acres in Ledyard," *New London Day*, May 11, 1976.

————, "Residents Fight Indian Land Claims," *New London Day*, May 15, 1976.

Thomas, Michael, "Wachau: A Publication from the Office of Michael Thomas," vol. 2, issue 1, January 1999.

Thorndike, Bill, "Indian Leader Downplays Gambling Parlor Option," *New London Day*, November 22, 1983.

United States Census, 1900.

————, 1910.

Vaughan, Kristi, "McGuigan Denies Request by Indians for Bingo Games," *Hartford Courant*, February 21, 1985.

Viafora, Susann, "All Decked Out: Mashantucket Pequots Celebrate Beginning of New Era with Casino," *Norwich Bulletin*, February 13, 1992.

————, "Crowds Small at Foxwoods Indian Festival," *Norwich Bulletin*, October 23, 1992.

Waldman, Hilary, "Mashantucket Pequot Chairman Revels in Foxwoods' Success," *Hartford Courant*, November 28, 1993.

————, "New Life for a Forgotten People," *Hartford Courant*, May 22, 1994.

Weicker, Lowell P., Jr., "Problems Created by Casino Gambling," undated.

————, "Letter to General Assembly Leadership," April 30, 1991.

————, "Press Release and Memorandum of Understanding on Slots Deal with Pequots," January 13, 1993.

Zielbauer, Paul, "Pequot Tribe Withdraws Annexation Plan Opposed by Neighboring Towns," *New York Times*, February 26, 2002.

Books

Avery, Rev. John, *History of the Town of Ledyard 1650–1900*, Norwich, Conn.: Noyes and Davis, 1901.

Barthelme, Frederick, and Steven Barthelme, *Double Down*, Boston: Houghton Mifflin Company, 1999.

Benedict, Jeff, *Without Reservation*, New York: HarperCollins, 2000.

Berkhofer, Robert F., *The White Man's Indian*, New York: Alfred A. Knopf, 1978.

Bordewich, Fergus M., *Killing the White Man's Indian*, New York: Doubleday, 1996.

Brodeur, Paul, *Restitution: The Land Claims of the Mashpee, Passamaquoddy, and Penobscot Indians of New England*, Boston: Northeastern University Press, 1985.

Brown, Dee, *Bury My Heart at Wounded Knee*, New York: Henry Holt, 1970.

Calloway, Colin G., *After King Philip's War*, Hanover, NH: University Press of New England, 1997.

————, ed., *After King Philip's War*, Hanover, NH: University Press of New England, 1997.

Cave, Alfred A., *The Pequot War*, Amherst, Mass.: University of Massachusetts Press, 1996.

Clifford, James, *The Predicament of Culture in Twentieth Century Ethnography, Literature and Art*, Cambridge, Mass.: Harvard University Press, 1988.

Clifton, James A., *Being and Becoming Indian*, Prospect Heights, Ill.: Waveland Press, 1989.

————, *The Invented Indian*, New Brunswick, NJ: Transaction Publishers, 1996.

Cornell, Stephen, *The Return of the Native*, New York: Oxford University Press, 1988.

Countryman, Edward, *Americans*, New York: Hill and Wang, 1996.

Debo, Angie, *A History of the Indians of the United States*, Norman, Okla.: University of Oklahoma Press, 1970.

DeForest, John W., *History of the Indians of Connecticut from the Earliest Known Period to 1850*, Hartford, Conn.: Wm. Jas. Hamersly, 1852.

Deloria, Vine, Jr., *Spirit and Reason*, Golden, Colo: Fulcrum Publishing, 1999.

————, and Clifford M. Lytle, *The Nations Within*, Austin: University of Texas Press, 1984.

Demos, John, *The Unredeemed Captive*, New York: Random House, 1994.

Eisler, Kim Isaac, *Revenge of the Pequots*, New York: Simon and Schuster, 2001.

Fey, Harold E., and D'Arcy McNickle, *Indians and Other Americans*, New York: Harper and Brothers, 1959.

Finch, Robert, *The Smithsonian Guide to Southern New England*, New York: Random House, 1996.

Frazier, Ian, *On the Rez*, New York: Farrar, Straus and Giroux, 2000.

Grumet, Robert S., *Northeastern Indian Lives, 1632–1816*, Amherst, Mass.: University of Massachusetts Press, 1996.

Hauptman, Laurence M., and James D. Wherry, eds., *The Pequots in Southern New England*, Norman, Okla.: University of Oklahoma Press, 1990.

Hobsbawm, Eric, and Terence Ranger, *The Invention of Tradition*, Cambridge, Eng.: Cambridge University Press, 2000.

Jennings, Francis, *The Invasion of America*, New York: W. W. Norton, 1975.

Josephy, Alvin M., Jr., *The Indian Heritage of America*, Boston: Houghton Mifflin Co., 1991.

Katz, William L., *Black Indians*, New York: Simon and Schuster, 1997.

Krech, Shepard III, *The Ecological Indian: Myth and History*, New York: W. W. Norton, 1999.

Lane, Ambrose I., *Return of the Buffalo: The Story Behind America's Indian Gaming Explosion*, Westport, Conn.: Bergin and Garvey, 1995.

Lepore, Jill, *The Name of War: King Philip's War and the Origins of American Identity*, New York: Knopf, 1998.

Malcomson, Scott L., *One Drop of Blood*, New York: Farrar, Straus and Giroux, 2000.

Marks, Paula Mitchell, *In a Barren Land: American Indian Dispossession and Survival*, New York: William Morrow, 1998.

Mason, John, *A Brief History of the Pequot War*, Boston: S. Kneeland and T. Green, 1736.

Morgan, Ted, *Wilderness at Dawn*, New York: Simon and Schuster, 1993.

Nagel, Joane, *American Indian Ethnic Renewal*, New York: Oxford University Press, 1996.

O'Brien, Timothy L., *Bad Bet: The Inside Story of the Glamour, Glitz, and Danger of America's Gambling Industry*, New York: Times Books, 1998.

Penn, William S., *As We Are Now*, Berkeley, Calif.: University of California Press, 1997.

Pevar, Stephen L., *The Rights of American Indians*, New York: Penguin Putnam Inc., 1997.

Prucha, Francis Paul, *American Indian Treaties: The History of a Political Anomaly*, Berkeley, Calif.: University of California Press, 1994.

Russell, Howard S., *Indian New England Before the Mayflower*, Hanover, NH: University Press of New England, 1980.

Salisbury, Neal, *Manitou and Providence*, Oxford, Eng.: Oxford University Press, 1982.

Spanier, David, *Inside the Gambler's Mind*, Reno, Nev.: University of Nevada Press, 1994.

Voight, Virginia Frances, *Mohegan Chief: The Story of Harold Tantaquidgeon*, New York: Funk and Wagnalls, 1965.

Weinstein, Laurie, *Enduring Traditions: The Native Peoples of New England*, Westport, Conn.: Bergin and Garvey, 1994.

White, Robert H., *Tribal Assets*, New York: Henry Holt, 1990.

Wilson, James, *The Earth Shall Weep: A History of Native America*, New York: Atlantic Monthly Press, 1999.

Court Records

Western Pequot Tribe of Indians v. Holdridge Enterprises et al., Civil Action No. 76/193.

Mashantucket Pequot Tribe v. State of Connecticut, Civil H-89-717 PCD.

Mashantucket Pequot Tribe v. State of Connecticut and William A. O'Neill, 90-7508.

State of Connecticut Superior Court Records, "Lake Spears Case," 1992.

————, "Ernest Reels Case," 1994–1998.

————, "Donricardo Sebastian, Jr. Case," 1999.

Transcripts

Hearing before the Senate Select Committee on Indian Affairs, United States Senate, July 14, 1982.

Hearing before the Committee on Interior and Insular Affairs, United States House of Representatives, July 15, 1982.

Report: "Authorizing Funds for the Settlement of Indian Claims in the Town of Ledyard, Conn.," Senate Select Committee on Indian Affairs, September 29, 1982.

Report: "Providing for the Settlement of Land Claims of the Mashantucket Pequot Indian Tribe of Connecticut, and for Other Purposes," House Committee on Interior and Insular Affairs, September 29, 1982.

Report: "Providing for the Settlement of Land Claims of the Mashantucket Pequot Indian Tribe of Connecticut, and for Other Purposes," House Committee on Interior and Insular Affairs, March 21, 1983.

Hearing before the Senate Select Committee on Indian Affairs, United States Senate, July 19, 1983.

Report: "Authorizing Funds for the Settlement of Indian Claims in the Town of Ledyard, Conn.," Senate Select Committee on Indian Affairs, September 14, 1983.

Connecticut Senate Debate on Las Vegas Nights Repeal Legislation, May 9, 1991.

Connecticut House Debate on Las Vegas Nights Repeal Legislation, May 16, 1991.

Statement of Senator Joseph Lieberman on Introduction of the Indian Trust Land Reform Act of 1997, October 1997.

Testimony of Robert Congdon, Wesley Johnson, and Nicholas Mullane before the Senate Committee on Indian Affairs, April 22, 1998.

Videotapes and CDs

CPTV, *The New Pequot: A Tribal Portrait*, 1988–1989.

Dobicki, Elizabeth, and Bruce Grant, *Brave One: A Mystical Journey of the Mashantucket Pequot Tribe*, 1995, Enchanted Entertainment.

James Stewart Polshek and Assoc., *Presentation of Museum Design During Pequot Days*, September 10, 1993.

Mashantucket Pequot Museum, *Overview of Museum*, January 1998.

Mashantucket Pequot Tribal Nation Creative Arts Services, *Educational Forum on Sovereignty*, May 14, 1999.

Mashantucket Pequot Tribe, *Schemitzun '96*, 1996.

TIMELINE

1635: English settlers arrive in Connecticut.

1637–38: War between English colonists and Pequots ending in defeat of the tribe. Colony divides tribe into two bands and places them under the control of rival Mohegan and Narragansett tribes.

1666: Connecticut Colony grants Pequots under Mohegan rule 2,000 acres of land in Ledyard for reservation.

1790: Passage of Indian Non-Intercourse Act by U.S. Congress.

1855: Sale of approximately 800 acres of reservation land by Connecticut to raise money for small remnant population of Pequots.

1973: Eliza George Plouffe, last full-time resident of reservation, dies. Later that year, one of her daughters, Theresa Hayward, moves onto reservation with family.

1974: Establishment of The Western Pequot Indians of Connecticut, Inc.

1975: U.S. District Judge Edward Ginoux of Maine rules that Non-Intercourse Act of 1790 applies to tribes in the eastern U.S.

1976: Pequots sue local landowners in federal court alleging the land was illegally sold by Connecticut in 1855.

1983: Via legislation, Congress settles the Pequot land-claim suit and grants the Pequots federal recognition.

1986: Pequots open high-stakes bingo parlor.

1988: Indian Gaming Regulatory Act gives federally recognized Indian tribes the right to negotiate gambling agreements with the States and build casinos on reservations.

1989: Pequots notify Connecticut of their intention to establish a casino on the reservation in Ledyard.

1991: Connecticut Gov. Lowell Weicker defeated in his attempt to repeal the state's charity gaming law, which tribal attorneys say gives the Pequots the right to establish a casino.

February 1992: Foxwoods High-Stakes Bingo & Casino opens.

August 1992: Pequots ask the Bureau of Indian Affairs to annex twenty-seven acres of land adjacent to the reservation.

January 1993: Attorneys for the Pequots negotiate a slot machine agreement with the State of Connecticut, and Foxwoods installs the first of over 2,000 machines that year.

February 1993: Pequots seek to annex another 247 acres to the reservation.

July 1993: Publication of map showing the Pequots' desire to annex thousands more acres to the reservation, including nearly 15 percent of North Stonington, 12 percent of Ledyard, and 5 percent of Preston.

August 1998: Mashantucket Pequot Museum opens.

November 1998: Skip Hayward defeated for the tribal chairmanship by Kenny Reels.

2000: Cumulative contributions to the State of Connecticut from Foxwoods slot machine revenue exceed $1 billion. Foxwoods employs nearly 11,500 workers and averages 40,000 gamblers a day.

February 2002: Pequots notify BIA they are withdrawing their nine-year land annexation request.

November 2002: Kenny Reels steps down as tribal chair and is replaced by his cousin Michael Thomas. Thomas served three years for felony drug possession in a prison in Rhode Island, and was released in 1991.

CANADA

MAINE

VERMONT

NEW HAMPSHIRE

MASS.

CONN.

R.I.

Montpelier

Concord

Hartford

Augusta

Portland

Boston

Providence

Mashpee

New London

Bridgeport

New York City

Penobscot Reservation

Calais

Passamaquoddy Reservation

Atlantic Ocean

Long Island

95

91

90

84

95